TEENAGE MU
TURTLES

ATTACK ON TECHNODROME
VOLUME 11

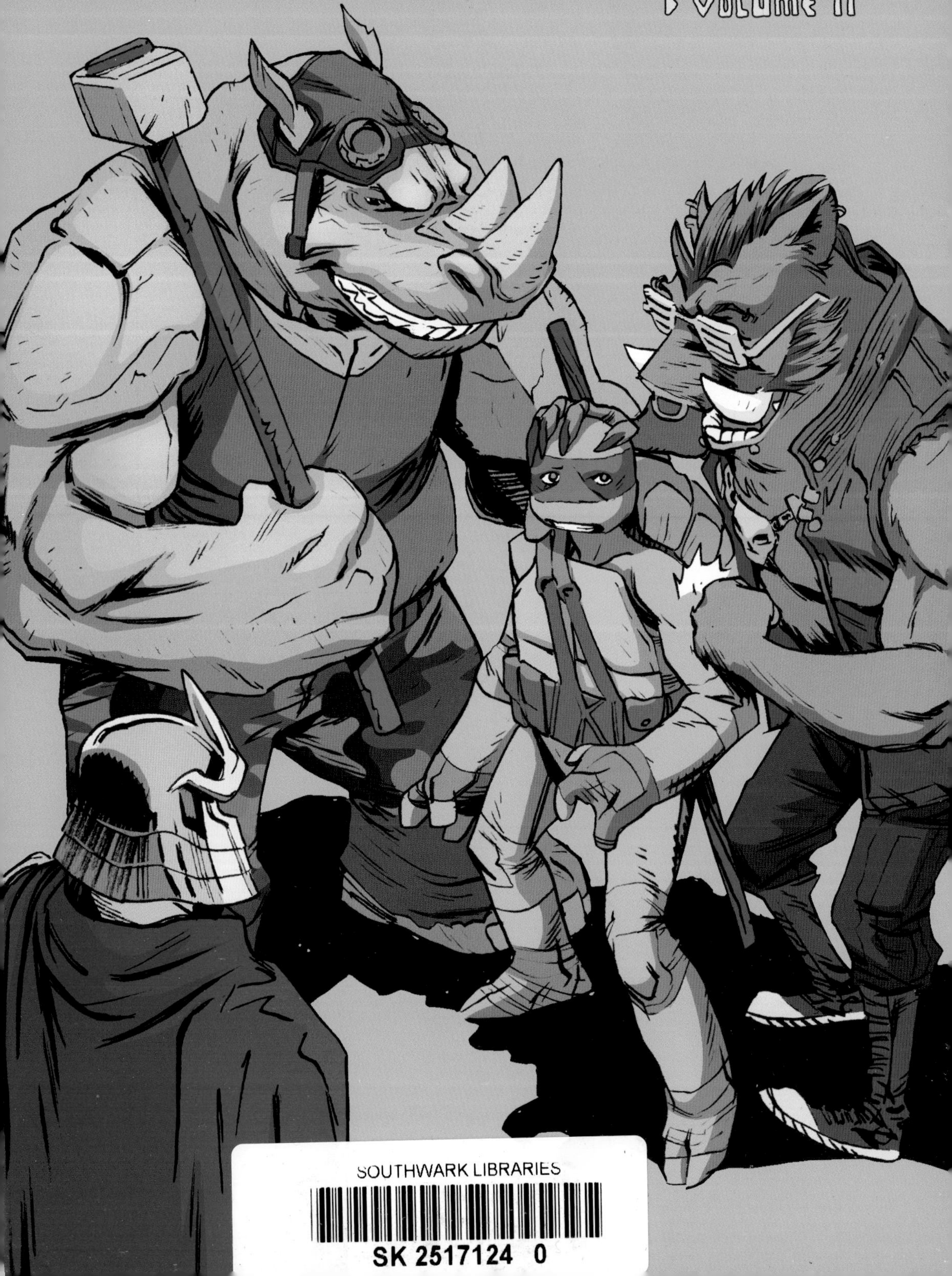

London Borough
of Southwark

CW

SK 2517124 0

Askews & Holts   12-Jun-2015

AF GRA   £13.50

Special thanks to Joan Hilty, Linda Lee, and Kat van Dam for their invaluable assistance.

ISBN: 978-1-63140-341-5

nickelodeon™

18 17 16 15   1 2 3 4

®

www.IDWPUBLISHING.com
IDW founded by Ted Adams, Alex Garner, Kris Oprisko, and Robbie Robbins

Ted Adams, CEO & Publisher
Greg Goldstein, President & COO
Robbie Robbins, EVP/Sr. Graphic Artist
Chris Ryall, Chief Creative Officer/Editor-in-Chief
Matthew Ruzicka, CPA, Chief Financial Officer
Alan Payne, VP of Sales
Dirk Wood, VP of Marketing
Lorelei Bunjes, VP of Digital Services
Jeff Webber, VP of Digital Publishing & Business Development

Facebook: **facebook.com/idwpublishing**
Twitter: **@idwpublishing**
YouTube: **youtube.com/idwpublishing**
Instagram: **instagram.com/idwpublishing**
deviantART: **idwpublishing.deviantart.com**
Pinterest: **pinterest.com/idwpublishing/idw-staff-faves**

Originally published as TEENAGE MUTANT NINJA TURTLES issues #41–44.

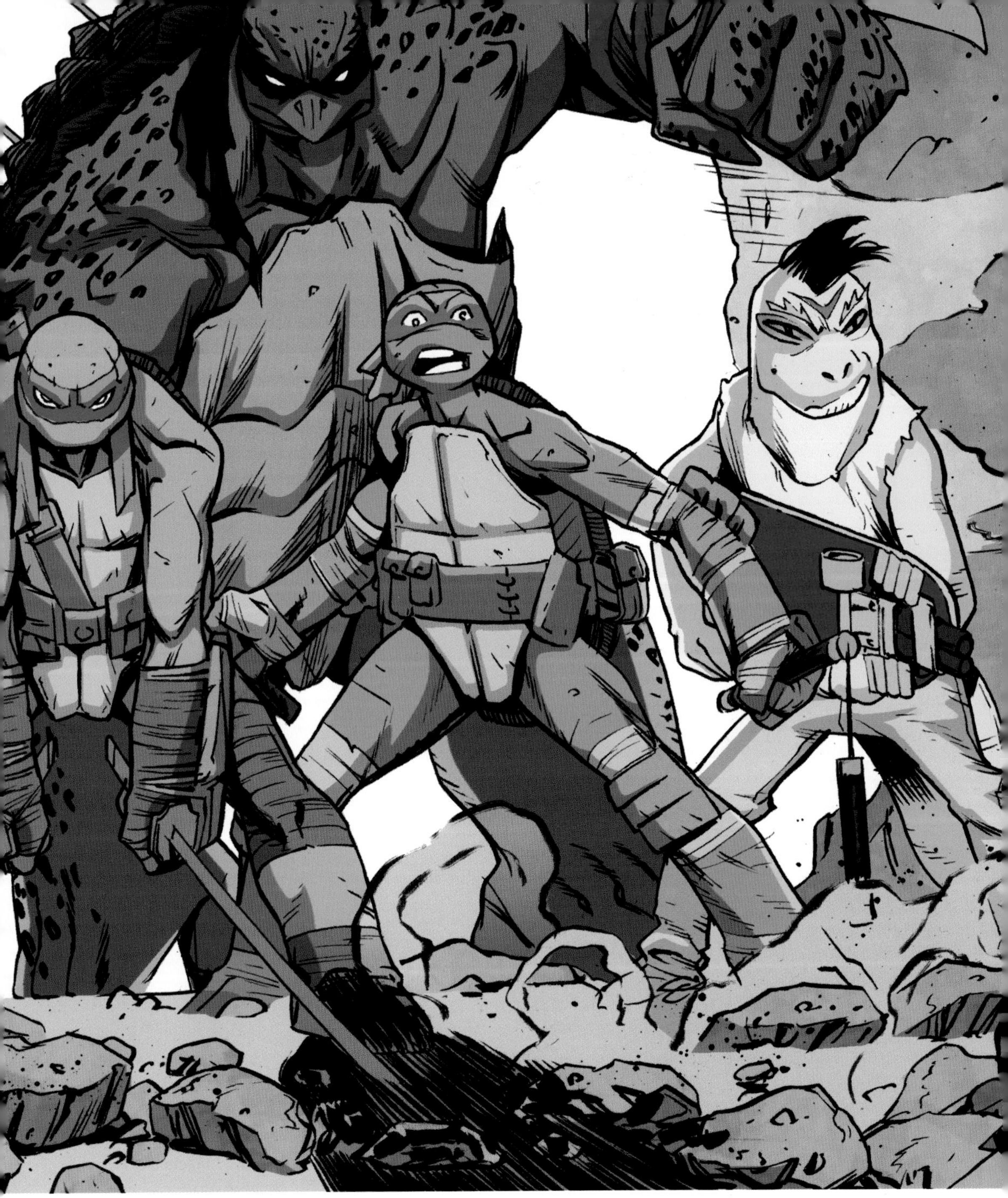

Story by Kevin Eastman, Bobby Curnow, and Tom Waltz • Script by Tom Waltz

Art by Cory Smith • Colors by Ronda Pattison

Letters by Shawn Lee • Series Edits by Bobby Curnow

Cover by Cory Smith • Cover Colors by Ronda Pattison

Collection Edits by Justin Eisinger & Alonzo Simon

Production by Shawn Lee

Based on characters created by Peter Laird and Kevin Eastman

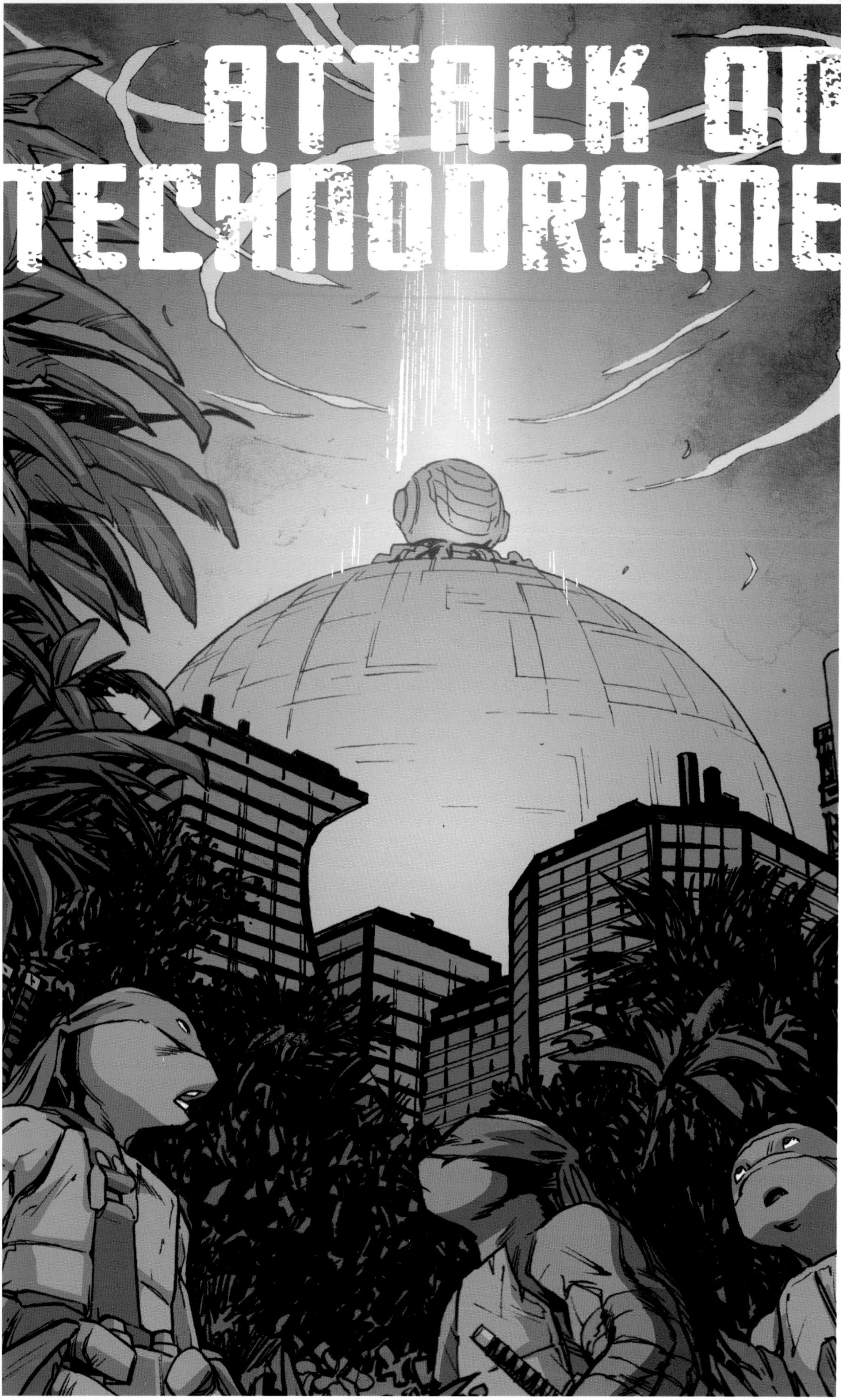
ATTACK ON
TECHNODROME

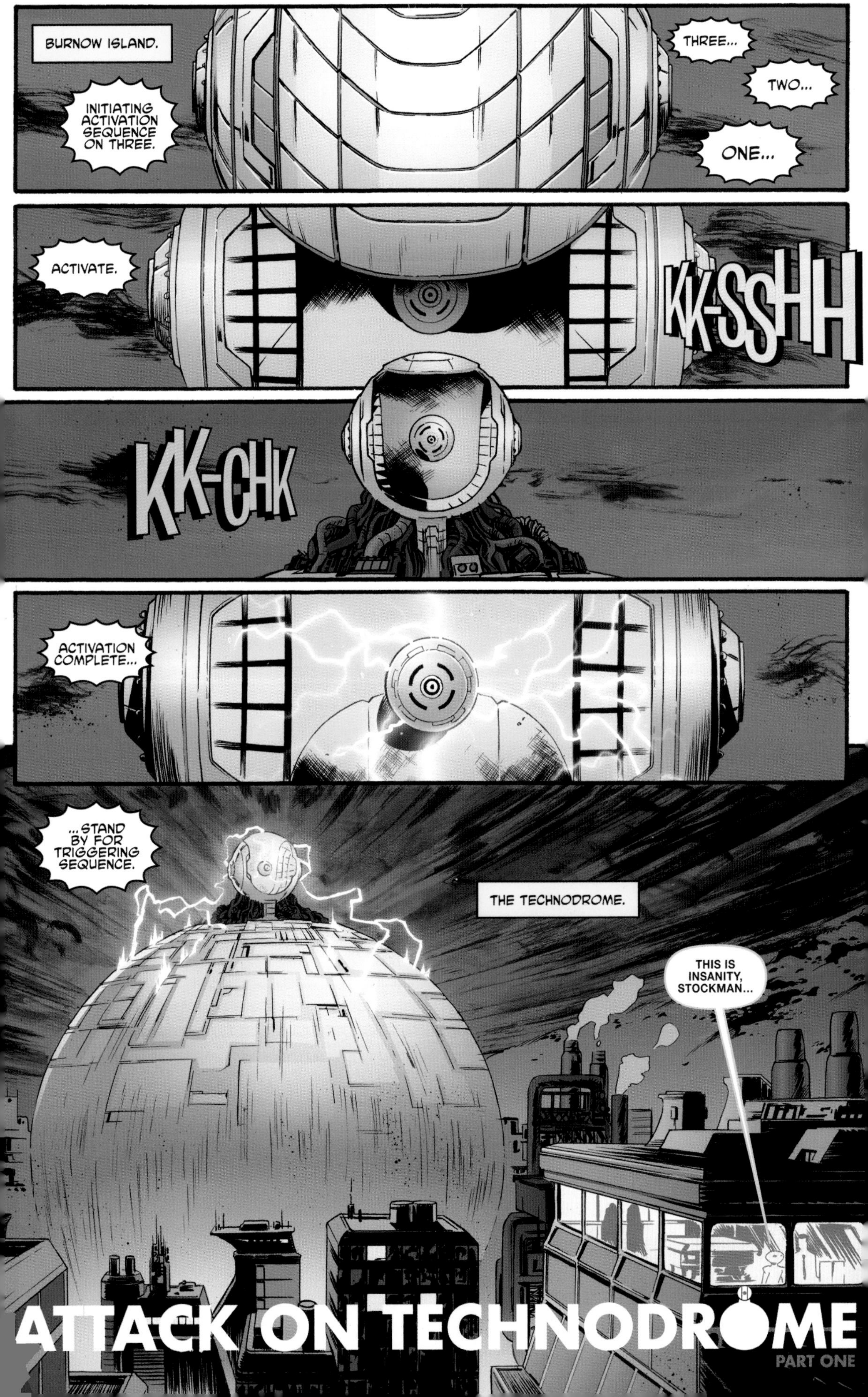
BURNOW ISLAND.
INITIATING ACTIVATION SEQUENCE ON THREE.
THREE...
TWO...
ONE...
ACTIVATE.
KK-SSHH
KK-CHK
ACTIVATION COMPLETE...
...STAND BY FOR TRIGGERING SEQUENCE.
THE TECHNODROME.
THIS IS INSANITY, STOCKMAN...
ATTACK ON TECHNODROME
PART ONE

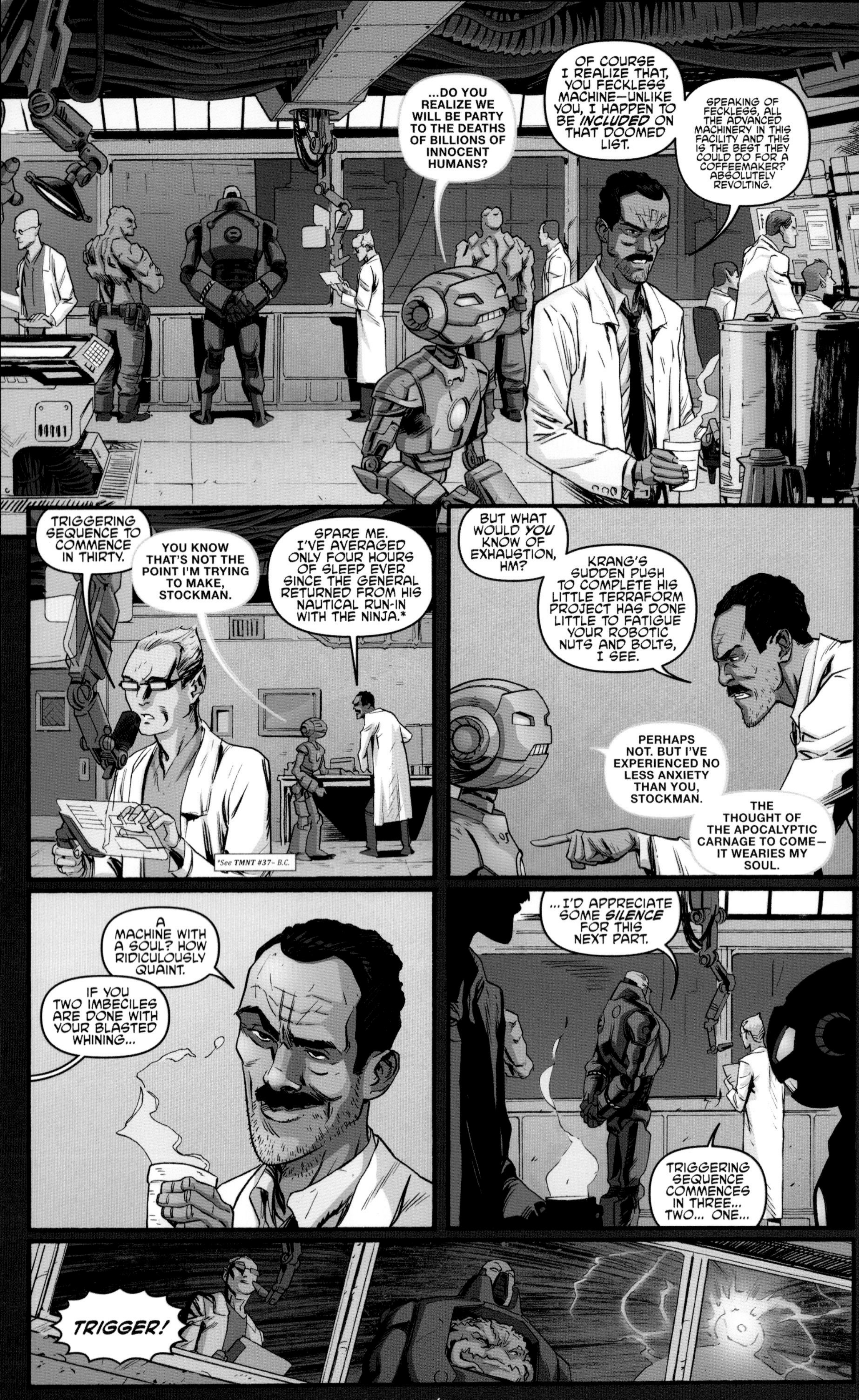

...DO YOU REALIZE WE WILL BE PARTY TO THE DEATHS OF BILLIONS OF INNOCENT HUMANS?
OF COURSE I REALIZE THAT, YOU FECKLESS MACHINE—UNLIKE YOU, I HAPPEN TO BE *INCLUDED* ON THAT DOOMED LIST.
SPEAKING OF FECKLESS, ALL THE ADVANCED MACHINERY IN THIS FACILITY AND THIS IS THE BEST THEY COULD DO FOR A COFFEEMAKER? ABSOLUTELY REVOLTING.
TRIGGERING SEQUENCE TO COMMENCE IN THIRTY.
YOU KNOW THAT'S NOT THE POINT I'M TRYING TO MAKE, STOCKMAN.
SPARE ME. I'VE AVERAGED ONLY FOUR HOURS OF SLEEP EVER SINCE THE GENERAL RETURNED FROM HIS NAUTICAL RUN-IN WITH THE NINJA.*
*See TMNT #37– B.C.
BUT WHAT WOULD *YOU* KNOW OF EXHAUSTION, HM?
KRANG'S SUDDEN PUSH TO COMPLETE HIS LITTLE TERRAFORM PROJECT HAS DONE LITTLE TO FATIGUE YOUR ROBOTIC NUTS AND BOLTS, I SEE.
PERHAPS NOT. BUT I'VE EXPERIENCED NO LESS ANXIETY THAN YOU, STOCKMAN.
THE THOUGHT OF THE APOCALYPTIC CARNAGE TO COME— IT WEARIES MY SOUL.
A MACHINE WITH A SOUL? HOW RIDICULOUSLY QUAINT.
IF YOU TWO IMBECILES ARE DONE WITH YOUR BLASTED WHINING...
...I'D APPRECIATE SOME *SILENCE* FOR THIS NEXT PART.
TRIGGERING SEQUENCE COMMENCES IN THREE... TWO... ONE...
TRIGGER!

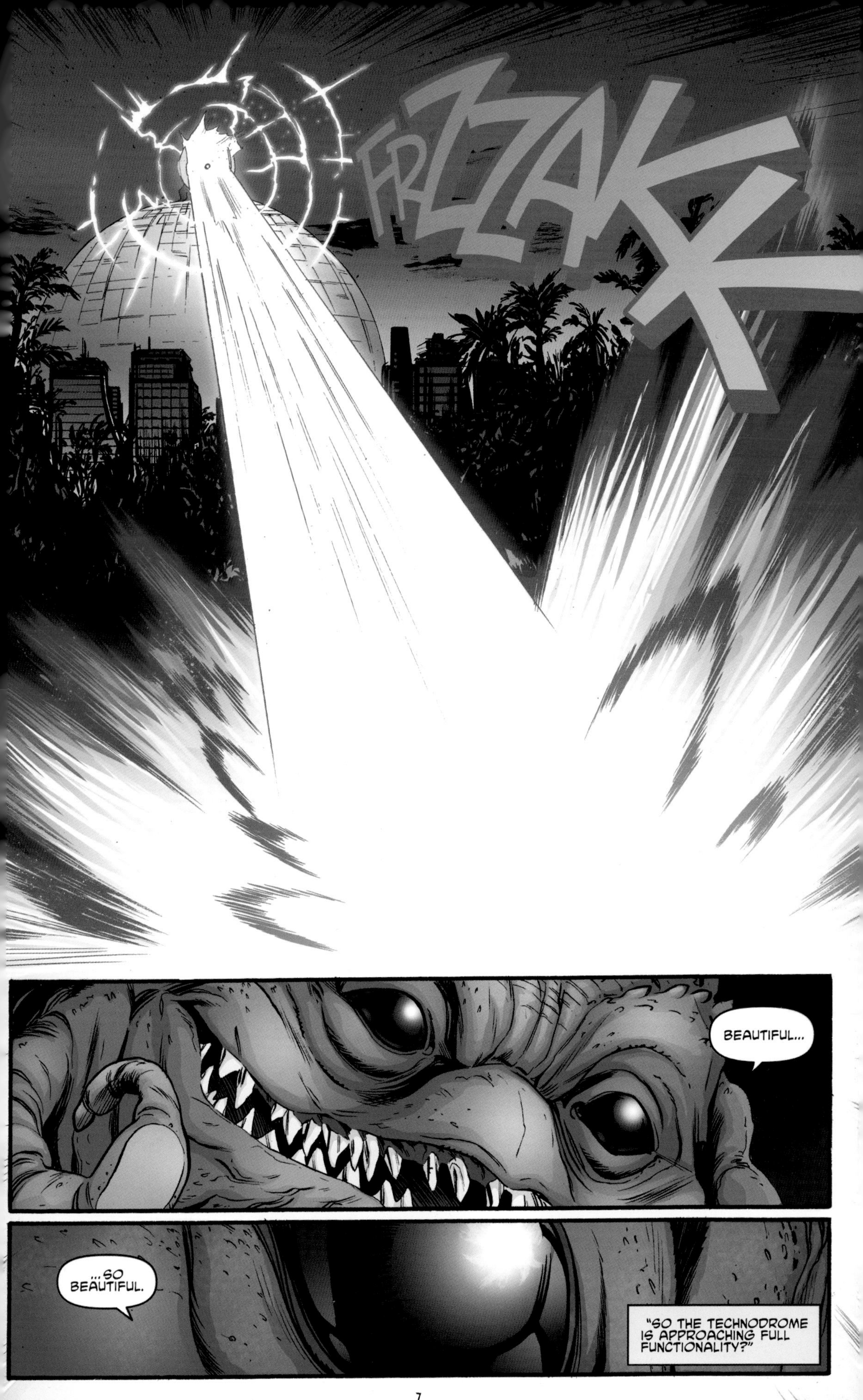
FRZZAKX
BEAUTIFUL...
...SO BEAUTIFUL.
"SO THE TECHNODROME IS APPROACHING FULL FUNCTIONALITY?"

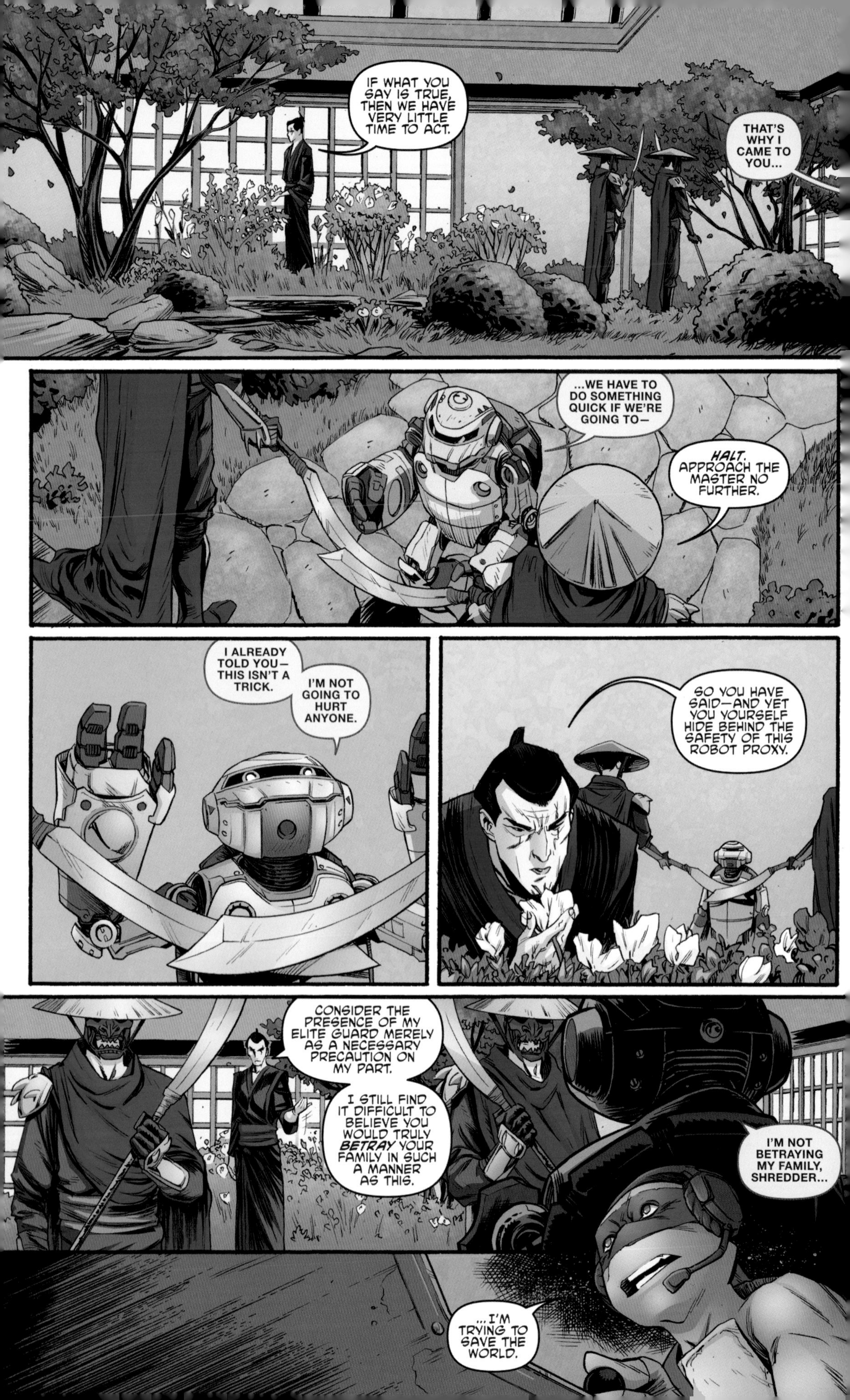
IF WHAT YOU SAY IS TRUE, THEN WE HAVE VERY LITTLE TIME TO ACT.
THAT'S WHY I CAME TO YOU...
...WE HAVE TO DO SOMETHING QUICK IF WE'RE GOING TO—
HALT. APPROACH THE MASTER NO FURTHER.
I ALREADY TOLD YOU— THIS ISN'T A TRICK.
I'M NOT GOING TO HURT ANYONE.
SO YOU HAVE SAID—AND YET YOU YOURSELF HIDE BEHIND THE SAFETY OF THIS ROBOT PROXY.
CONSIDER THE PRESENCE OF MY ELITE GUARD MERELY AS A NECESSARY PRECAUTION ON MY PART.
I STILL FIND IT DIFFICULT TO BELIEVE YOU WOULD TRULY BETRAY YOUR FAMILY IN SUCH A MANNER AS THIS.
I'M NOT BETRAYING MY FAMILY, SHREDDER...
...I'M TRYING TO SAVE THE WORLD.

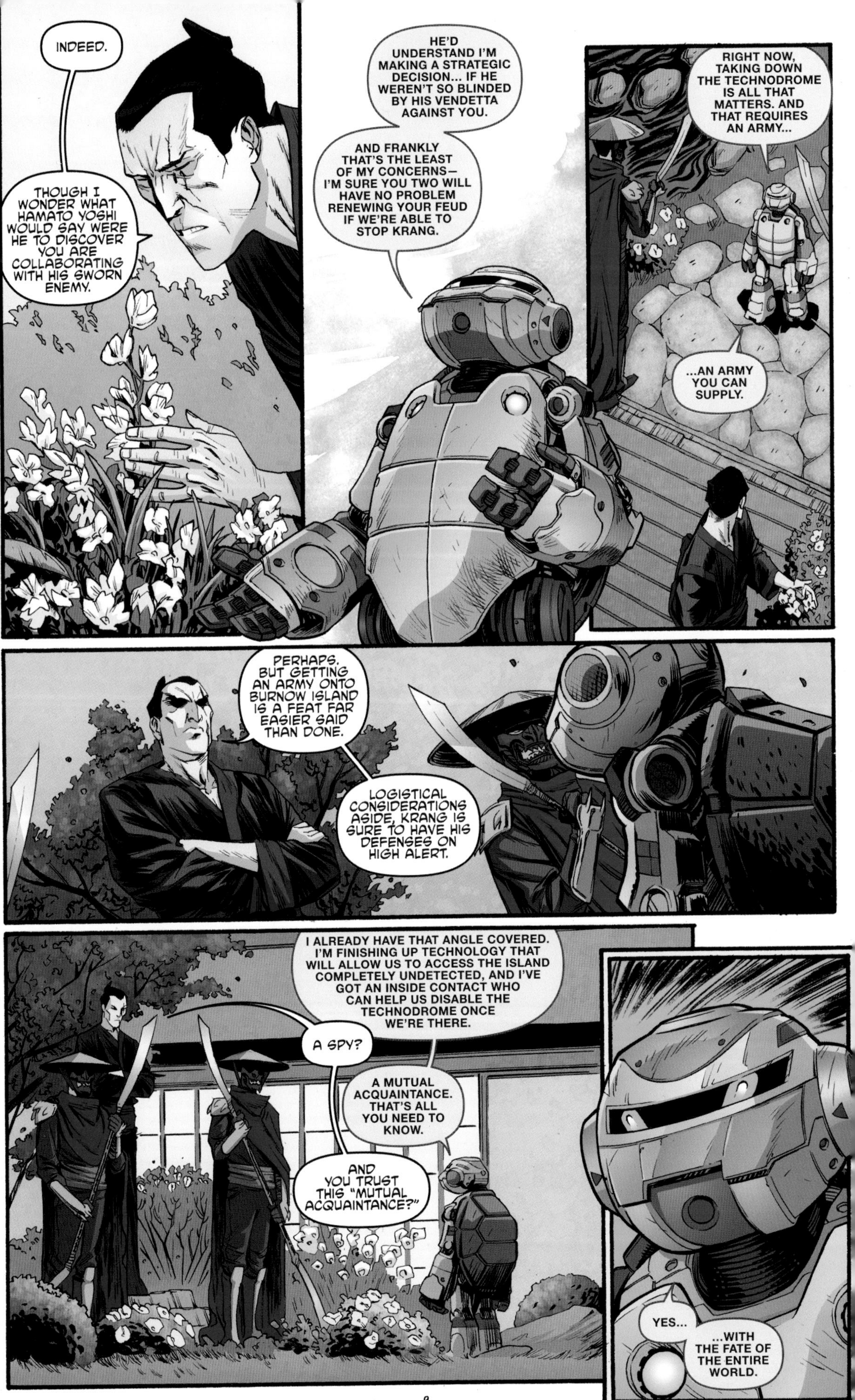
INDEED.
THOUGH I WONDER WHAT HAMATO YOSHI WOULD SAY WERE HE TO DISCOVER YOU ARE COLLABORATING WITH HIS SWORN ENEMY.
HE'D UNDERSTAND I'M MAKING A STRATEGIC DECISION... IF HE WEREN'T SO BLINDED BY HIS VENDETTA AGAINST YOU.
AND FRANKLY THAT'S THE LEAST OF MY CONCERNS— I'M SURE YOU TWO WILL HAVE NO PROBLEM RENEWING YOUR FEUD IF WE'RE ABLE TO STOP KRANG.
RIGHT NOW, TAKING DOWN THE TECHNODROME IS ALL THAT MATTERS. AND THAT REQUIRES AN ARMY...
...AN ARMY YOU CAN SUPPLY.
PERHAPS. BUT GETTING AN ARMY ONTO BURNOW ISLAND IS A FEAT FAR EASIER SAID THAN DONE.
LOGISTICAL CONSIDERATIONS ASIDE, KRANG IS SURE TO HAVE HIS DEFENSES ON HIGH ALERT.
I ALREADY HAVE THAT ANGLE COVERED. I'M FINISHING UP TECHNOLOGY THAT WILL ALLOW US TO ACCESS THE ISLAND COMPLETELY UNDETECTED, AND I'VE GOT AN INSIDE CONTACT WHO CAN HELP US DISABLE THE TECHNODROME ONCE WE'RE THERE.
A SPY?
A MUTUAL ACQUAINTANCE. THAT'S ALL YOU NEED TO KNOW.
AND YOU TRUST THIS "MUTUAL ACQUAINTANCE?"
YES...
...WITH THE FATE OF THE ENTIRE WORLD.

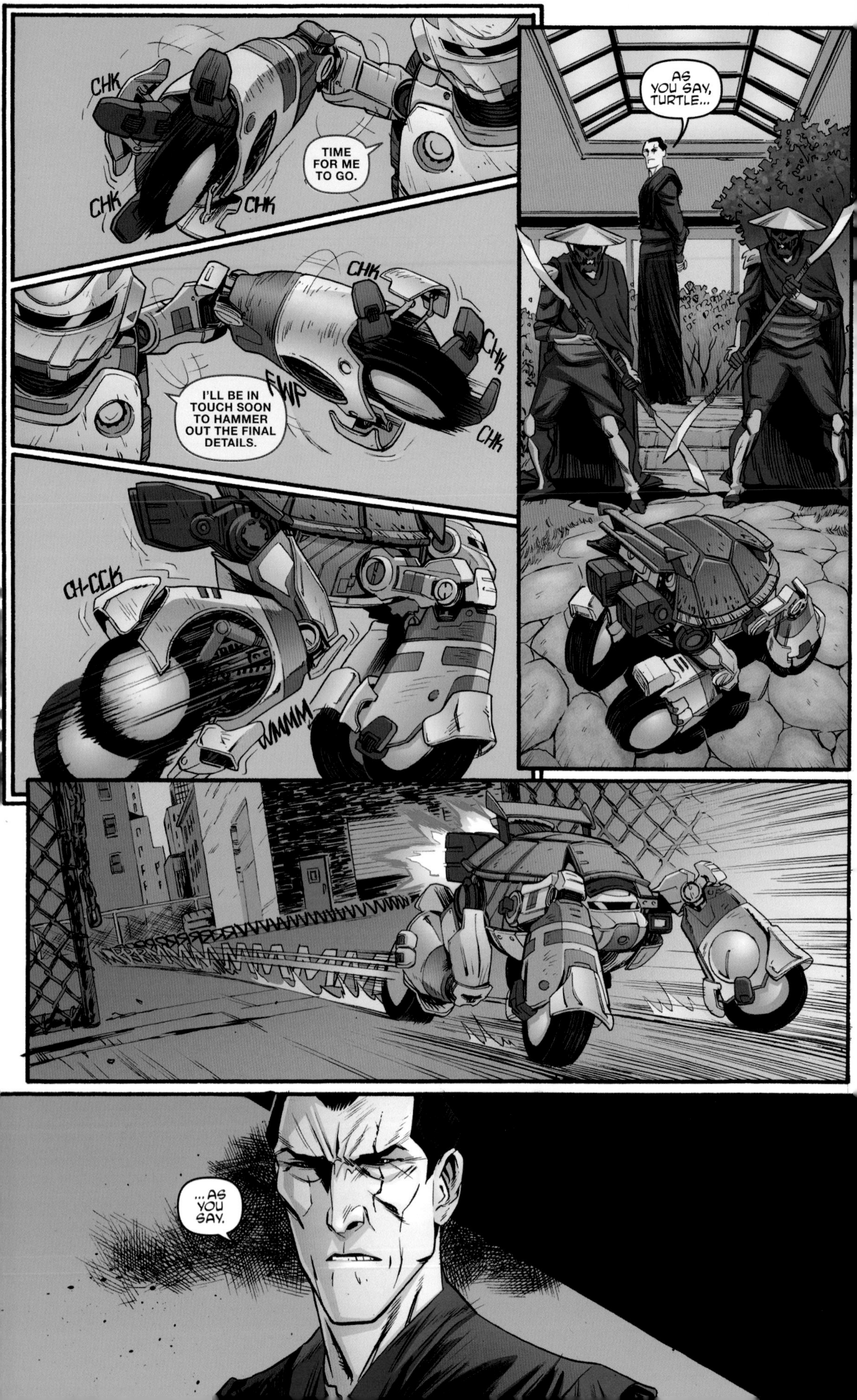
CHK
TIME FOR ME TO GO.
CHK
CHK
AS YOU SAY, TURTLE...
CHK
CHK
FWP
I'LL BE IN TOUCH SOON TO HAMMER OUT THE FINAL DETAILS.
CHK
CH-CCK
WMMM
...AS YOU SAY.

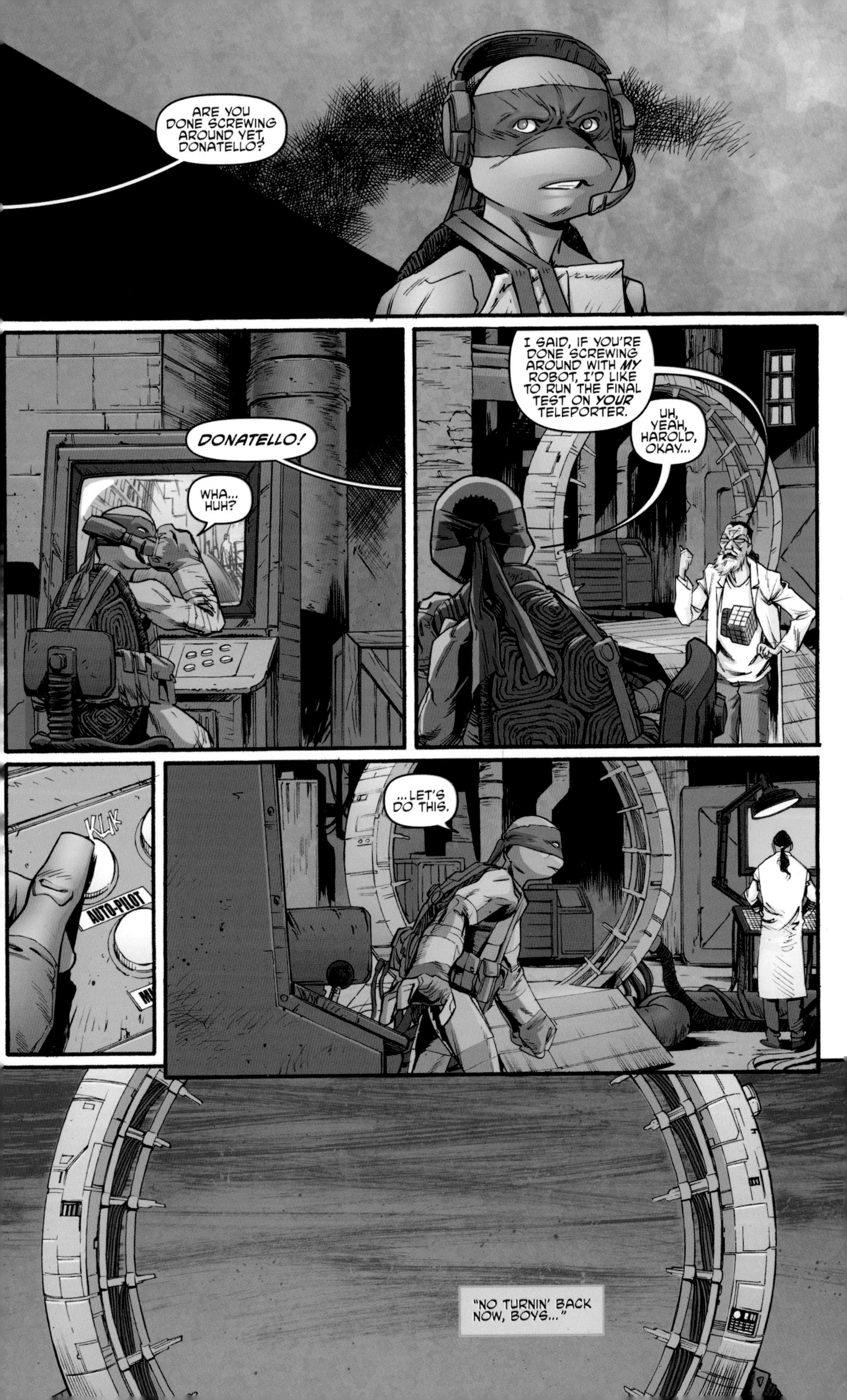

ARE YOU DONE SCREWING AROUND YET, DONATELLO?
DONATELLO!
WHA... HUH?
I SAID, IF YOU'RE DONE SCREWING AROUND WITH MY ROBOT, I'D LIKE TO RUN THE FINAL TEST ON YOUR TELEPORTER.
UH, YEAH, HAROLD, OKAY...
KLIK
AUTO-PILOT
...LET'S DO THIS.
"NO TURNIN' BACK NOW, BOYS..."

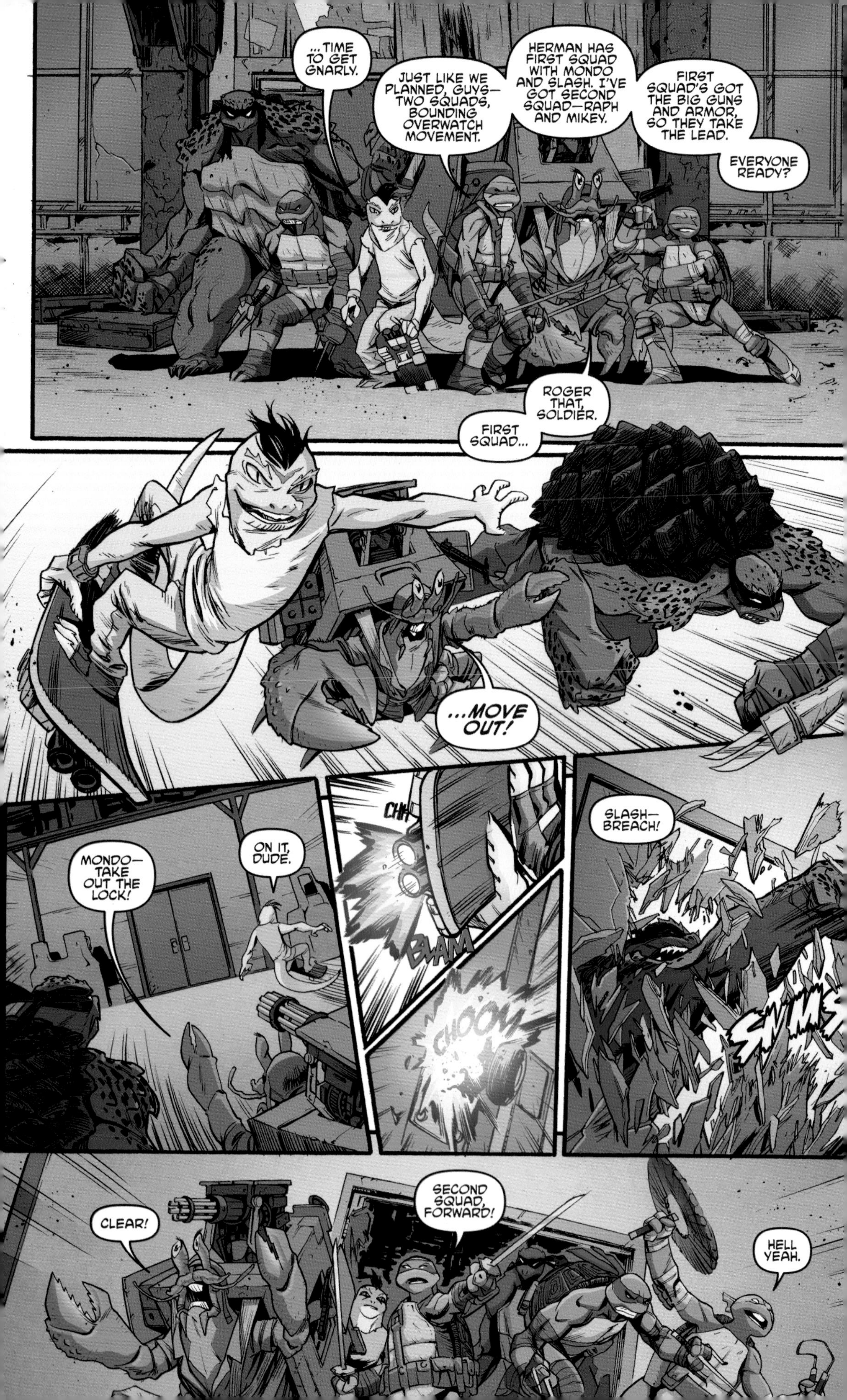
...TIME TO GET GNARLY.
JUST LIKE WE PLANNED, GUYS— TWO SQUADS, BOUNDING OVERWATCH MOVEMENT.
HERMAN HAS FIRST SQUAD WITH MONDO AND SLASH. I'VE GOT SECOND SQUAD—RAPH AND MIKEY.
FIRST SQUAD'S GOT THE BIG GUNS AND ARMOR, SO THEY TAKE THE LEAD.
EVERYONE READY?
ROGER THAT, SOLDIER.
FIRST SQUAD...
...MOVE OUT!
MONDO— TAKE OUT THE LOCK!
ON IT, DUDE.
CHK
BLAM
CHOOM
SLASH— BREACH!
SMASH
CLEAR!
SECOND SQUAD, FORWARD!
HELL YEAH.

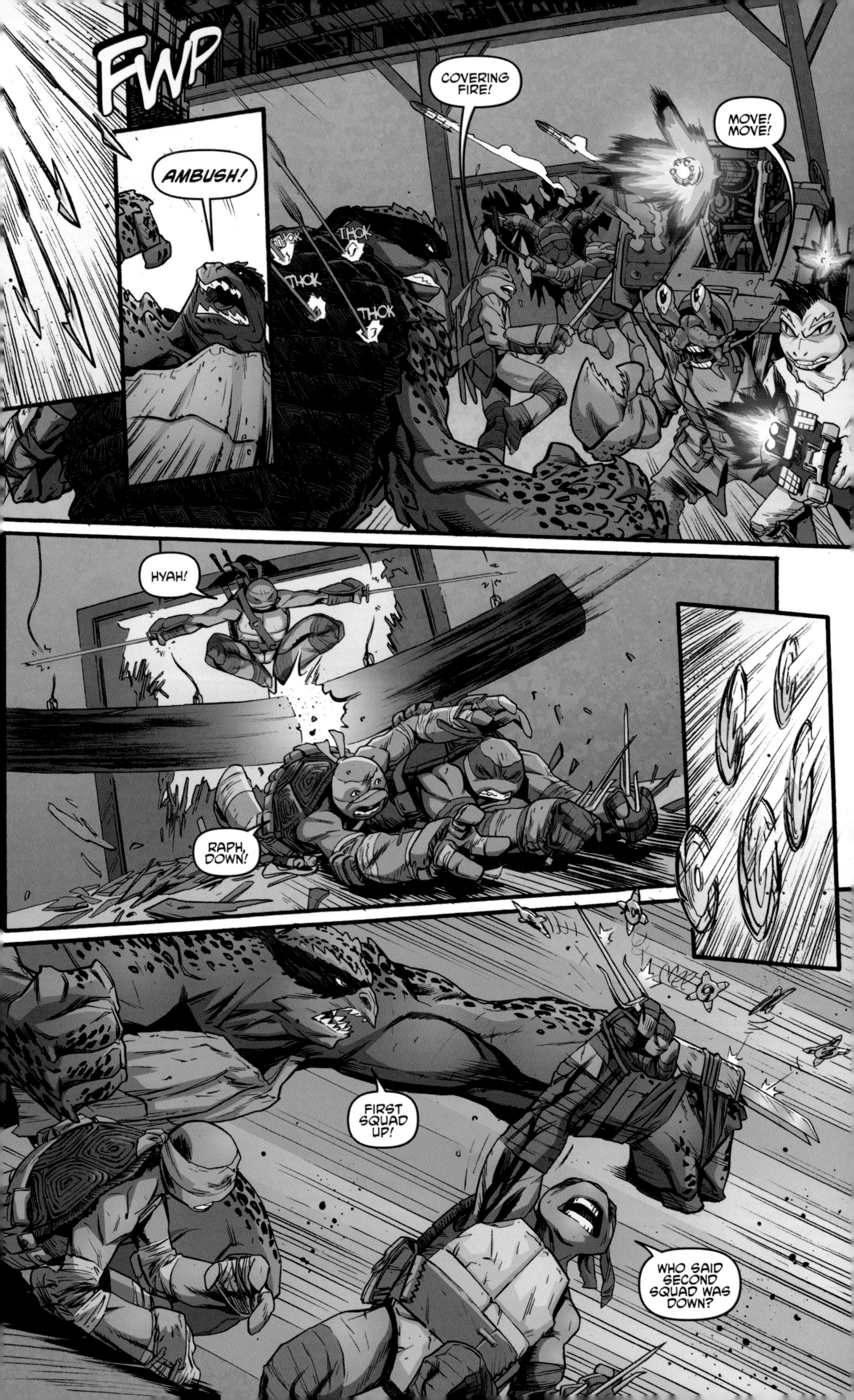
FWP
AMBUSH!
THOK
THOK
THOK
THOK
COVERING FIRE!
MOVE! MOVE!
HYAH!
RAPH, DOWN!
FIRST SQUAD UP!
WHO SAID SECOND SQUAD WAS DOWN?

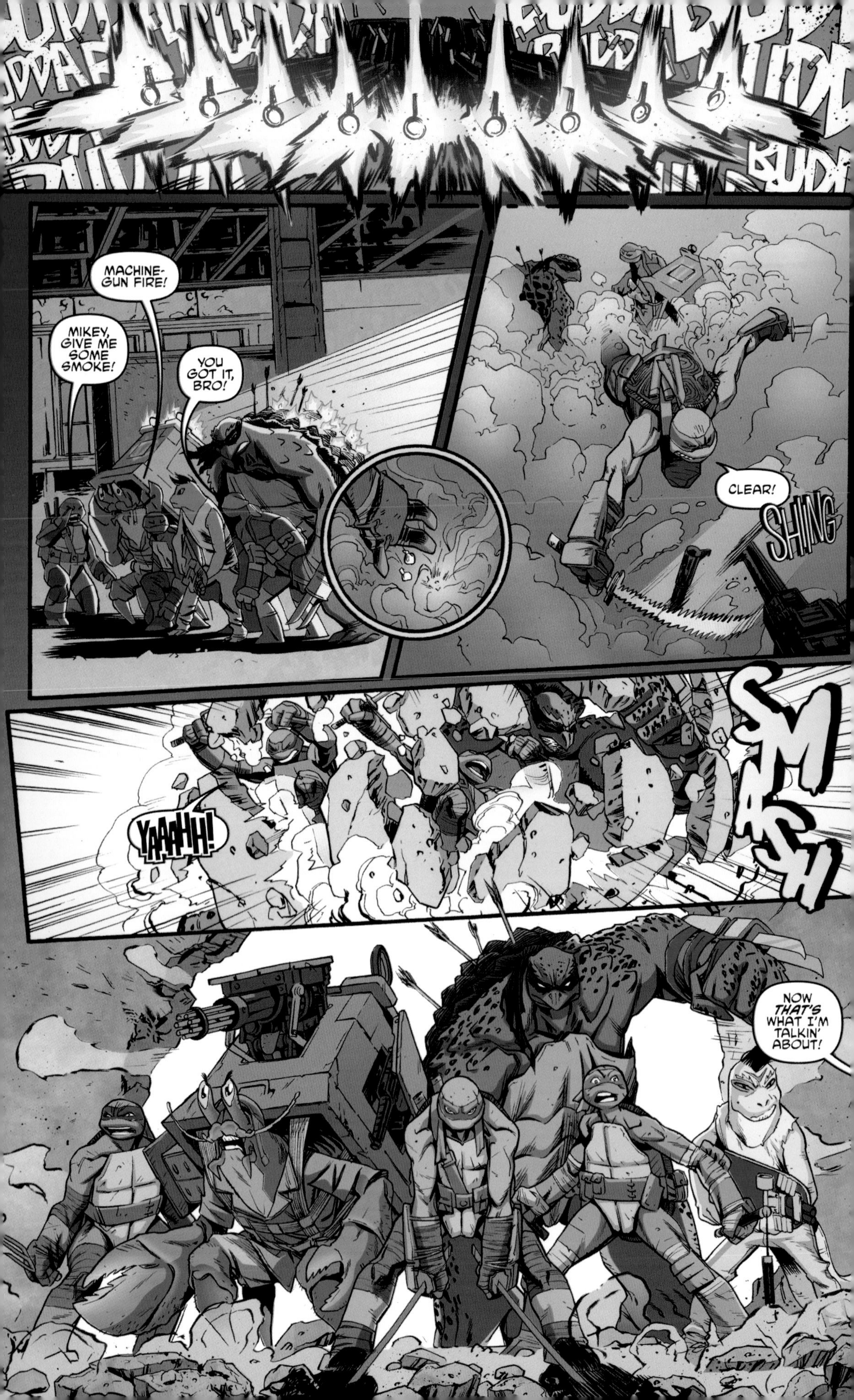
MACHINE-GUN FIRE!
MIKEY, GIVE ME SOME SMOKE!
YOU GOT IT, BRO!
CLEAR!
SHING
YAAAHH!
SMASH
NOW THAT'S WHAT I'M TALKIN' ABOUT!

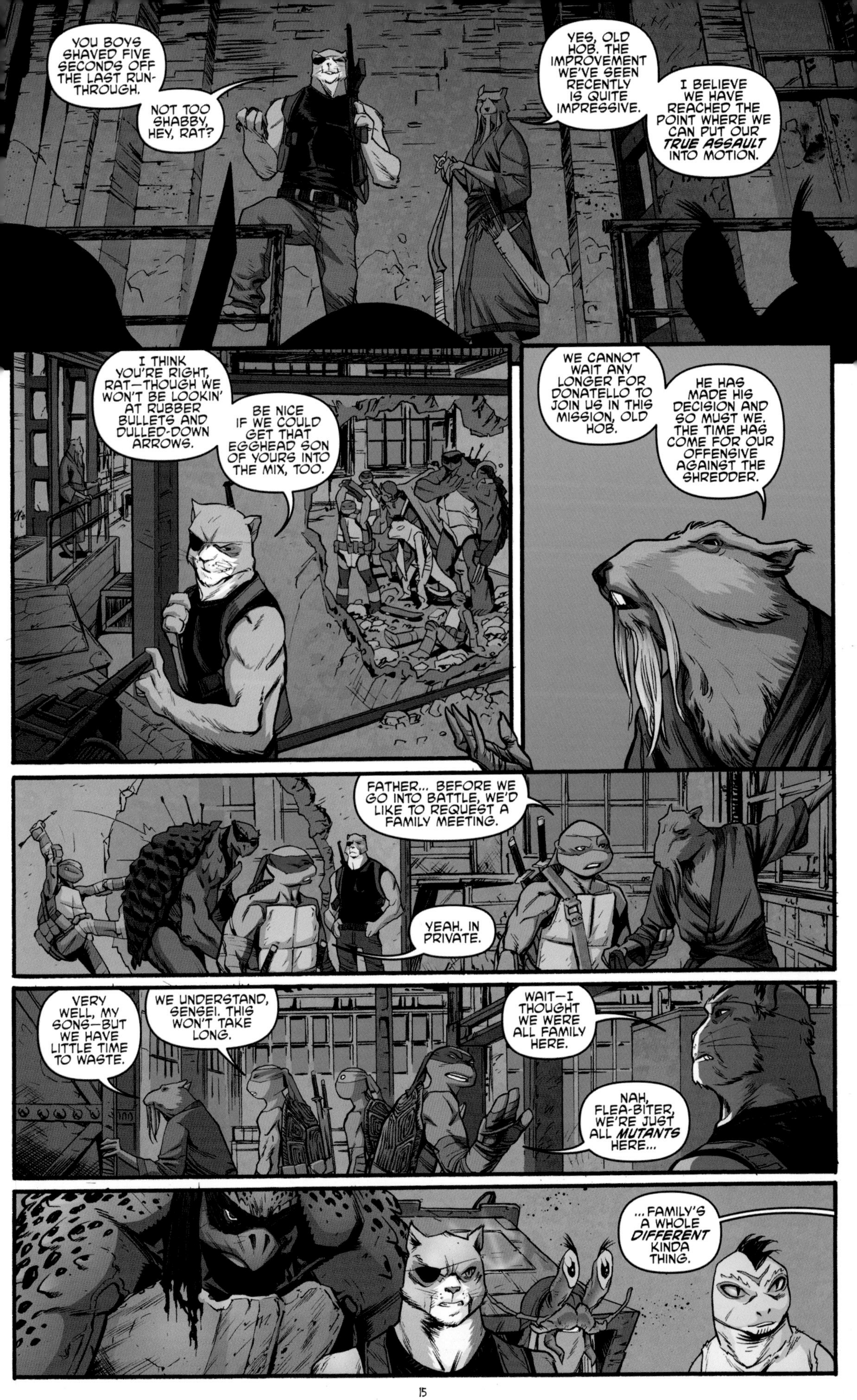
YOU BOYS SHAVED FIVE SECONDS OFF THE LAST RUN-THROUGH.
NOT TOO SHABBY, HEY, RAT?
YES, OLD HOB. THE IMPROVEMENT WE'VE SEEN RECENTLY IS QUITE IMPRESSIVE.
I BELIEVE WE HAVE REACHED THE POINT WHERE WE CAN PUT OUR *TRUE ASSAULT* INTO MOTION.
I THINK YOU'RE RIGHT, RAT—THOUGH WE WON'T BE LOOKIN' AT RUBBER BULLETS AND DULLED-DOWN ARROWS.
BE NICE IF WE COULD GET THAT EGGHEAD SON OF YOURS INTO THE MIX, TOO.
WE CANNOT WAIT ANY LONGER FOR DONATELLO TO JOIN US IN THIS MISSION, OLD HOB.
HE HAS MADE HIS DECISION AND SO MUST WE. THE TIME HAS COME FOR OUR OFFENSIVE AGAINST THE SHREDDER.
FATHER... BEFORE WE GO INTO BATTLE, WE'D LIKE TO REQUEST A FAMILY MEETING.
YEAH. IN PRIVATE.
VERY WELL, MY SONS—BUT WE HAVE LITTLE TIME TO WASTE.
WE UNDERSTAND, SENSEI. THIS WON'T TAKE LONG.
WAIT—I THOUGHT WE WERE ALL FAMILY HERE.
NAH, FLEA-BITER, WE'RE JUST ALL *MUTANTS* HERE...
...FAMILY'S A WHOLE *DIFFERENT* KINDA THING.

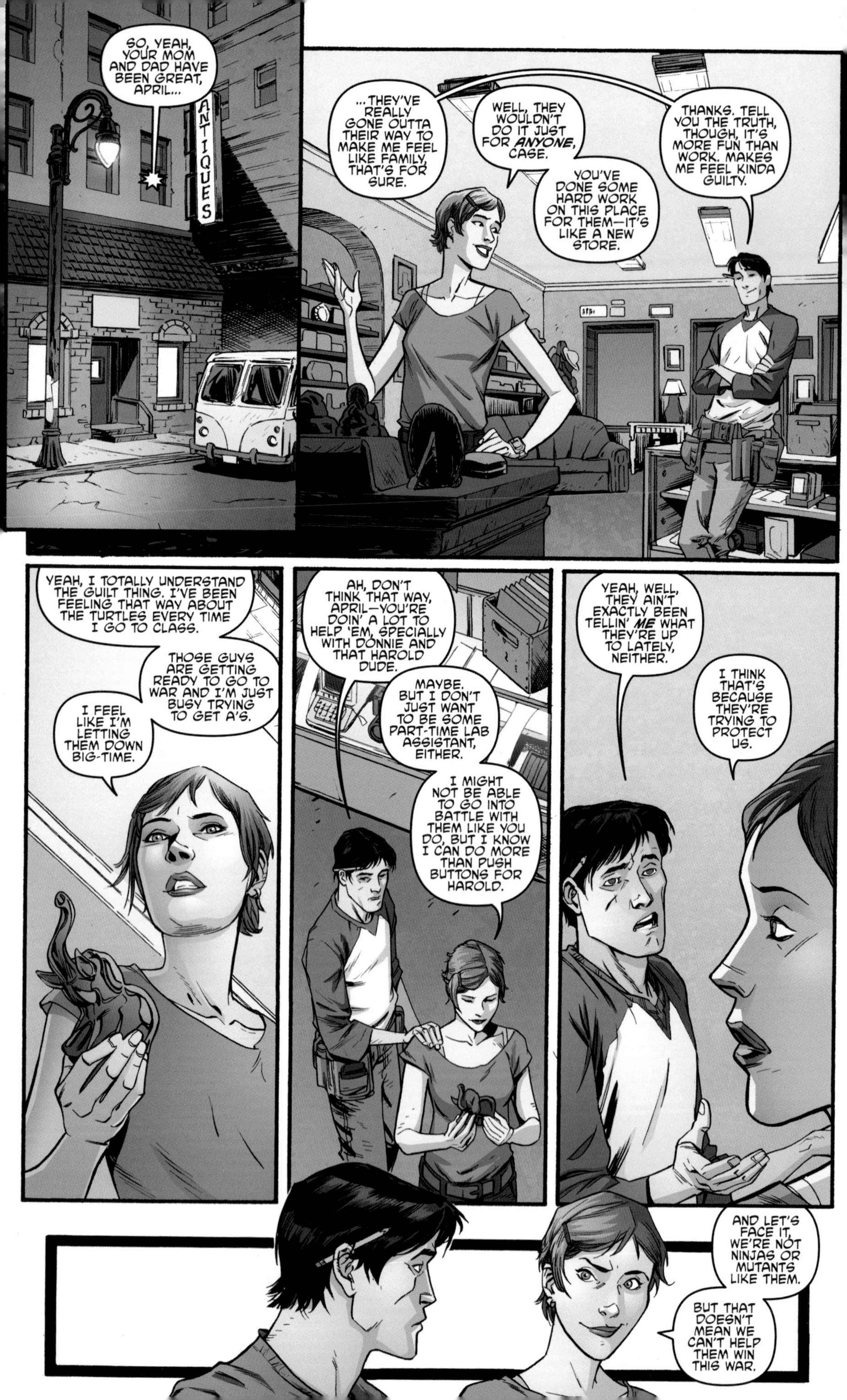

SO, YEAH, YOUR MOM AND DAD HAVE BEEN GREAT, APRIL...
ANTIQUES
...THEY'VE REALLY GONE OUTTA THEIR WAY TO MAKE ME FEEL LIKE FAMILY, THAT'S FOR SURE.
WELL, THEY WOULDN'T DO IT JUST FOR ANYONE, CASE.
YOU'VE DONE SOME HARD WORK ON THIS PLACE FOR THEM—IT'S LIKE A NEW STORE.
THANKS. TELL YOU THE TRUTH, THOUGH, IT'S MORE FUN THAN WORK. MAKES ME FEEL KINDA GUILTY.
YEAH, I TOTALLY UNDERSTAND THE GUILT THING. I'VE BEEN FEELING THAT WAY ABOUT THE TURTLES EVERY TIME I GO TO CLASS.
THOSE GUYS ARE GETTING READY TO GO TO WAR AND I'M JUST BUSY TRYING TO GET A'S.
I FEEL LIKE I'M LETTING THEM DOWN BIG-TIME.
AH, DON'T THINK THAT WAY, APRIL—YOU'RE DOIN' A LOT TO HELP 'EM, SPECIALLY WITH DONNIE AND THAT HAROLD DUDE.
MAYBE. BUT I DON'T JUST WANT TO BE SOME PART-TIME LAB ASSISTANT, EITHER.
I MIGHT NOT BE ABLE TO GO INTO BATTLE WITH THEM LIKE YOU DO, BUT I KNOW I CAN DO MORE THAN PUSH BUTTONS FOR HAROLD.
YEAH, WELL, THEY AIN'T EXACTLY BEEN TELLIN' ME WHAT THEY'RE UP TO LATELY, NEITHER.
I THINK THAT'S BECAUSE THEY'RE TRYING TO PROTECT US.
AND LET'S FACE IT, WE'RE NOT NINJAS OR MUTANTS LIKE THEM.
BUT THAT DOESN'T MEAN WE CAN'T HELP THEM WIN THIS WAR.

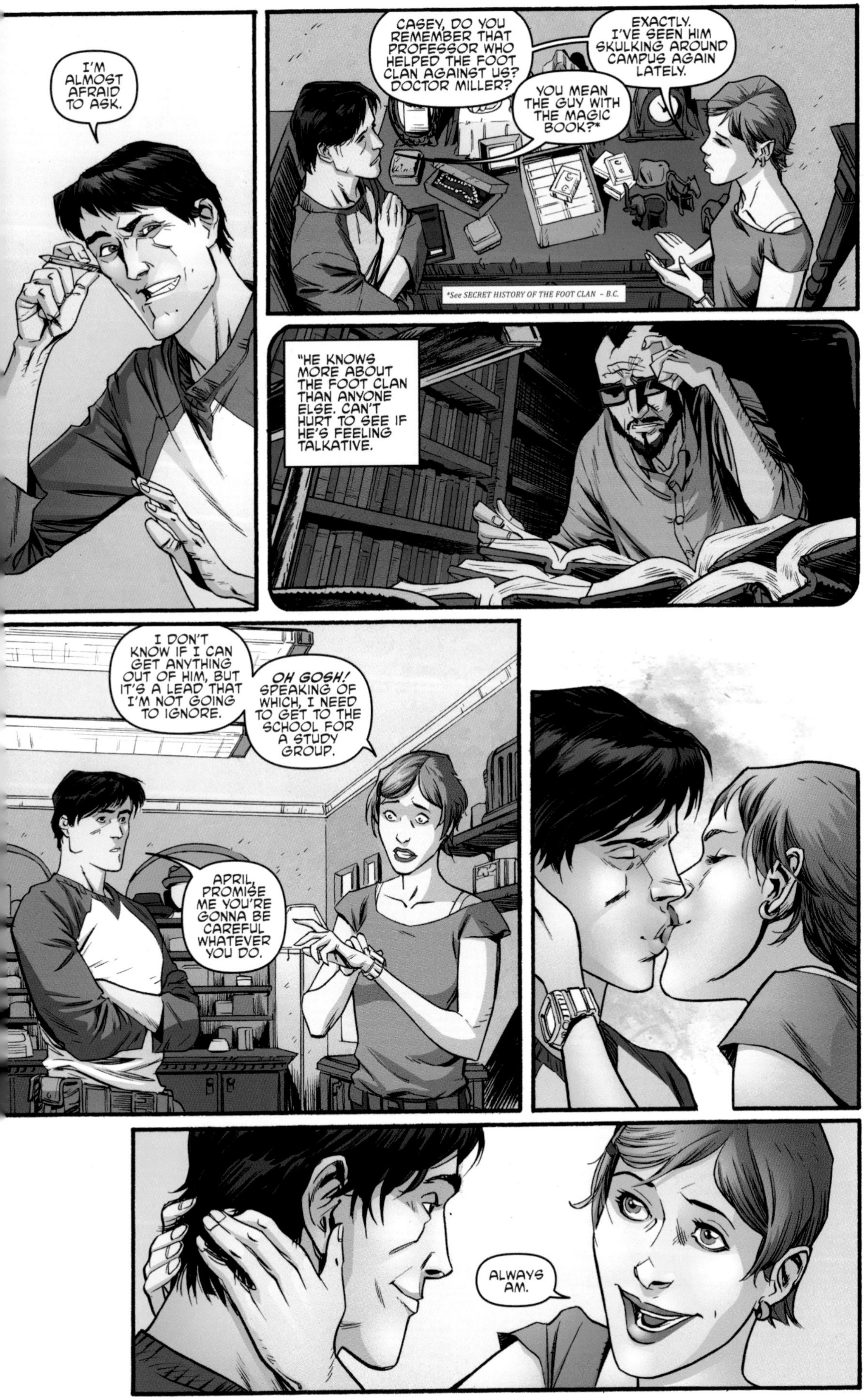
I'M ALMOST AFRAID TO ASK.
CASEY, DO YOU REMEMBER THAT PROFESSOR WHO HELPED THE FOOT CLAN AGAINST US? DOCTOR MILLER?
YOU MEAN THE GUY WITH THE MAGIC BOOK?*
EXACTLY. I'VE SEEN HIM SKULKING AROUND CAMPUS AGAIN LATELY.
*See SECRET HISTORY OF THE FOOT CLAN – B.C.
"HE KNOWS MORE ABOUT THE FOOT CLAN THAN ANYONE ELSE. CAN'T HURT TO SEE IF HE'S FEELING TALKATIVE.
I DON'T KNOW IF I CAN GET ANYTHING OUT OF HIM, BUT IT'S A LEAD THAT I'M NOT GOING TO IGNORE.
OH GOSH! SPEAKING OF WHICH, I NEED TO GET TO THE SCHOOL FOR A STUDY GROUP.
APRIL, PROMISE ME YOU'RE GONNA BE CAREFUL WHATEVER YOU DO.
ALWAYS AM.

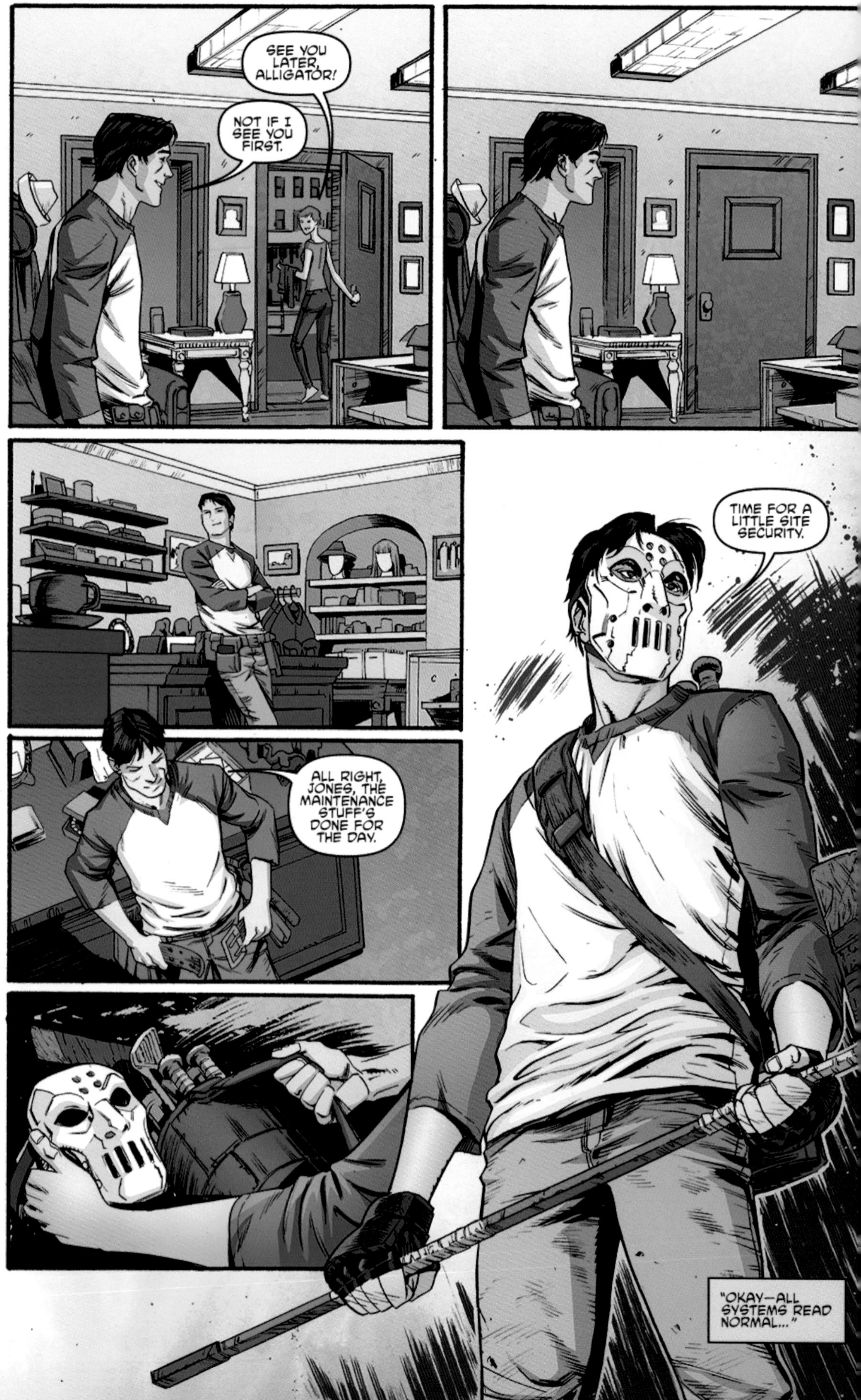
NOT IF I SEE YOU FIRST.
SEE YOU LATER, ALLIGATOR!
ALL RIGHT, JONES, THE MAINTENANCE STUFF'S DONE FOR THE DAY.
TIME FOR A LITTLE SITE SECURITY.
"OKAY—ALL SYSTEMS READ NORMAL..."

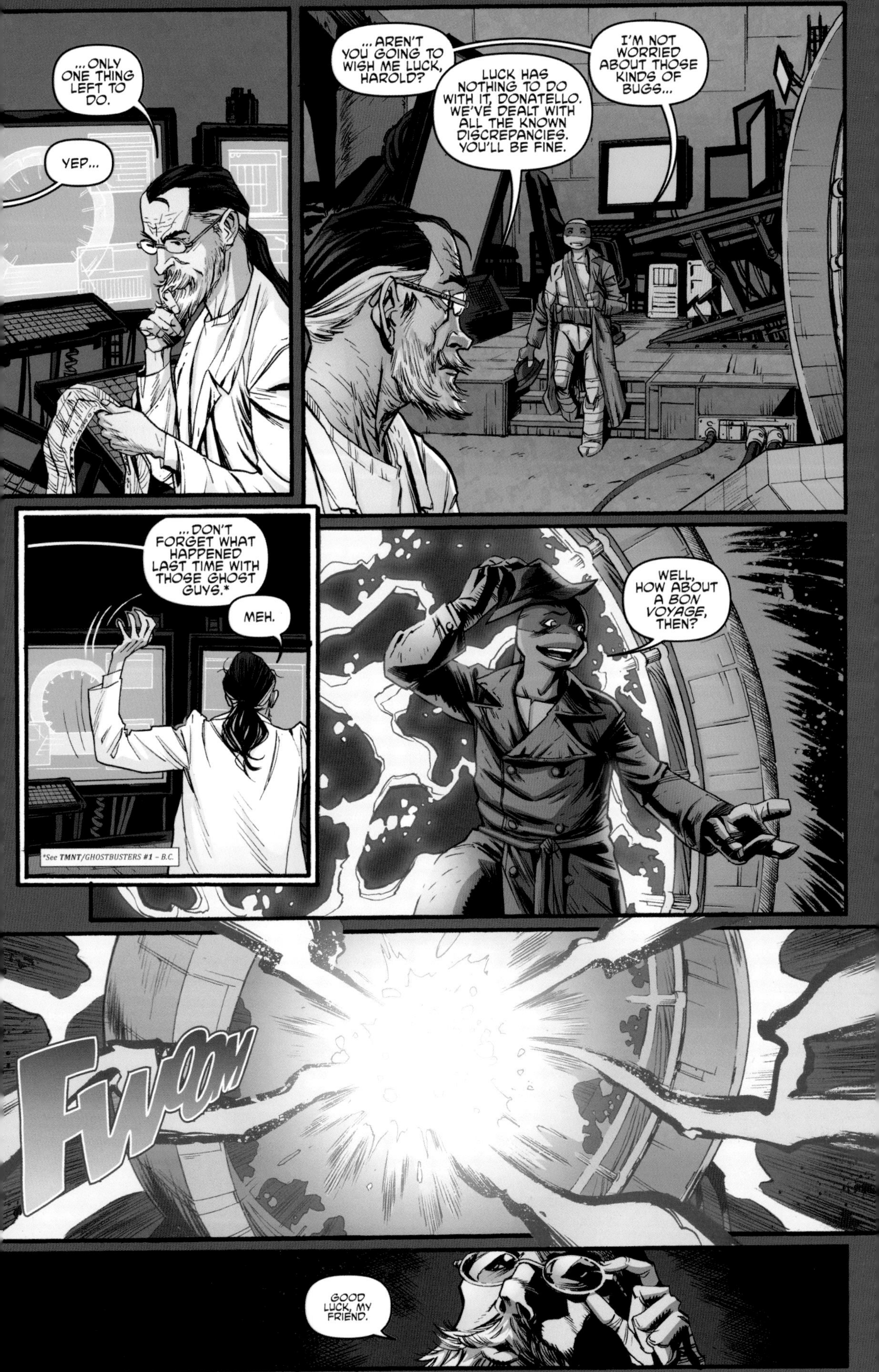
...ONLY ONE THING LEFT TO DO.
YEP...
...AREN'T YOU GOING TO WISH ME LUCK, HAROLD?
LUCK HAS NOTHING TO DO WITH IT, DONATELLO. WE'VE DEALT WITH ALL THE KNOWN DISCREPANCIES. YOU'LL BE FINE.
I'M NOT WORRIED ABOUT THOSE KINDS OF BUGS...
...DON'T FORGET WHAT HAPPENED LAST TIME WITH THOSE GHOST GUYS.*
MEH.
*See TMNT/GHOSTBUSTERS #1 – B.C.
WELL, HOW ABOUT A BON VOYAGE, THEN?
FWOOM
GOOD LUCK, MY FRIEND.

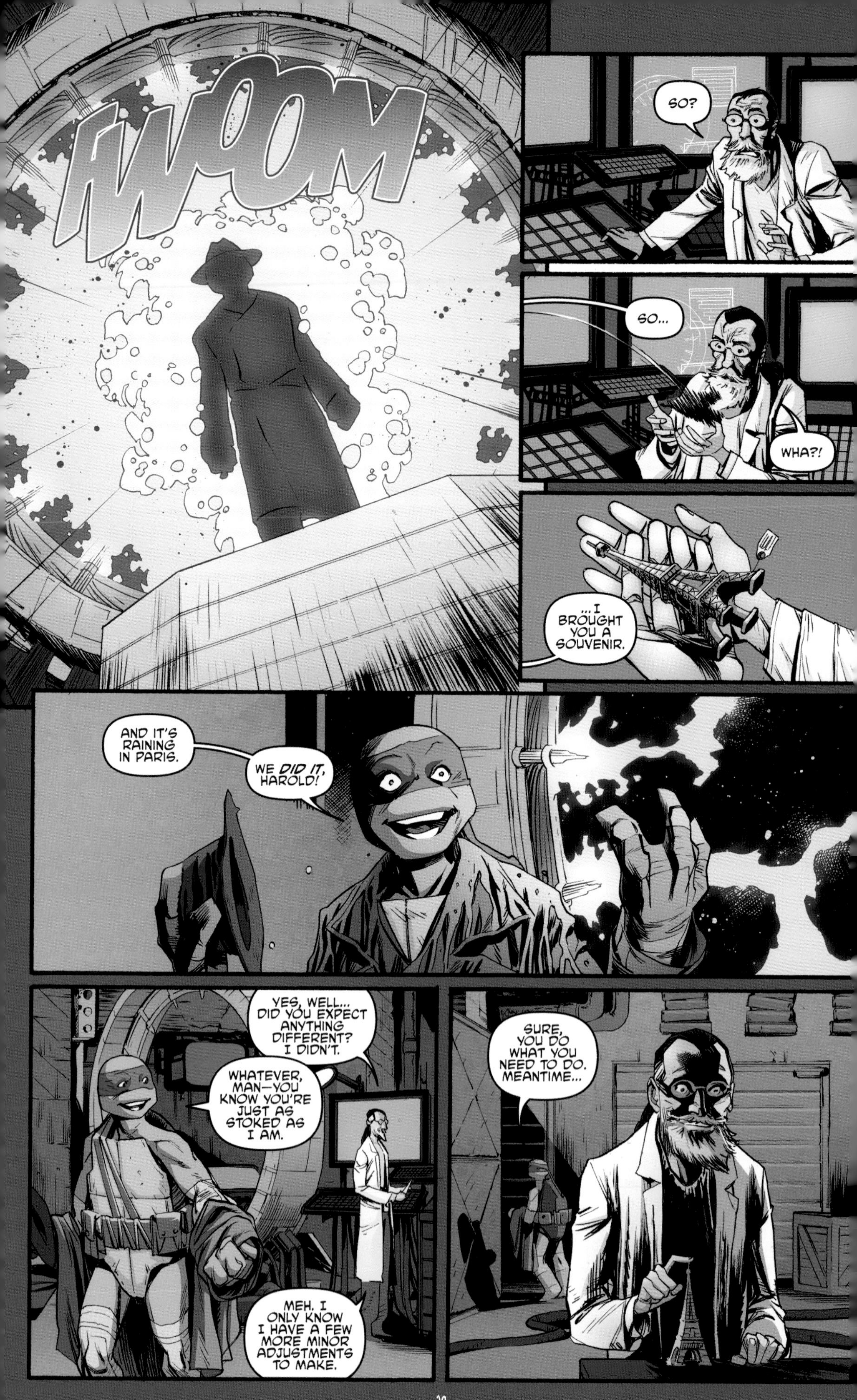
FWOOM
SO?
SO...
WHA?!
...I BROUGHT YOU A SOUVENIR.
AND IT'S RAINING IN PARIS.
WE DID IT, HAROLD!
YES, WELL... DID YOU EXPECT ANYTHING DIFFERENT? I DIDN'T.
WHATEVER, MAN—YOU KNOW YOU'RE JUST AS STOKED AS I AM.
MEH. I ONLY KNOW I HAVE A FEW MORE MINOR ADJUSTMENTS TO MAKE.
SURE, YOU DO WHAT YOU NEED TO DO. MEANTIME...

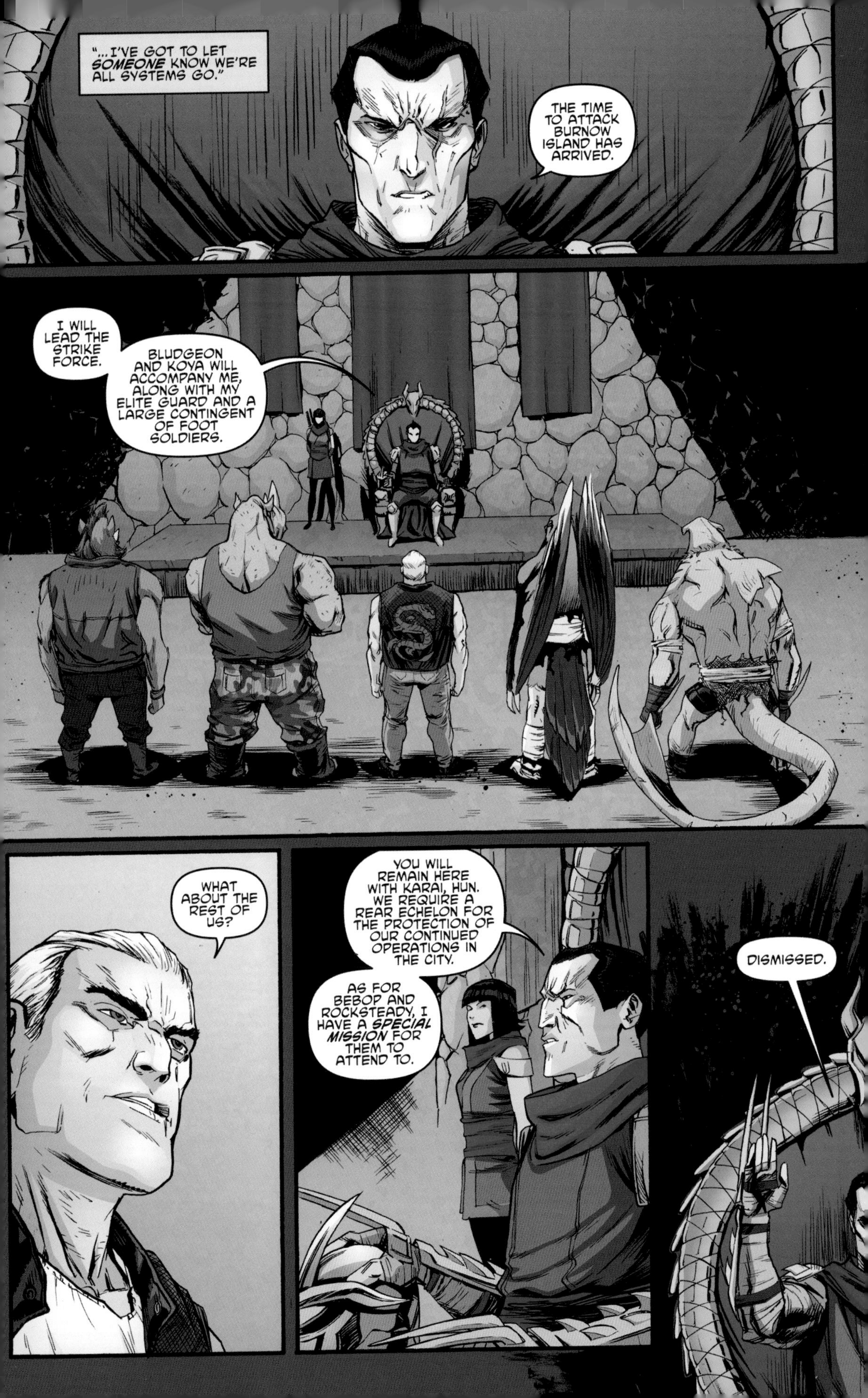
"...I'VE GOT TO LET SOMEONE KNOW WE'RE ALL SYSTEMS GO."
THE TIME TO ATTACK BURNOW ISLAND HAS ARRIVED.
I WILL LEAD THE STRIKE FORCE.
BLUDGEON AND KOYA WILL ACCOMPANY ME, ALONG WITH MY ELITE GUARD AND A LARGE CONTINGENT OF FOOT SOLDIERS.
WHAT ABOUT THE REST OF US?
YOU WILL REMAIN HERE WITH KARAI, HUN. WE REQUIRE A REAR ECHELON FOR THE PROTECTION OF OUR CONTINUED OPERATIONS IN THE CITY.
AS FOR BEBOP AND ROCKSTEADY, I HAVE A SPECIAL MISSION FOR THEM TO ATTEND TO.
DISMISSED.

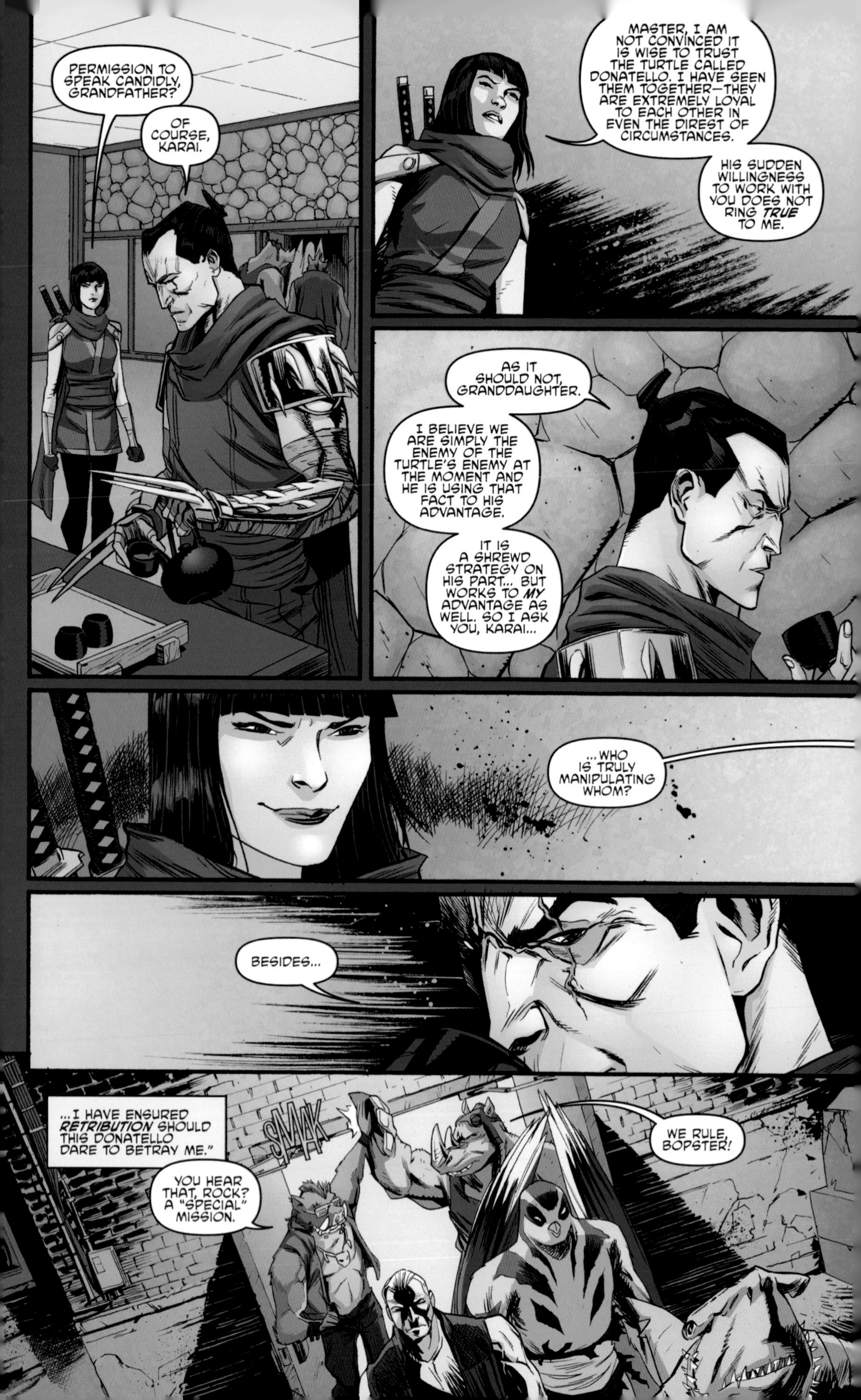
PERMISSION TO SPEAK CANDIDLY, GRANDFATHER?
OF COURSE, KARAI.
MASTER, I AM NOT CONVINCED IT IS WISE TO TRUST THE TURTLE CALLED DONATELLO. I HAVE SEEN THEM TOGETHER—THEY ARE EXTREMELY LOYAL TO EACH OTHER IN EVEN THE DIREST OF CIRCUMSTANCES.
HIS SUDDEN WILLINGNESS TO WORK WITH YOU DOES NOT RING *TRUE* TO ME.
AS IT SHOULD NOT, GRANDDAUGHTER.
I BELIEVE WE ARE SIMPLY THE ENEMY OF THE TURTLE'S ENEMY AT THE MOMENT AND HE IS USING THAT FACT TO HIS ADVANTAGE.
IT IS A SHREWD STRATEGY ON HIS PART... BUT WORKS TO *MY* ADVANTAGE AS WELL. SO I ASK YOU, KARAI...
...WHO IS TRULY MANIPULATING WHOM?
BESIDES...
...I HAVE ENSURED *RETRIBUTION* SHOULD THIS DONATELLO DARE TO BETRAY ME."
SKVAAK
WE RULE, BOPSTER!
YOU HEAR THAT, ROCK? A "SPECIAL" MISSION.

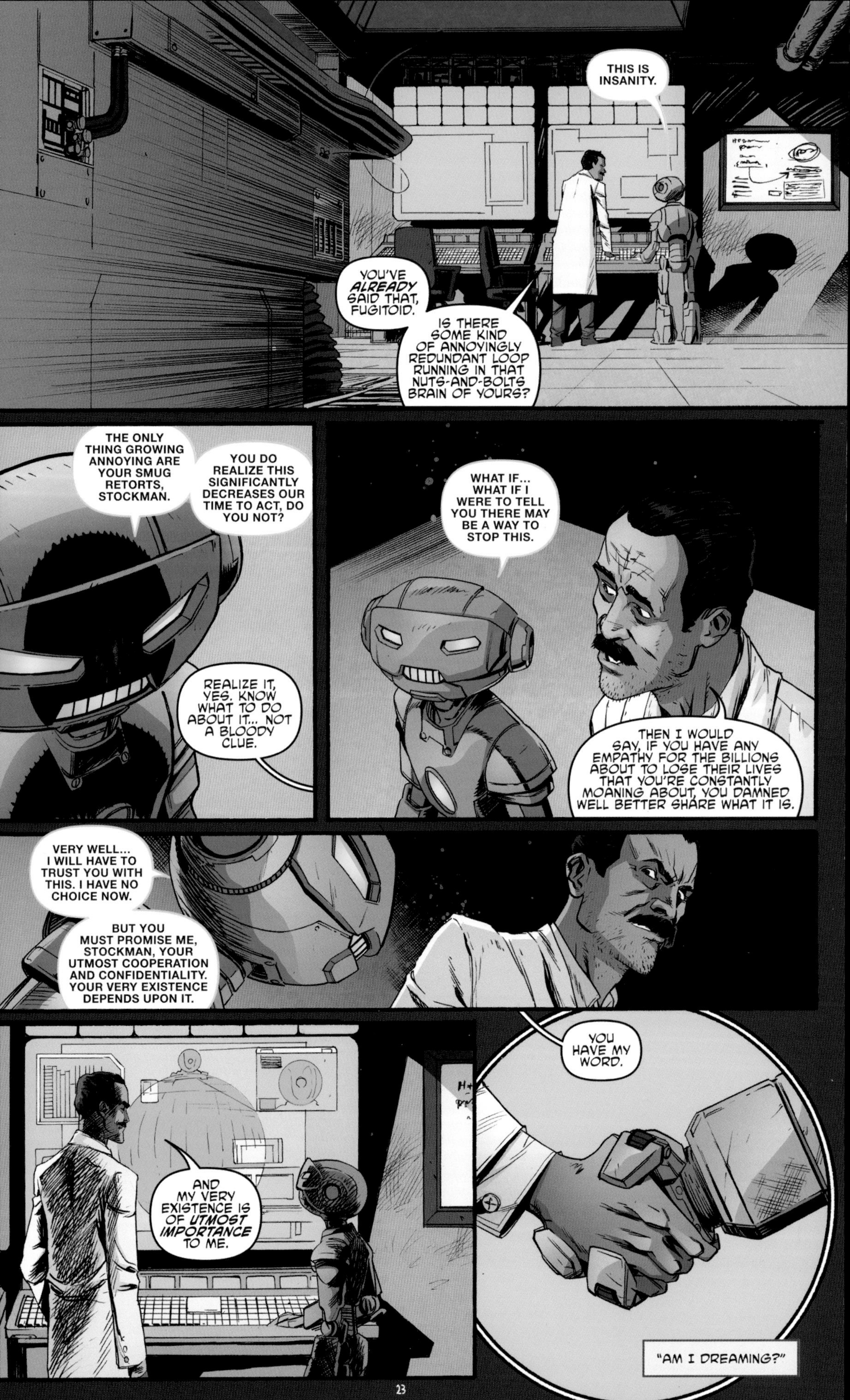
THIS IS INSANITY.
YOU'VE ALREADY SAID THAT, FUGITOID.
IS THERE SOME KIND OF ANNOYINGLY REDUNDANT LOOP RUNNING IN THAT NUTS-AND-BOLTS BRAIN OF YOURS?
THE ONLY THING GROWING ANNOYING ARE YOUR SMUG RETORTS, STOCKMAN.
YOU DO REALIZE THIS SIGNIFICANTLY DECREASES OUR TIME TO ACT, DO YOU NOT?
REALIZE IT, YES. KNOW WHAT TO DO ABOUT IT... NOT A BLOODY CLUE.
WHAT IF... WHAT IF I WERE TO TELL YOU THERE MAY BE A WAY TO STOP THIS.
THEN I WOULD SAY, IF YOU HAVE ANY EMPATHY FOR THE BILLIONS ABOUT TO LOSE THEIR LIVES THAT YOU'RE CONSTANTLY MOANING ABOUT, YOU DAMNED WELL BETTER SHARE WHAT IT IS.
VERY WELL... I WILL HAVE TO TRUST YOU WITH THIS. I HAVE NO CHOICE NOW.
BUT YOU MUST PROMISE ME, STOCKMAN, YOUR UTMOST COOPERATION AND CONFIDENTIALITY. YOUR VERY EXISTENCE DEPENDS UPON IT.
AND MY VERY EXISTENCE IS OF UTMOST IMPORTANCE TO ME.
YOU HAVE MY WORD.
"AM I DREAMING?"

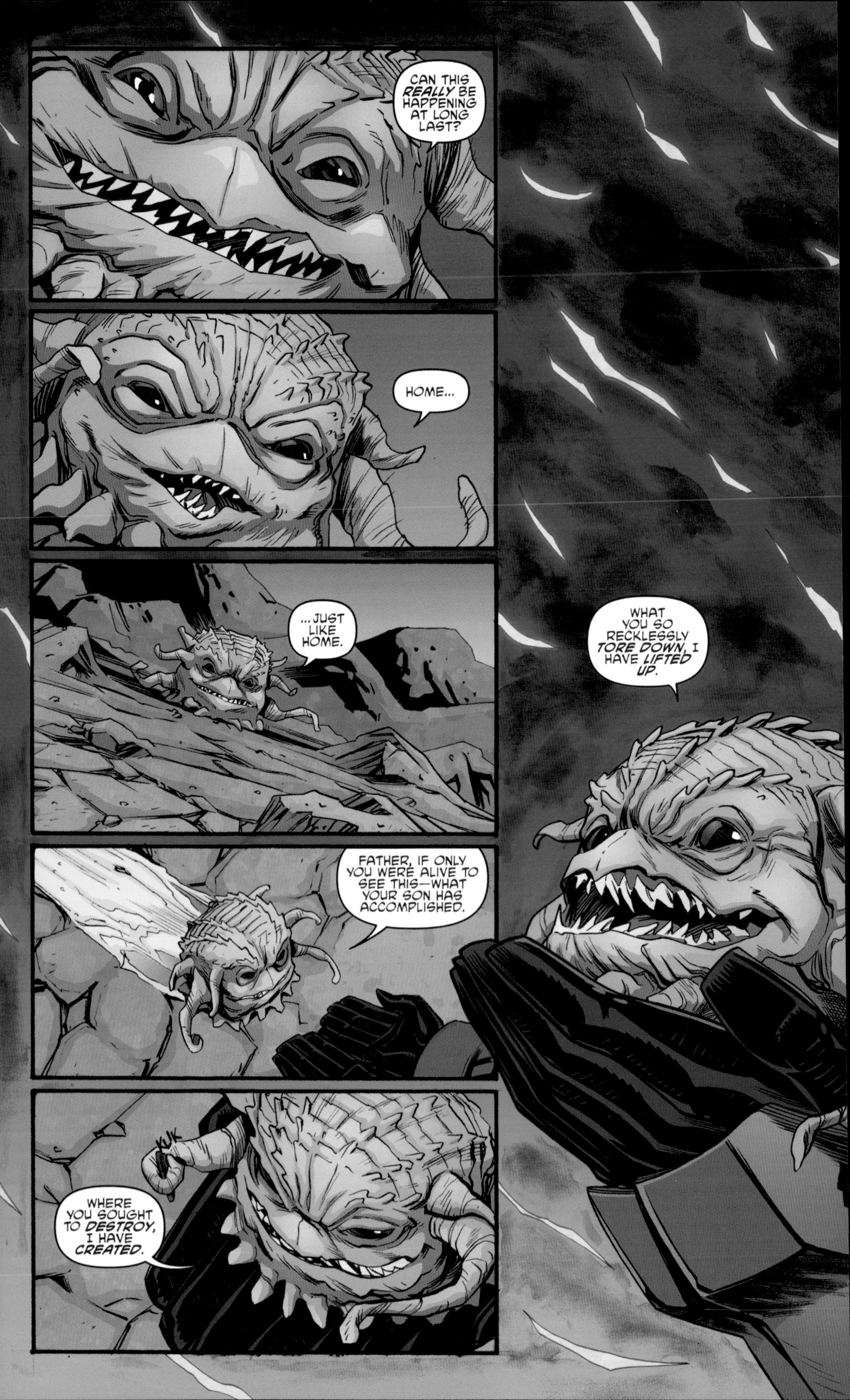
CAN THIS REALLY BE HAPPENING AT LONG LAST?
HOME...
...JUST LIKE HOME.
FATHER, IF ONLY YOU WERE ALIVE TO SEE THIS—WHAT YOUR SON HAS ACCOMPLISHED.
KUK
WHERE YOU SOUGHT TO DESTROY, I HAVE CREATED.
WHAT YOU SO RECKLESSLY TORE DOWN, I HAVE LIFTED UP.

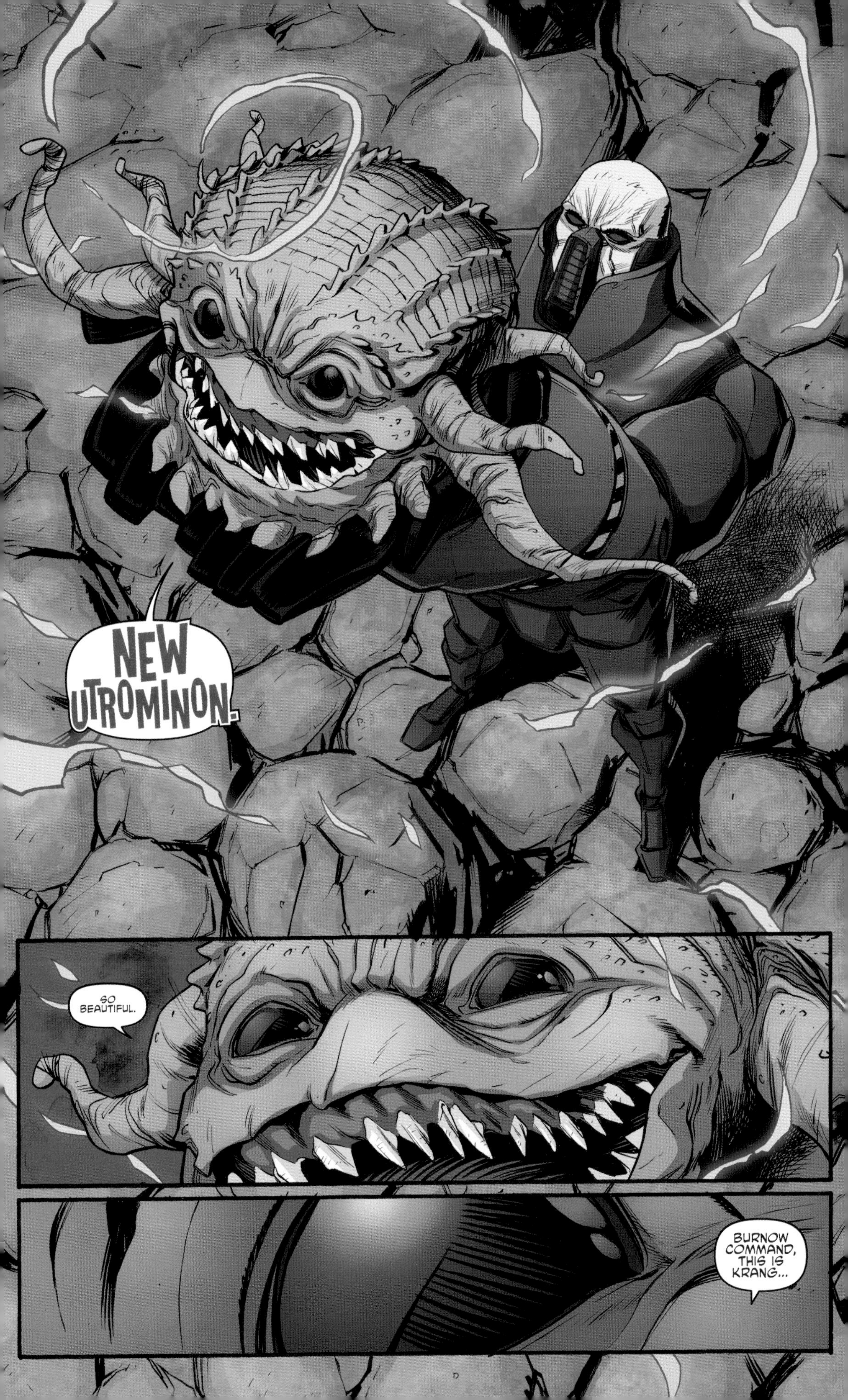
NEW UTROMINON.
SO BEAUTIFUL.
BURNOW COMMAND, THIS IS KRANG...

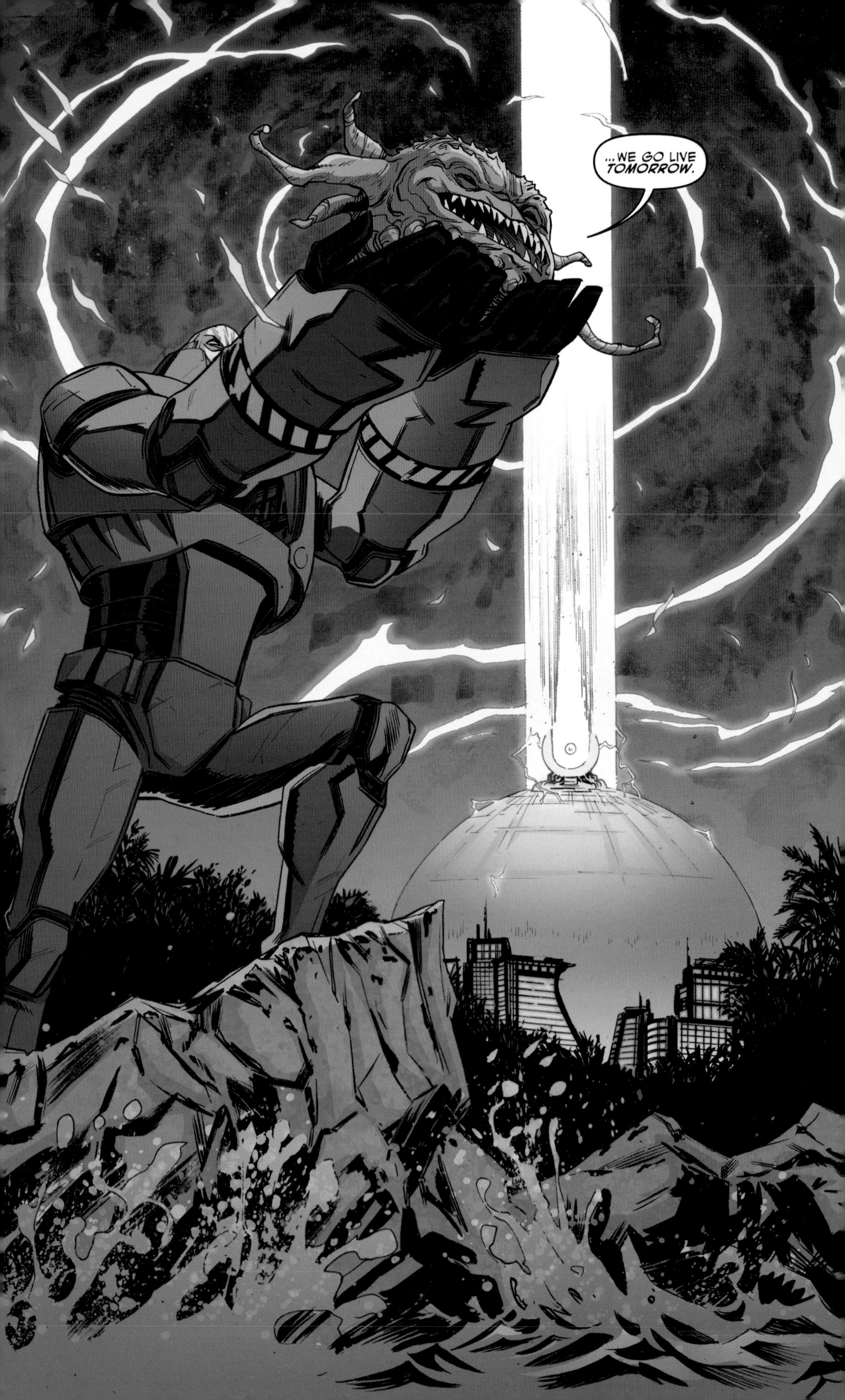
...WE GO LIVE TOMORROW.

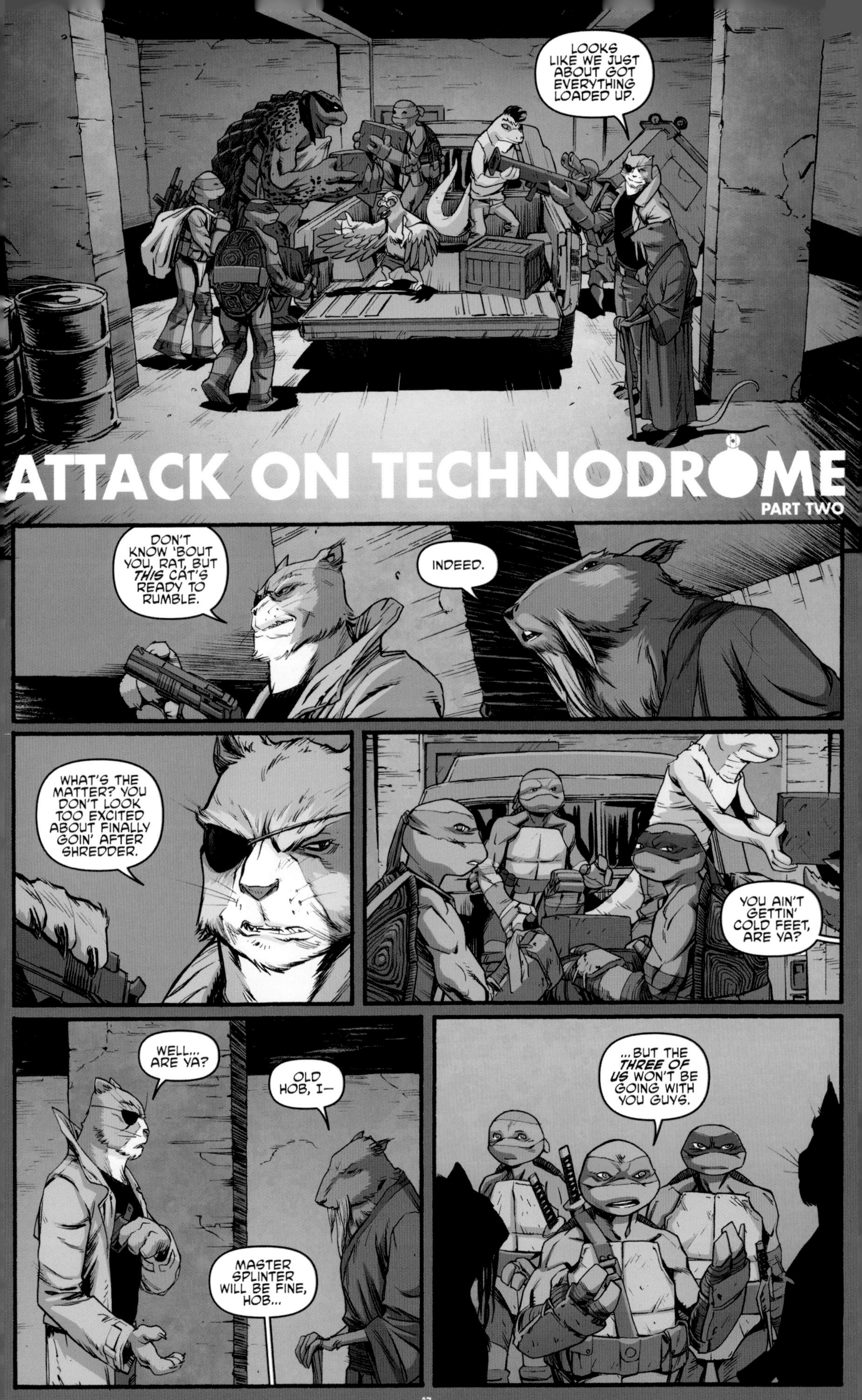
LOOKS LIKE WE JUST ABOUT GOT EVERYTHING LOADED UP.
ATTACK ON TECHNODROME
PART TWO
DON'T KNOW 'BOUT YOU, RAT, BUT THIS CAT'S READY TO RUMBLE.
INDEED.
WHAT'S THE MATTER? YOU DON'T LOOK TOO EXCITED ABOUT FINALLY GOIN' AFTER SHREDDER.
YOU AIN'T GETTIN' COLD FEET, ARE YA?
WELL... ARE YA?
OLD HOB, I—
MASTER SPLINTER WILL BE FINE, HOB...
...BUT THE THREE OF US WON'T BE GOING WITH YOU GUYS.

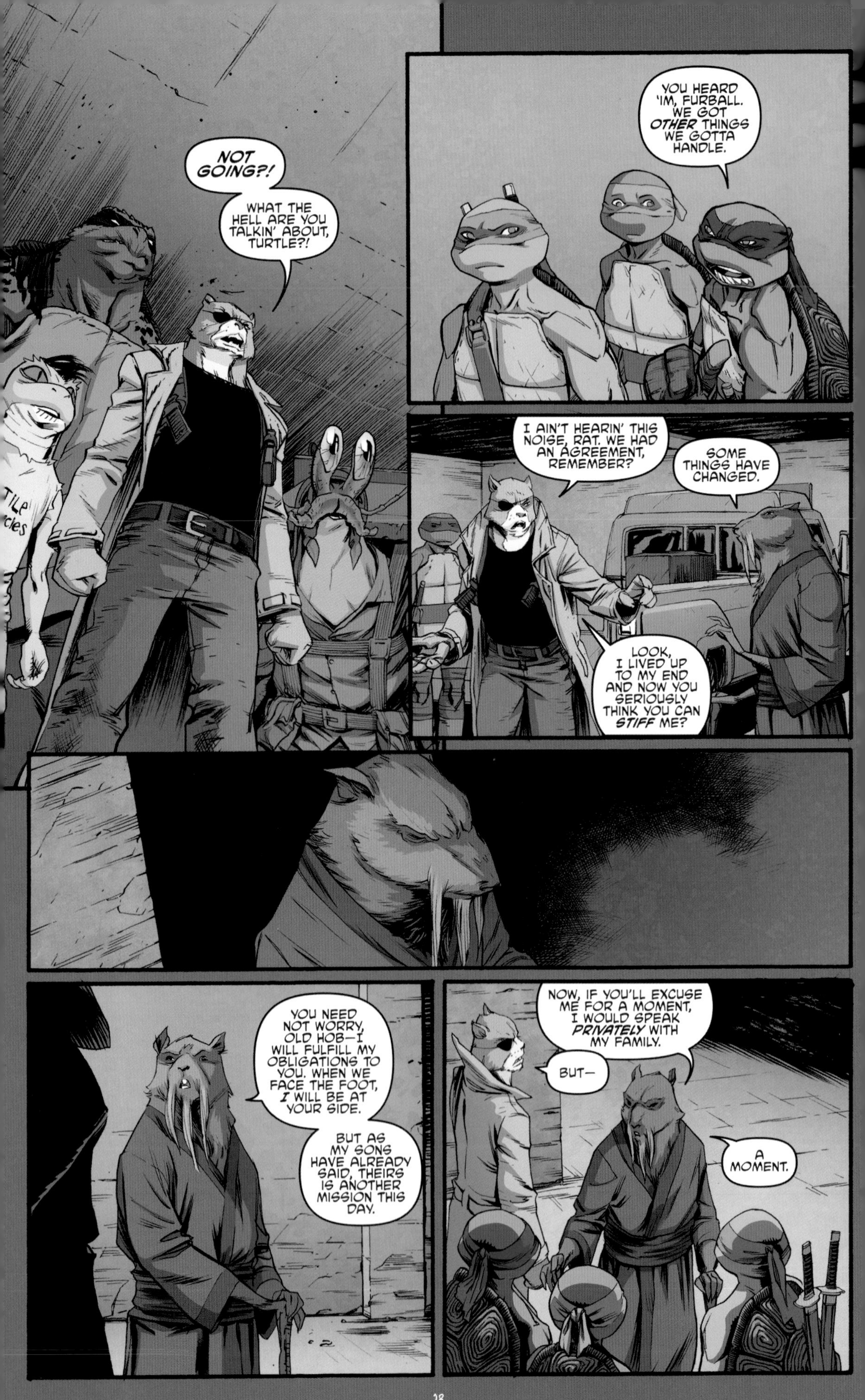
NOT GOING?!
WHAT THE HELL ARE YOU TALKIN' ABOUT, TURTLE?!
YOU HEARD 'IM, FURBALL. WE GOT *OTHER* THINGS WE GOTTA HANDLE.
I AIN'T HEARIN' THIS NOISE, RAT. WE HAD AN AGREEMENT, REMEMBER?
SOME THINGS HAVE CHANGED.
LOOK, I LIVED UP TO MY END AND NOW YOU SERIOUSLY THINK YOU CAN *STIFF* ME?
YOU NEED NOT WORRY, OLD HOB—I WILL FULFILL MY OBLIGATIONS TO YOU. WHEN WE FACE THE FOOT, *I* WILL BE AT YOUR SIDE.
BUT AS MY SONS HAVE ALREADY SAID, THEIRS IS ANOTHER MISSION THIS DAY.
NOW, IF YOU'LL EXCUSE ME FOR A MOMENT, I WOULD SPEAK *PRIVATELY* WITH MY FAMILY.
BUT—
A MOMENT.

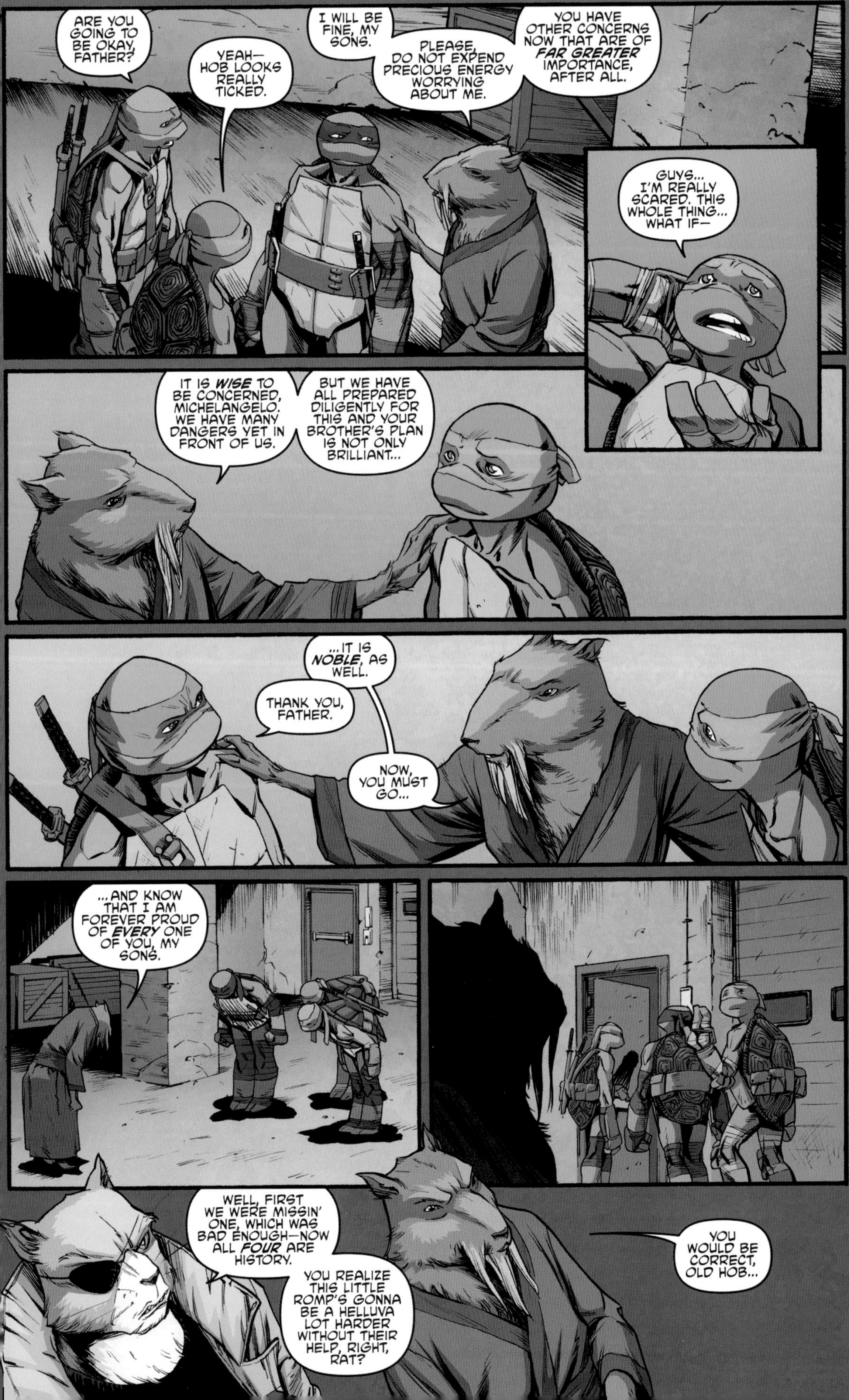

ARE YOU GOING TO BE OKAY, FATHER?
YEAH— HOB LOOKS REALLY TICKED.
I WILL BE FINE, MY SONS.
PLEASE, DO NOT EXPEND PRECIOUS ENERGY WORRYING ABOUT ME.
YOU HAVE OTHER CONCERNS NOW THAT ARE OF FAR GREATER IMPORTANCE, AFTER ALL.
GUYS... I'M REALLY SCARED. THIS WHOLE THING... WHAT IF—
IT IS WISE TO BE CONCERNED, MICHELANGELO. WE HAVE MANY DANGERS YET IN FRONT OF US.
BUT WE HAVE ALL PREPARED DILIGENTLY FOR THIS AND YOUR BROTHER'S PLAN IS NOT ONLY BRILLIANT...
...IT IS NOBLE, AS WELL.
THANK YOU, FATHER.
NOW, YOU MUST GO...
...AND KNOW THAT I AM FOREVER PROUD OF EVERY ONE OF YOU, MY SONS.
WELL, FIRST WE WERE MISSIN' ONE, WHICH WAS BAD ENOUGH—NOW ALL FOUR ARE HISTORY.
YOU REALIZE THIS LITTLE ROMP'S GONNA BE A HELLUVA LOT HARDER WITHOUT THEIR HELP, RIGHT, RAT?
YOU WOULD BE CORRECT, OLD HOB...

"...IF IT WERE *TRUE* THAT MY SONS ARE NO LONGER HELPING US."

GENERAL KRANG, MUCH AS I HATE TO INTERRUPT YOUR REVERIE...

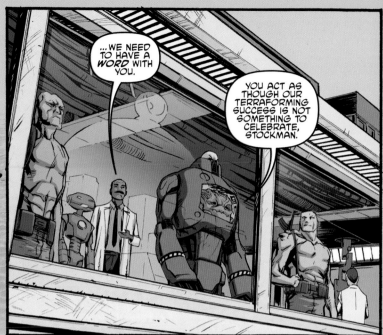

...WE NEED TO HAVE A *WORD* WITH YOU.

YOU ACT AS THOUGH OUR TERRAFORMING SUCCESS IS NOT SOMETHING TO CELEBRATE, STOCKMAN.

VERY WELL, BUT MAKE IT QUICK. I WANT TO INITIATE THE FINAL PHASE SOON, SO SPEAK NOW WHILE YOU *STILL* CAN.

AS ALWAYS, YOU RADIATE BENEVOLENCE, GENERAL.

WELL, FUGITOID... HE'S LISTENING. TELL HIM.

I... THAT IS... I...

AGAIN, I SUGGEST YOU SPEAK *NOW*, HONEYCUTT. YOU MAY NOT HAVE THE OPPORTUNITY LATER.

I HAVE INTELLIGENCE THAT SHREDDER AND THE FOOT ARE ATTACKING THE ISLAND TODAY!

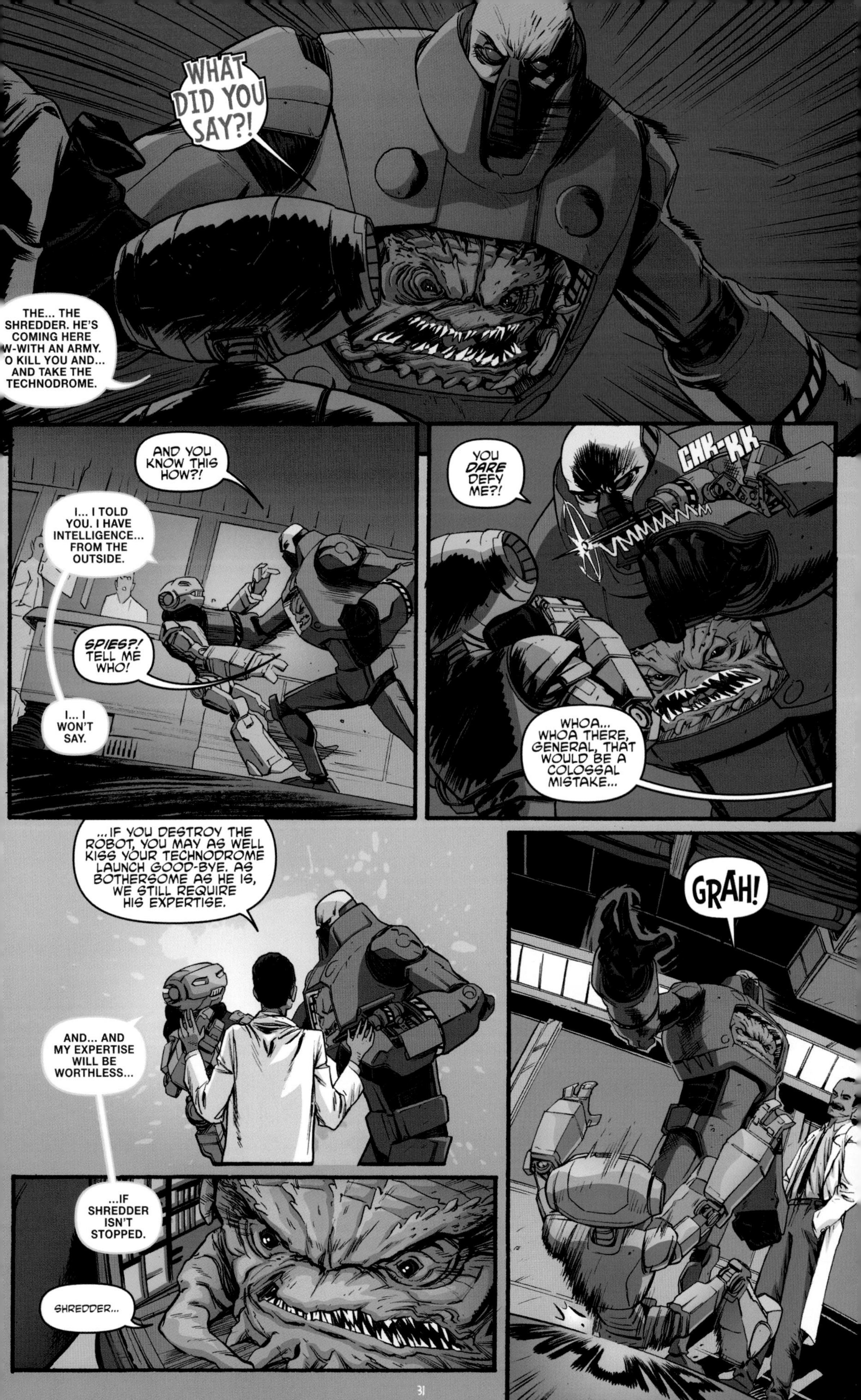
WHAT DID YOU SAY?!
THE... THE SHREDDER. HE'S COMING HERE W-WITH AN ARMY. O KILL YOU AND... AND TAKE THE TECHNODROME.
AND YOU KNOW THIS HOW?!
I... I TOLD YOU. I HAVE INTELLIGENCE... FROM THE OUTSIDE.
SPIES?! TELL ME WHO!
I... I WON'T SAY.
YOU DARE DEFY ME?!
CHK-KK
WHOA... WHOA THERE, GENERAL, THAT WOULD BE A COLOSSAL MISTAKE...
...IF YOU DESTROY THE ROBOT, YOU MAY AS WELL KISS YOUR TECHNODROME LAUNCH GOOD-BYE. AS BOTHERSOME AS HE IS, WE STILL REQUIRE HIS EXPERTISE.
AND... AND MY EXPERTISE WILL BE WORTHLESS...
...IF SHREDDER ISN'T STOPPED.
SHREDDER...
GRAH!

CAPTAIN TRAGG, PUT OUR FORCES ON FULL ALERT. IF WHAT THIS DAMNED MACHINE CLAIMS IS TRUE, I WANT TO BE SURE WE'RE PREPARED TO CRUSH OUR UNINVITED GUESTS.

I WILL ALLOW *NOTHING* TO STAND IN THE WAY OF MY NEW UTROMINON, LEAST OF ALL THAT BASTARD SAKI.

YES, GENERAL!

GENERAL, IF I MAY, THERE IS SOMETHING ELSE.

WHAT NOW, STOCKMAN?

WELL, AS IT TURNS OUT, OUR FRIEND HONEYCUTT HERE IS NOT THE *ONLY ONE* WITH SPIES, AND I HAVE IT ON GOOD FAITH HE'S MERELY PROVIDING YOU HALF THE STORY.

MEANING?

SHREDDER IS NOT THE ONLY THREAT MAKING ITS WAY TO THE ISLAND.

H-HOW COULD YOU KNOW?

A FLY ON THE WALL, OF COURSE.

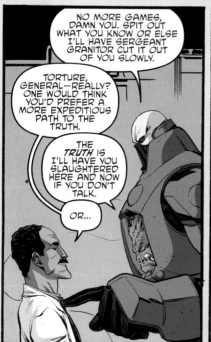

NO MORE GAMES, DAMN YOU. SPIT OUT WHAT YOU KNOW OR ELSE I'LL HAVE SERGEANT GRANITOR CUT IT OUT OF YOU SLOWLY.

TORTURE, GENERAL—REALLY? ONE WOULD THINK YOU'D PREFER A MORE EXPEDITIOUS PATH TO THE TRUTH.

THE *TRUTH* IS I'LL HAVE YOU SLAUGHTERED HERE AND NOW IF YOU DON'T TALK.

OR...

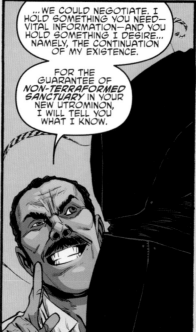

...WE COULD NEGOTIATE. I HOLD SOMETHING YOU NEED—VITAL INFORMATION—AND YOU HOLD SOMETHING I DESIRE... NAMELY, THE CONTINUATION OF MY EXISTENCE.

FOR THE GUARANTEE OF *NON-TERRAFORMED SANCTUARY* IN YOUR NEW UTROMINON, I WILL TELL YOU WHAT I KNOW.

BLASTED HUMAN... FINE! DONE!

YOU WILL HAVE YOUR SANCTUARY. *NOW SPEAK!*

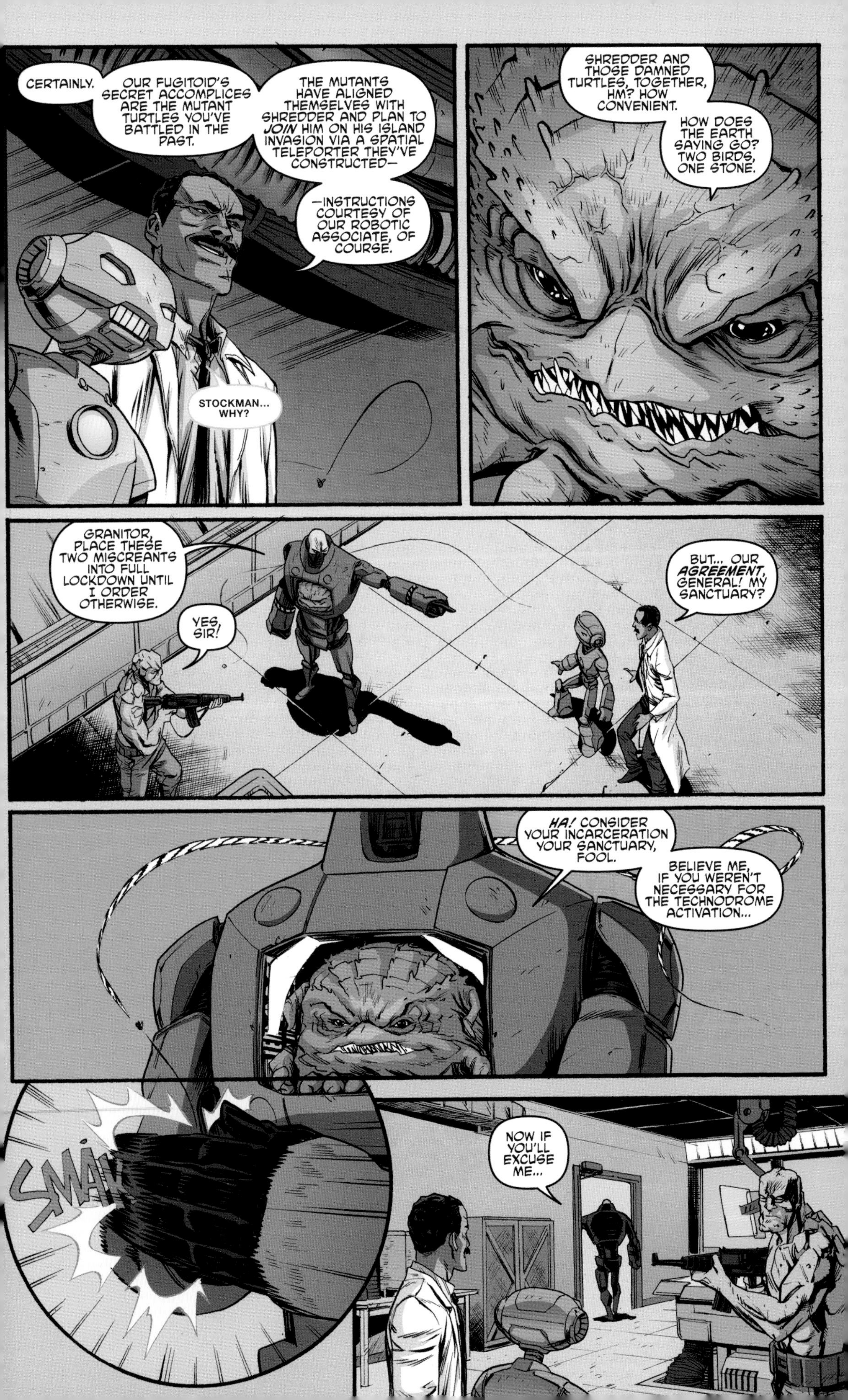
CERTAINLY.
OUR FUGITOID'S SECRET ACCOMPLICES ARE THE MUTANT TURTLES YOU'VE BATTLED IN THE PAST.
THE MUTANTS HAVE ALIGNED THEMSELVES WITH SHREDDER AND PLAN TO JOIN HIM ON HIS ISLAND INVASION VIA A SPATIAL TELEPORTER THEY'VE CONSTRUCTED—
—INSTRUCTIONS COURTESY OF OUR ROBOTIC ASSOCIATE, OF COURSE.
STOCKMAN... WHY?
SHREDDER AND THOSE DAMNED TURTLES, TOGETHER, HM? HOW CONVENIENT.
HOW DOES THE EARTH SAYING GO? TWO BIRDS, ONE STONE.
GRANITOR, PLACE THESE TWO MISCREANTS INTO FULL LOCKDOWN UNTIL I ORDER OTHERWISE.
YES, SIR!
BUT... OUR AGREEMENT, GENERAL! MY SANCTUARY?
HA! CONSIDER YOUR INCARCERATION YOUR SANCTUARY, FOOL.
BELIEVE ME, IF YOU WEREN'T NECESSARY FOR THE TECHNODROME ACTIVATION...
SMAK
NOW IF YOU'LL EXCUSE ME...

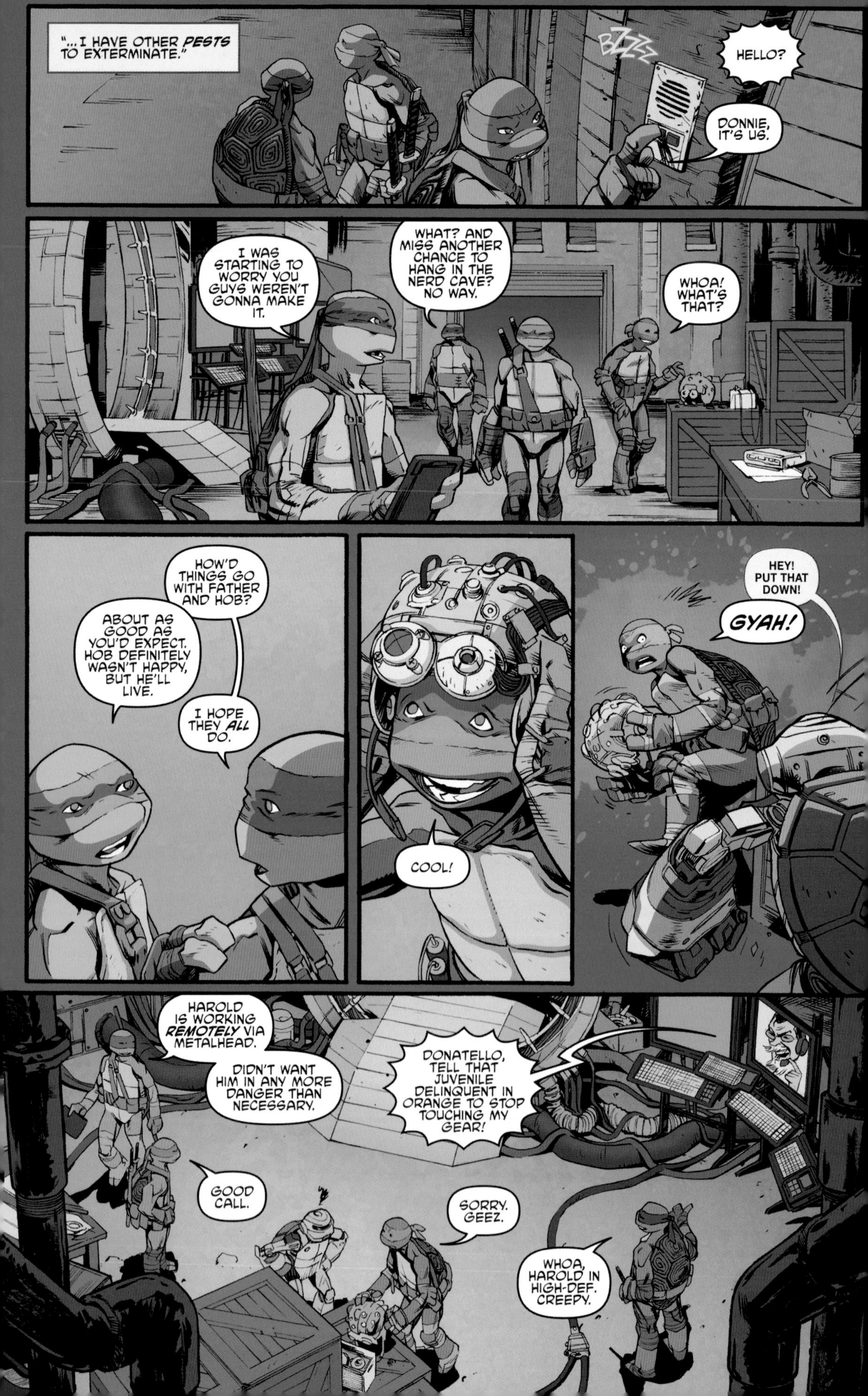
"...I HAVE OTHER PESTS TO EXTERMINATE."
BZZZZ
HELLO?
DONNIE, IT'S US.
I WAS STARTING TO WORRY YOU GUYS WEREN'T GONNA MAKE IT.
WHAT? AND MISS ANOTHER CHANCE TO HANG IN THE NERD CAVE? NO WAY.
WHOA! WHAT'S THAT?
HOW'D THINGS GO WITH FATHER AND HOB?
ABOUT AS GOOD AS YOU'D EXPECT. HOB DEFINITELY WASN'T HAPPY, BUT HE'LL LIVE.
I HOPE THEY ALL DO.
COOL!
HEY! PUT THAT DOWN!
GYAH!
HAROLD IS WORKING REMOTELY VIA METALHEAD.
DIDN'T WANT HIM IN ANY MORE DANGER THAN NECESSARY.
DONATELLO, TELL THAT JUVENILE DELINQUENT IN ORANGE TO STOP TOUCHING MY GEAR!
GOOD CALL.
SORRY. GEEZ.
WHOA, HAROLD IN HIGH-DEF. CREEPY.

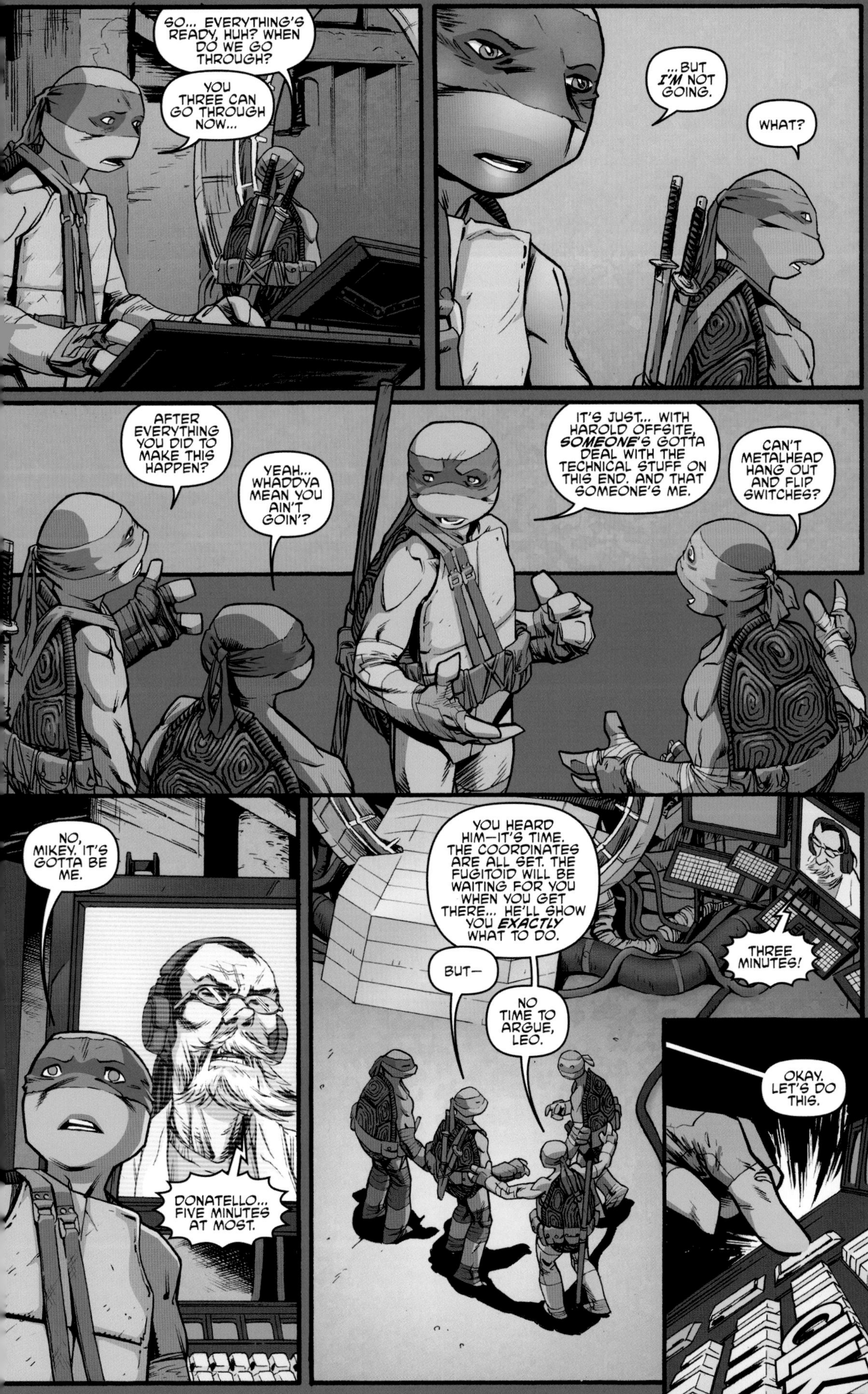
SO... EVERYTHING'S READY, HUH? WHEN DO WE GO THROUGH?
YOU THREE CAN GO THROUGH NOW...
...BUT I'M NOT GOING.
WHAT?
AFTER EVERYTHING YOU DID TO MAKE THIS HAPPEN?
YEAH... WHADDYA MEAN YOU AIN'T GOIN'?
IT'S JUST... WITH HAROLD OFFSITE, SOMEONE'S GOTTA DEAL WITH THE TECHNICAL STUFF ON THIS END. AND THAT SOMEONE'S ME.
CAN'T METALHEAD HANG OUT AND FLIP SWITCHES?
NO, MIKEY. IT'S GOTTA BE ME.
DONATELLO... FIVE MINUTES AT MOST.
YOU HEARD HIM—IT'S TIME. THE COORDINATES ARE ALL SET. THE FUGITOID WILL BE WAITING FOR YOU WHEN YOU GET THERE... HE'LL SHOW YOU EXACTLY WHAT TO DO.
THREE MINUTES!
BUT—
NO TIME TO ARGUE, LEO.
OKAY. LET'S DO THIS.

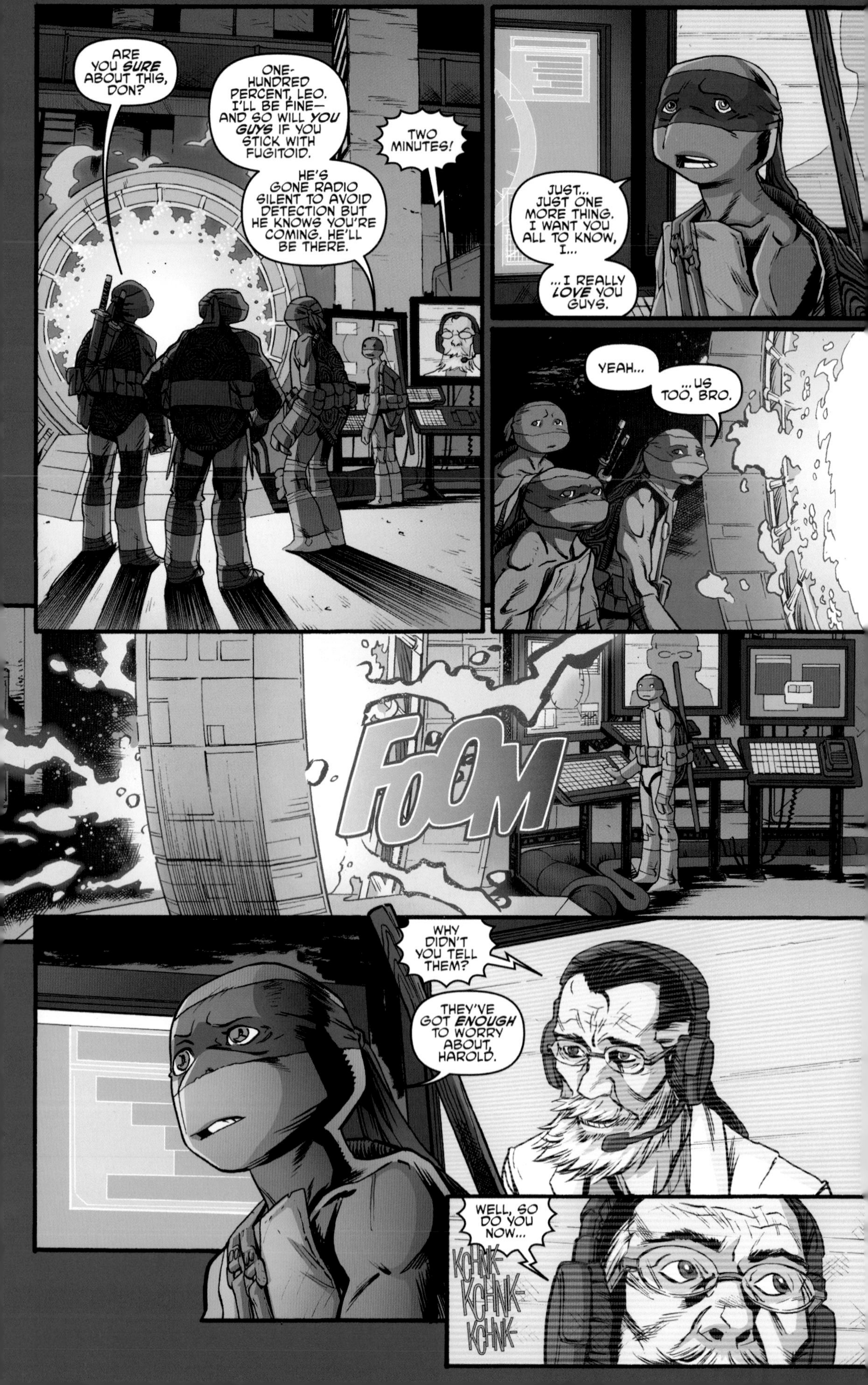

ARE YOU SURE ABOUT THIS, DON?
ONE-HUNDRED PERCENT, LEO. I'LL BE FINE— AND SO WILL YOU GUYS IF YOU STICK WITH FUGITOID.
HE'S GONE RADIO SILENT TO AVOID DETECTION BUT HE KNOWS YOU'RE COMING. HE'LL BE THERE.
TWO MINUTES!
JUST... JUST ONE MORE THING. I WANT YOU ALL TO KNOW, I...
...I REALLY LOVE YOU GUYS.
YEAH...
...US TOO, BRO.
FOOM
WHY DIDN'T YOU TELL THEM?
THEY'VE GOT ENOUGH TO WORRY ABOUT, HAROLD.
WELL, SO DO YOU NOW...
KCHNK-
KCHNK-
KCHNK-

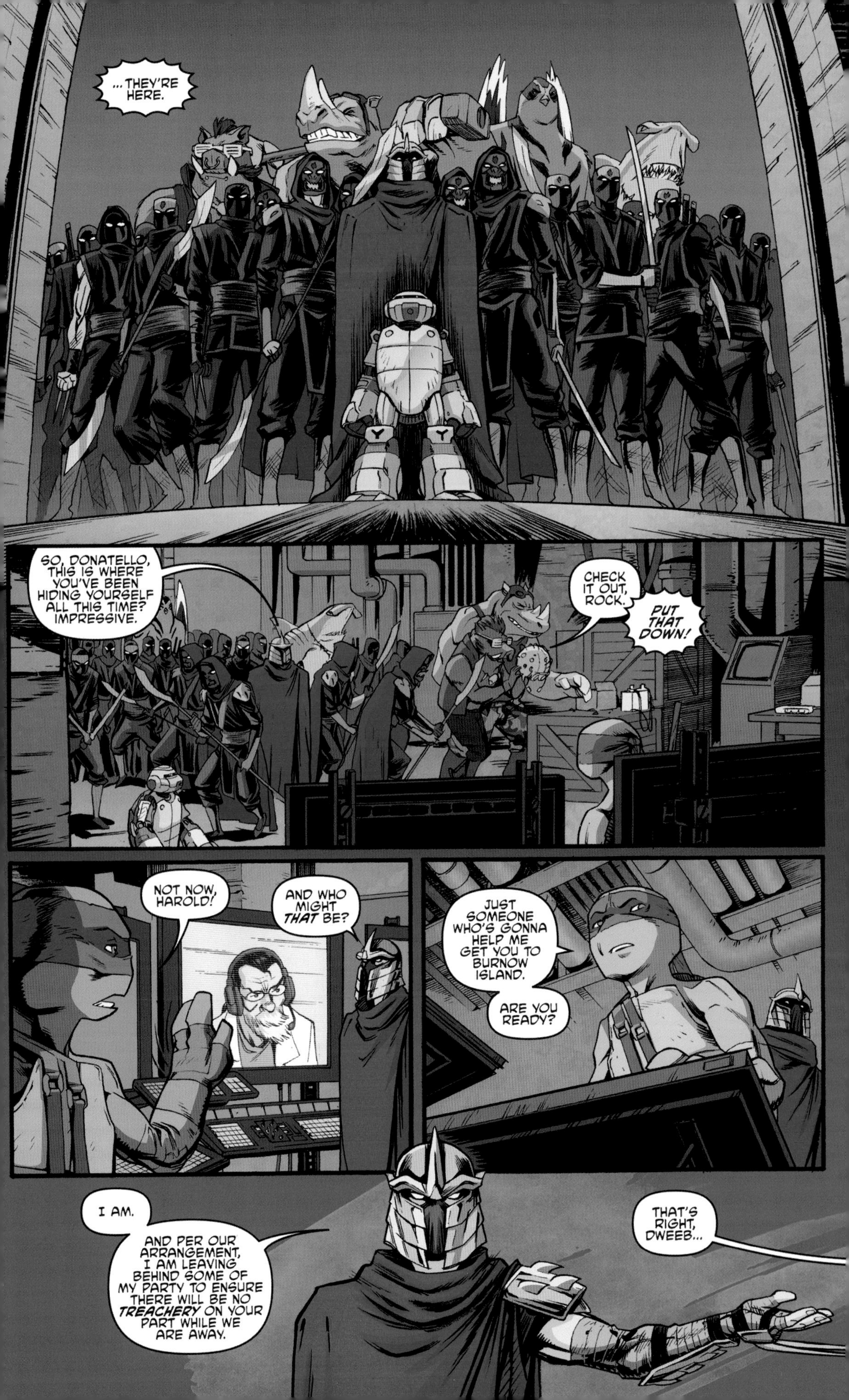

...THEY'RE HERE.
SO, DONATELLO, THIS IS WHERE YOU'VE BEEN HIDING YOURSELF ALL THIS TIME? IMPRESSIVE.
CHECK IT OUT, ROCK.
PUT THAT DOWN!
NOT NOW, HAROLD!
AND WHO MIGHT *THAT* BE?
JUST SOMEONE WHO'S GONNA HELP ME GET YOU TO BURNOW ISLAND.
ARE YOU READY?
I AM.
AND PER OUR ARRANGEMENT, I AM LEAVING BEHIND SOME OF MY PARTY TO ENSURE THERE WILL BE NO *TREACHERY* ON YOUR PART WHILE WE ARE AWAY.
THAT'S RIGHT, DWEEB...

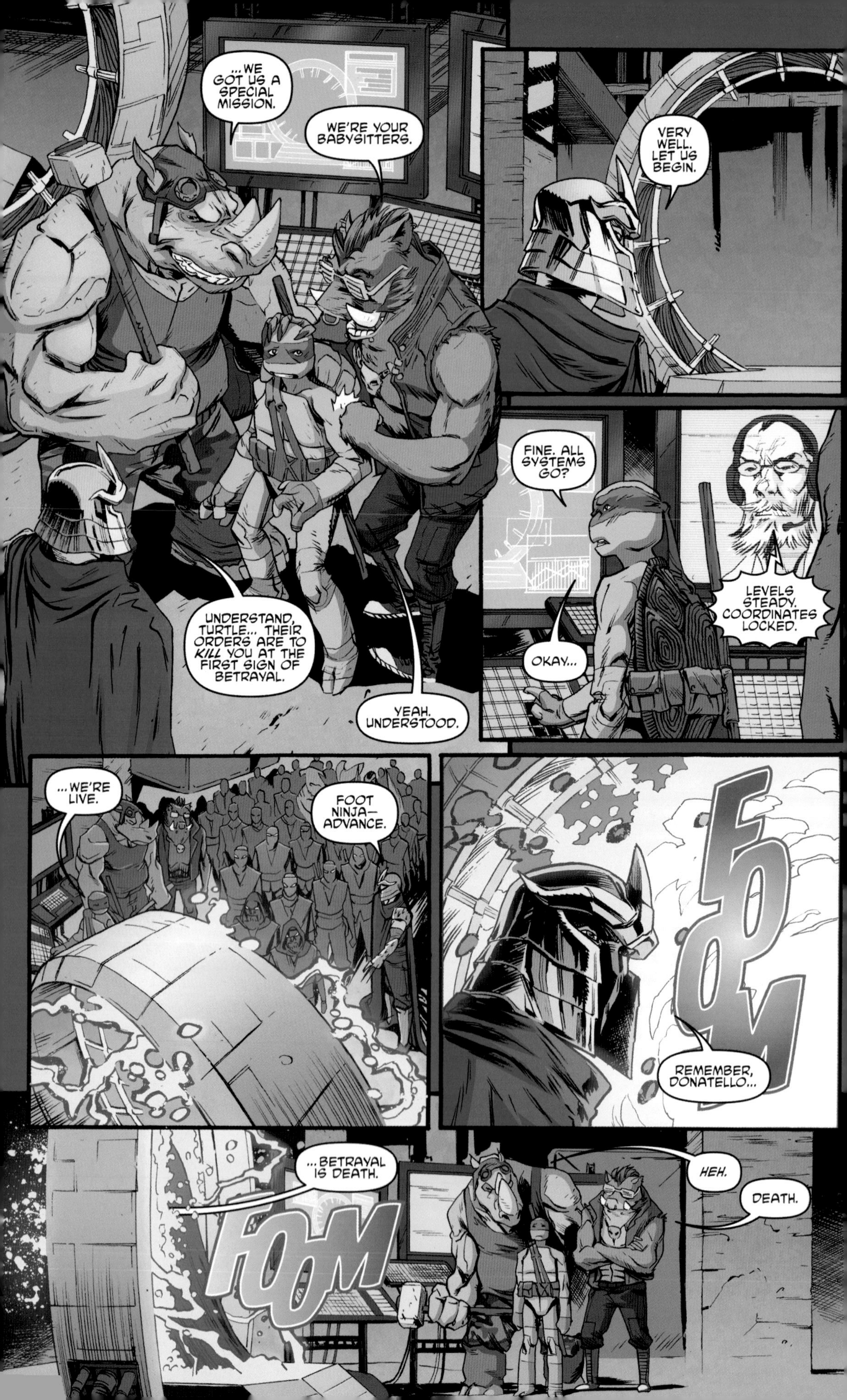
...WE GOT US A SPECIAL MISSION.
WE'RE YOUR BABYSITTERS.
VERY WELL. LET US BEGIN.
UNDERSTAND, TURTLE... THEIR ORDERS ARE TO KILL YOU AT THE FIRST SIGN OF BETRAYAL.
YEAH. UNDERSTOOD.
FINE. ALL SYSTEMS GO?
LEVELS STEADY. COORDINATES LOCKED.
OKAY...
...WE'RE LIVE.
FOOT NINJA— ADVANCE.
FOOM
REMEMBER, DONATELLO...
...BETRAYAL IS DEATH.
FOOM
HEH.
DEATH.

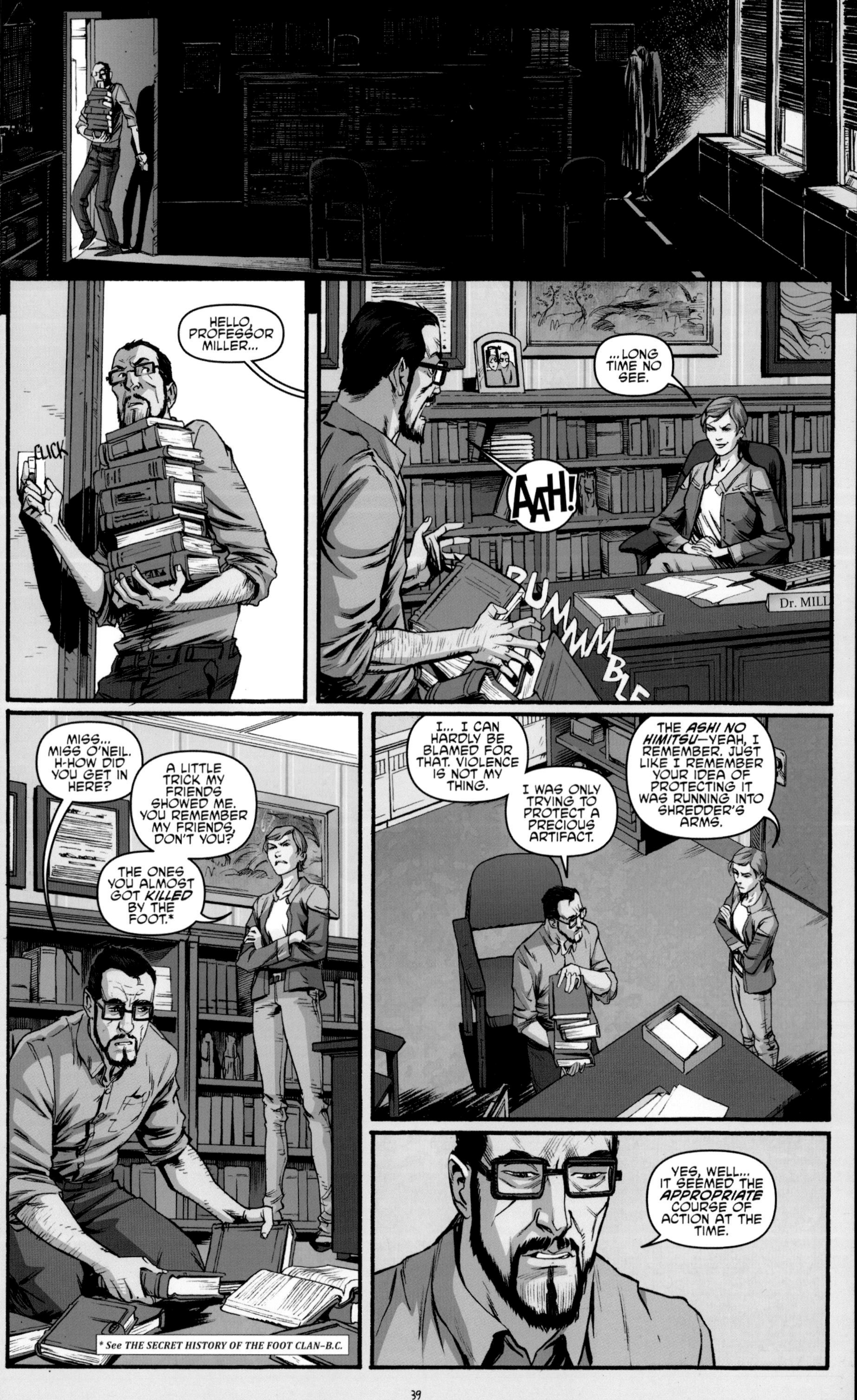

HELLO, PROFESSOR MILLER...
CLICK
...LONG TIME NO SEE.
AAH!
DUMMMBLE
Dr. MILL
MISS... MISS O'NEIL. H-HOW DID YOU GET IN HERE?
A LITTLE TRICK MY FRIENDS SHOWED ME. YOU REMEMBER MY FRIENDS, DON'T YOU?
THE ONES YOU ALMOST GOT *KILLED* BY THE FOOT.*
I... I CAN HARDLY BE BLAMED FOR THAT. VIOLENCE IS NOT MY THING.
I WAS ONLY TRYING TO PROTECT A PRECIOUS ARTIFACT.
THE *ASHI NO HIMITSU*—YEAH, I REMEMBER. JUST LIKE I REMEMBER YOUR IDEA OF PROTECTING IT WAS RUNNING INTO SHREDDER'S ARMS.
YES, WELL... IT SEEMED THE *APPROPRIATE* COURSE OF ACTION AT THE TIME.

*** See THE SECRET HISTORY OF THE FOOT CLAN–B.C.**

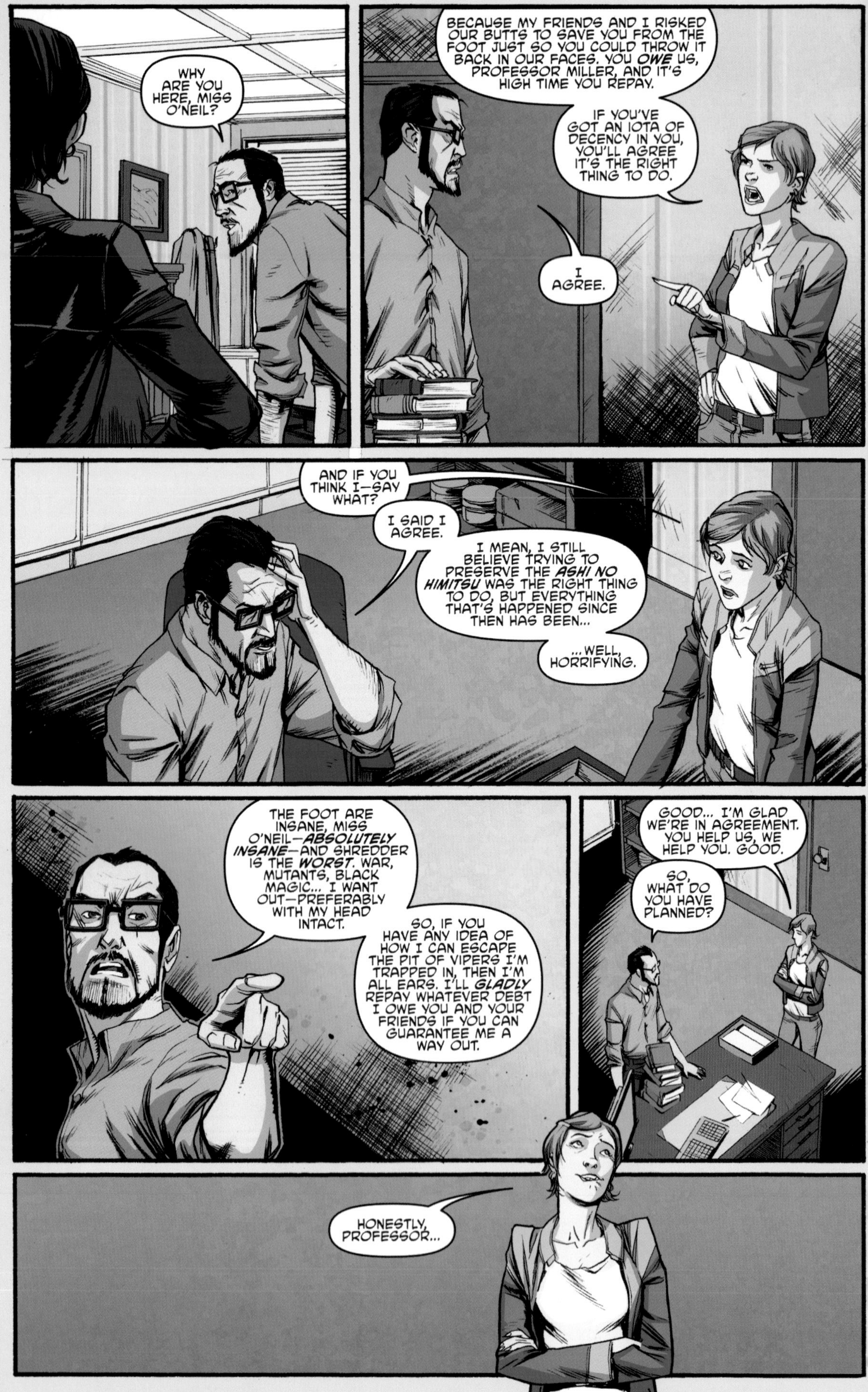
WHY ARE YOU HERE, MISS O'NEIL?
BECAUSE MY FRIENDS AND I RISKED OUR BUTTS TO SAVE YOU FROM THE FOOT JUST SO YOU COULD THROW IT BACK IN OUR FACES. YOU OWE US, PROFESSOR MILLER, AND IT'S HIGH TIME YOU REPAY.
IF YOU'VE GOT AN IOTA OF DECENCY IN YOU, YOU'LL AGREE IT'S THE RIGHT THING TO DO.
I AGREE.
AND IF YOU THINK I—SAY WHAT?
I SAID I AGREE.
I MEAN, I STILL BELIEVE TRYING TO PRESERVE THE ASHI NO HIMITSU WAS THE RIGHT THING TO DO, BUT EVERYTHING THAT'S HAPPENED SINCE THEN HAS BEEN...
...WELL, HORRIFYING.
THE FOOT ARE INSANE, MISS O'NEIL—ABSOLUTELY INSANE—AND SHREDDER IS THE WORST. WAR, MUTANTS, BLACK MAGIC... I WANT OUT—PREFERABLY WITH MY HEAD INTACT.
SO, IF YOU HAVE ANY IDEA OF HOW I CAN ESCAPE THE PIT OF VIPERS I'M TRAPPED IN, THEN I'M ALL EARS. I'LL GLADLY REPAY WHATEVER DEBT I OWE YOU AND YOUR FRIENDS IF YOU CAN GUARANTEE ME A WAY OUT.
GOOD... I'M GLAD WE'RE IN AGREEMENT. YOU HELP US, WE HELP YOU. GOOD.
SO, WHAT DO YOU HAVE PLANNED?
HONESTLY, PROFESSOR...

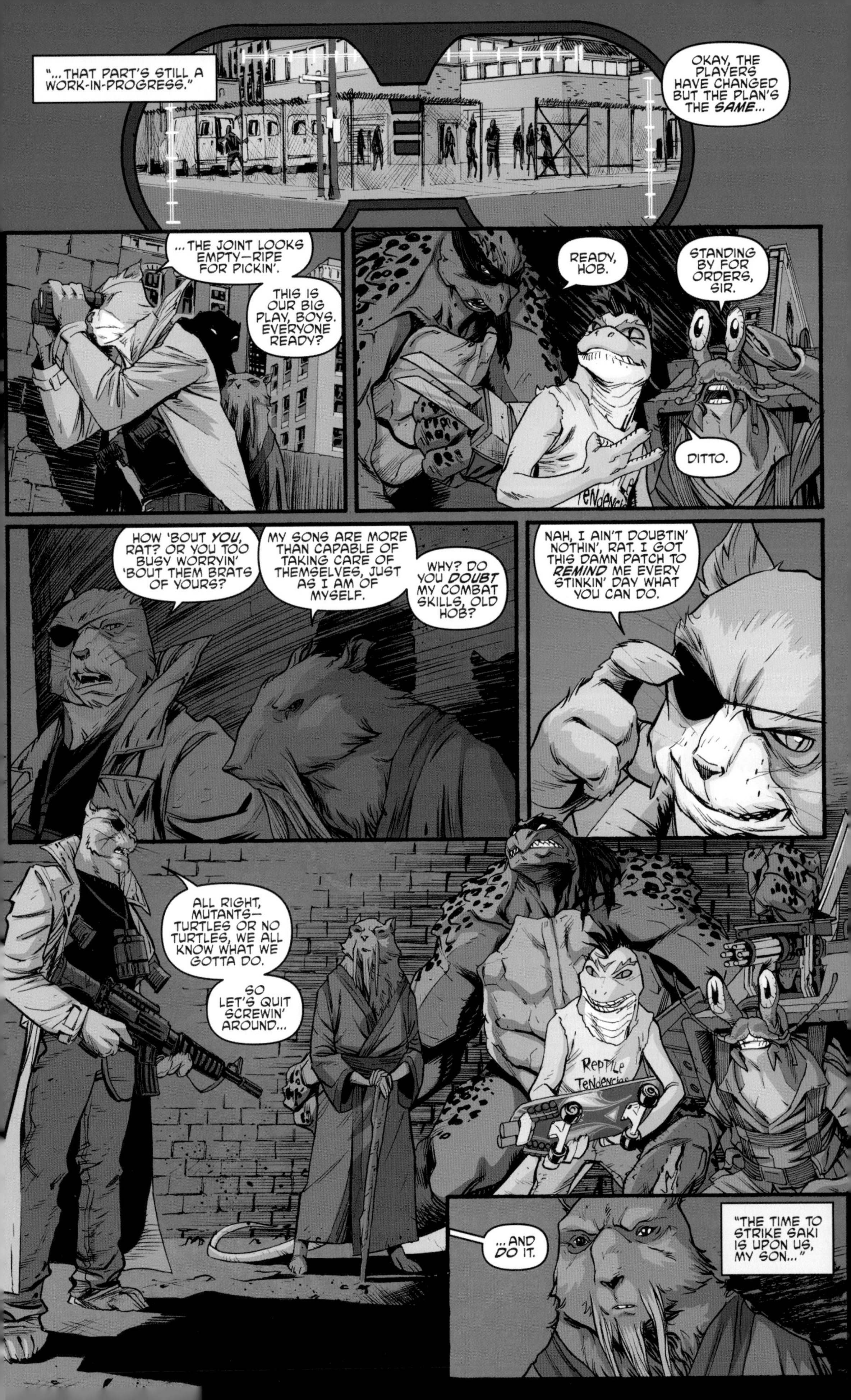
"...THAT PART'S STILL A WORK-IN-PROGRESS."
OKAY, THE PLAYERS HAVE CHANGED BUT THE PLAN'S THE *SAME*...
...THE JOINT LOOKS EMPTY—RIPE FOR PICKIN'.
THIS IS OUR BIG PLAY, BOYS. EVERYONE READY?
READY, HOB.
STANDING BY FOR ORDERS, SIR.
DITTO.
HOW 'BOUT *YOU*, RAT? OR YOU TOO BUSY WORRYIN' 'BOUT THEM BRATS OF YOURS?
MY SONS ARE MORE THAN CAPABLE OF TAKING CARE OF THEMSELVES, JUST AS I AM OF MYSELF.
WHY? DO YOU *DOUBT* MY COMBAT SKILLS, OLD HOB?
NAH, I AIN'T DOUBTIN' NOTHIN', RAT. I GOT THIS DAMN PATCH TO *REMIND* ME EVERY STINKIN' DAY WHAT YOU CAN DO.
ALL RIGHT, MUTANTS—TURTLES OR NO TURTLES, WE ALL KNOW WHAT WE GOTTA DO.
SO LET'S QUIT SCREWIN' AROUND...
REPTILE TENDENCIES
...AND *DO* IT.
"THE TIME TO STRIKE SAKI IS UPON US, MY SON..."

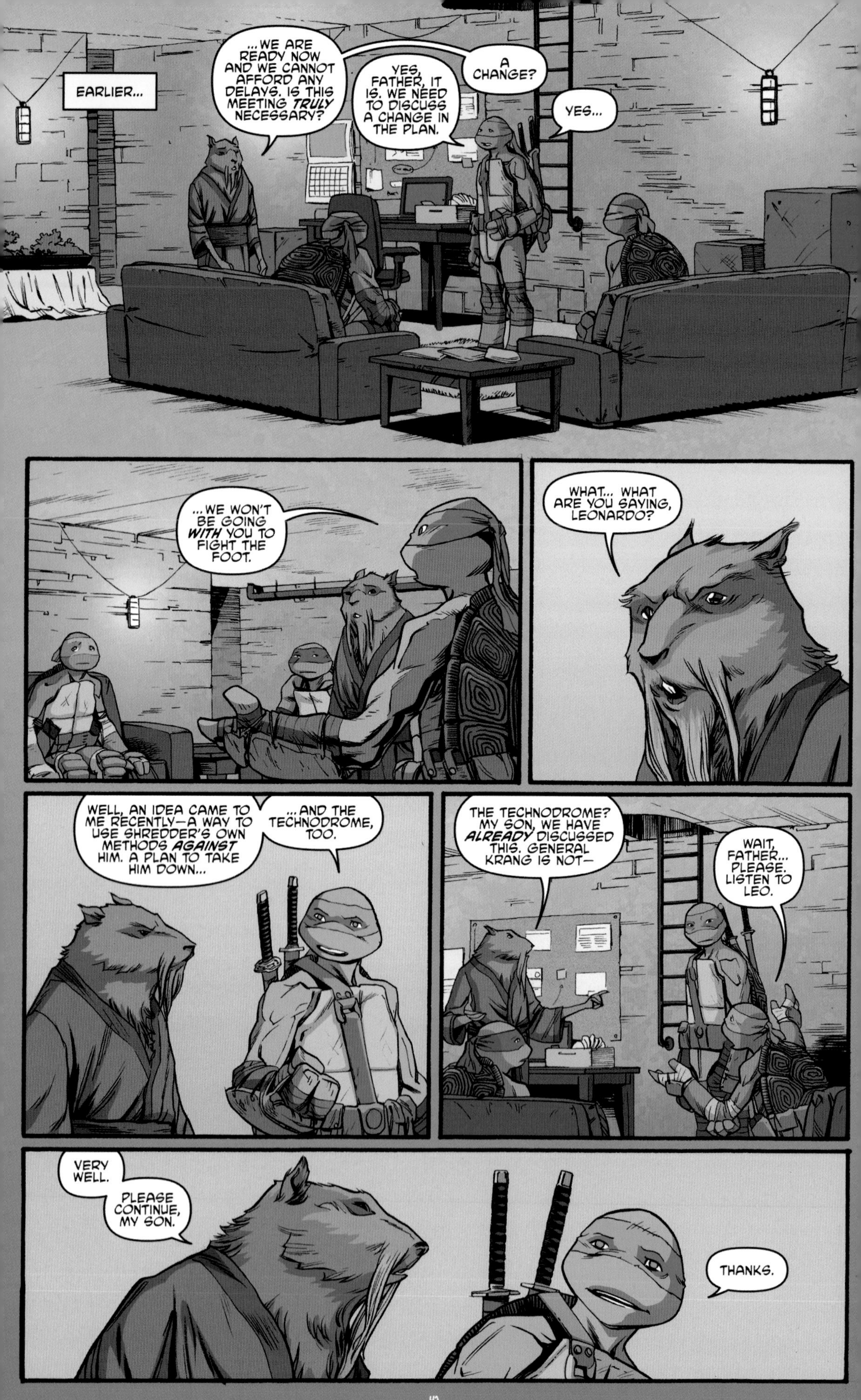
EARLIER...
...WE ARE READY NOW AND WE CANNOT AFFORD ANY DELAYS. IS THIS MEETING TRULY NECESSARY?
YES, FATHER, IT IS. WE NEED TO DISCUSS A CHANGE IN THE PLAN.
A CHANGE?
YES...
...WE WON'T BE GOING WITH YOU TO FIGHT THE FOOT.
WHAT... WHAT ARE YOU SAYING, LEONARDO?
WELL, AN IDEA CAME TO ME RECENTLY—A WAY TO USE SHREDDER'S OWN METHODS AGAINST HIM. A PLAN TO TAKE HIM DOWN...
...AND THE TECHNODROME, TOO.
THE TECHNODROME? MY SON, WE HAVE ALREADY DISCUSSED THIS. GENERAL KRANG IS NOT—
WAIT, FATHER... PLEASE. LISTEN TO LEO.
VERY WELL.
PLEASE CONTINUE, MY SON.
THANKS.

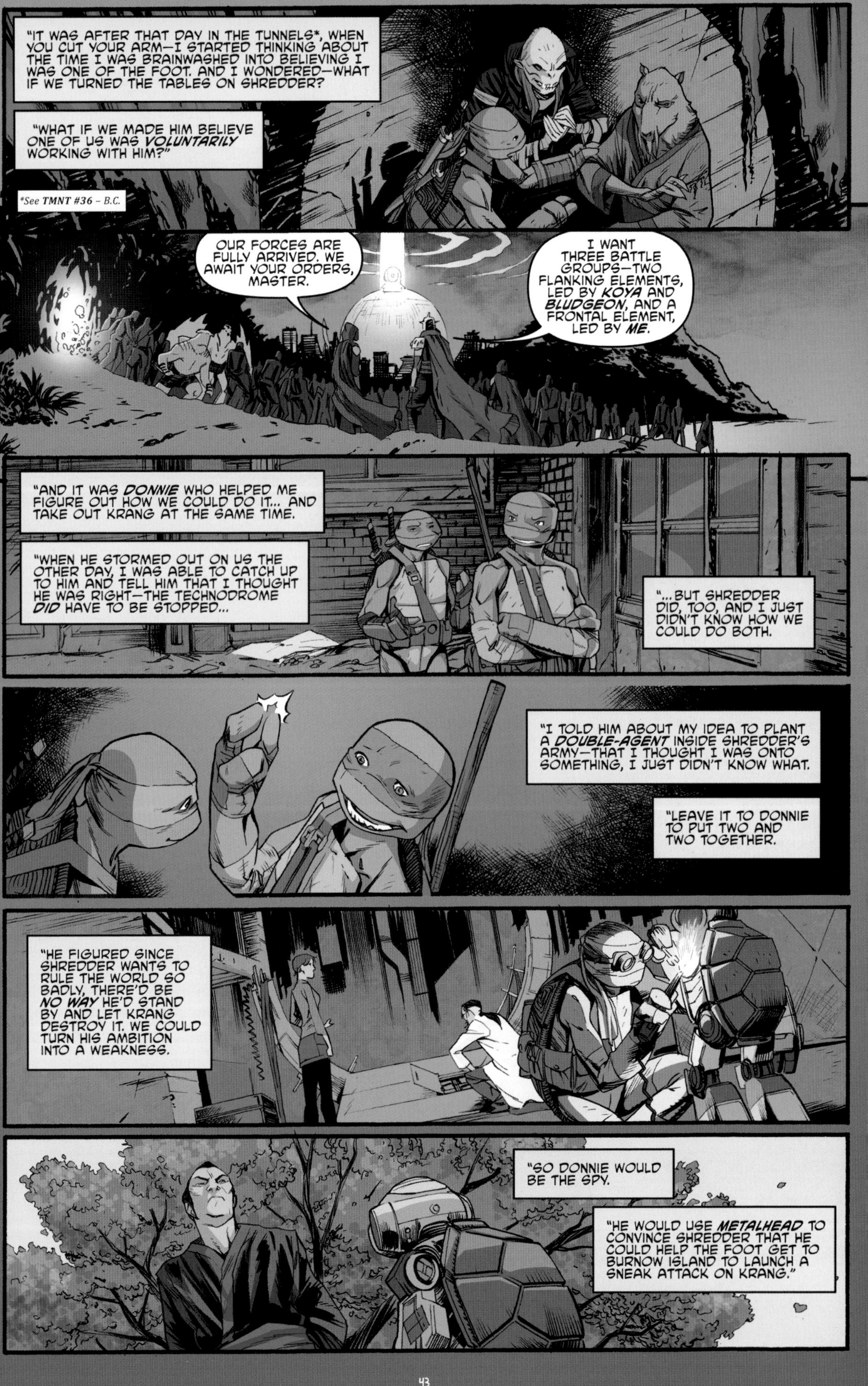
"IT WAS AFTER THAT DAY IN THE TUNNELS*, WHEN YOU CUT YOUR ARM—I STARTED THINKING ABOUT THE TIME I WAS BRAINWASHED INTO BELIEVING I WAS ONE OF THE FOOT. AND I WONDERED—WHAT IF WE TURNED THE TABLES ON SHREDDER?
"WHAT IF WE MADE HIM BELIEVE ONE OF US WAS *VOLUNTARILY* WORKING WITH HIM?"
*See TMNT #36 – B.C.
OUR FORCES ARE FULLY ARRIVED. WE AWAIT YOUR ORDERS, MASTER.
I WANT THREE BATTLE GROUPS—TWO FLANKING ELEMENTS, LED BY *KOYA* AND *BLUDGEON*, AND A FRONTAL ELEMENT, LED BY *ME*.
"AND IT WAS *DONNIE* WHO HELPED ME FIGURE OUT HOW WE COULD DO IT... AND TAKE OUT KRANG AT THE SAME TIME.
"WHEN HE STORMED OUT ON US THE OTHER DAY, I WAS ABLE TO CATCH UP TO HIM AND TELL HIM THAT I THOUGHT HE WAS RIGHT—THE TECHNODROME *DID* HAVE TO BE STOPPED...
"...BUT SHREDDER DID, TOO, AND I JUST DIDN'T KNOW HOW WE COULD DO BOTH.
"I TOLD HIM ABOUT MY IDEA TO PLANT A *DOUBLE-AGENT* INSIDE SHREDDER'S ARMY—THAT I THOUGHT I WAS ONTO SOMETHING, I JUST DIDN'T KNOW WHAT.
"LEAVE IT TO DONNIE TO PUT TWO AND TWO TOGETHER.
"HE FIGURED SINCE SHREDDER WANTS TO RULE THE WORLD SO BADLY, THERE'D BE *NO WAY* HE'D STAND BY AND LET KRANG DESTROY IT. WE COULD TURN HIS AMBITION INTO A WEAKNESS.
"SO DONNIE WOULD BE THE SPY.
"HE WOULD USE *METALHEAD* TO CONVINCE SHREDDER THAT HE COULD HELP THE FOOT GET TO BURNOW ISLAND TO LAUNCH A SNEAK ATTACK ON KRANG."

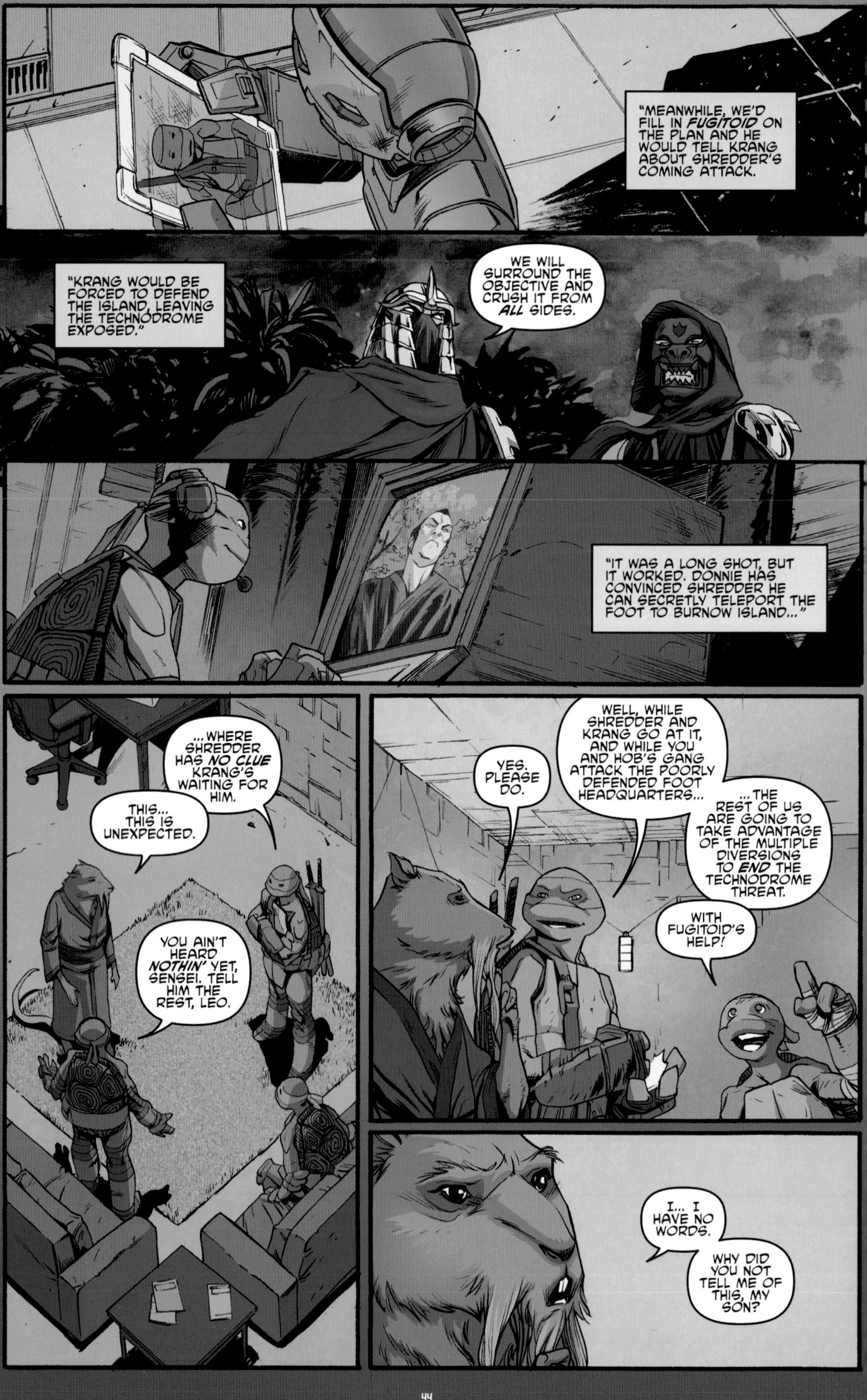
"MEANWHILE, WE'D FILL IN FUGITOID ON THE PLAN AND HE WOULD TELL KRANG ABOUT SHREDDER'S COMING ATTACK.
"KRANG WOULD BE FORCED TO DEFEND THE ISLAND, LEAVING THE TECHNODROME EXPOSED."
WE WILL SURROUND THE OBJECTIVE AND CRUSH IT FROM ALL SIDES.
"IT WAS A LONG SHOT, BUT IT WORKED. DONNIE HAS CONVINCED SHREDDER HE CAN SECRETLY TELEPORT THE FOOT TO BURNOW ISLAND..."
...WHERE SHREDDER HAS NO CLUE KRANG'S WAITING FOR HIM.
THIS... THIS IS UNEXPECTED.
YOU AIN'T HEARD NOTHIN' YET, SENSEI. TELL HIM THE REST, LEO.
YES. PLEASE DO.
WELL, WHILE SHREDDER AND KRANG GO AT IT, AND WHILE YOU AND HOB'S GANG ATTACK THE POORLY DEFENDED FOOT HEADQUARTERS...
...THE REST OF US ARE GOING TO TAKE ADVANTAGE OF THE MULTIPLE DIVERSIONS TO END THE TECHNODROME THREAT.
WITH FUGITOID'S HELP!
I... I HAVE NO WORDS.
WHY DID YOU NOT TELL ME OF THIS, MY SON?

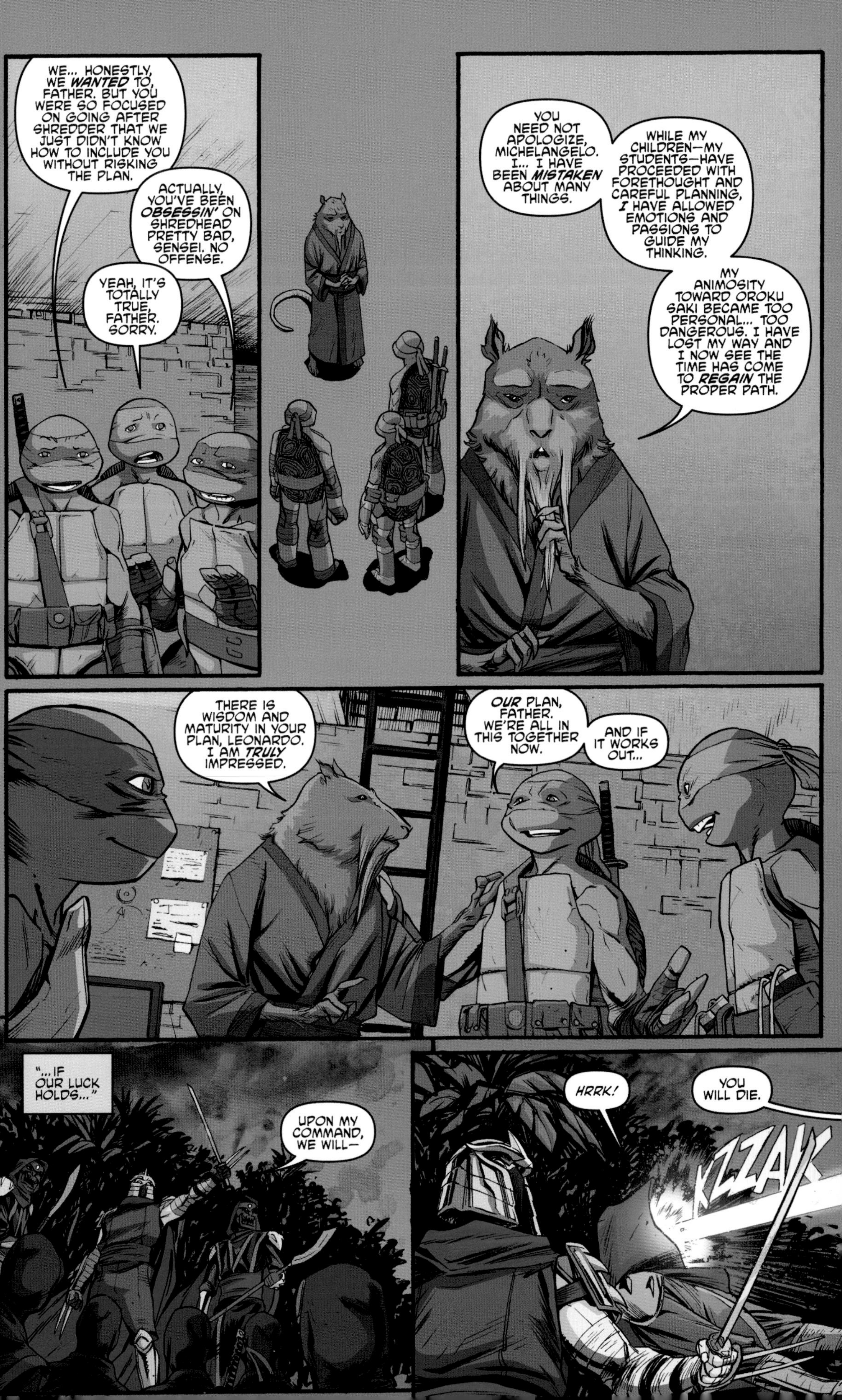
WE... HONESTLY, WE WANTED TO, FATHER. BUT YOU WERE SO FOCUSED ON GOING AFTER SHREDDER THAT WE JUST DIDN'T KNOW HOW TO INCLUDE YOU WITHOUT RISKING THE PLAN.
ACTUALLY, YOU'VE BEEN OBSESSIN' ON SHREDHEAD PRETTY BAD, SENSEI. NO OFFENSE.
YEAH, IT'S TOTALLY TRUE, FATHER. SORRY.
YOU NEED NOT APOLOGIZE, MICHELANGELO. I... I HAVE BEEN MISTAKEN ABOUT MANY THINGS.
WHILE MY CHILDREN—MY STUDENTS—HAVE PROCEEDED WITH FORETHOUGHT AND CAREFUL PLANNING, I HAVE ALLOWED EMOTIONS AND PASSIONS TO GUIDE MY THINKING.
MY ANIMOSITY TOWARD OROKU SAKI BECAME TOO PERSONAL... TOO DANGEROUS. I HAVE LOST MY WAY AND I NOW SEE THE TIME HAS COME TO REGAIN THE PROPER PATH.
THERE IS WISDOM AND MATURITY IN YOUR PLAN, LEONARDO. I AM TRULY IMPRESSED.
OUR PLAN, FATHER. WE'RE ALL IN THIS TOGETHER NOW.
AND IF IT WORKS OUT...
"...IF OUR LUCK HOLDS..."
UPON MY COMMAND, WE WILL—
HRRK!
YOU WILL DIE.
KZZAK

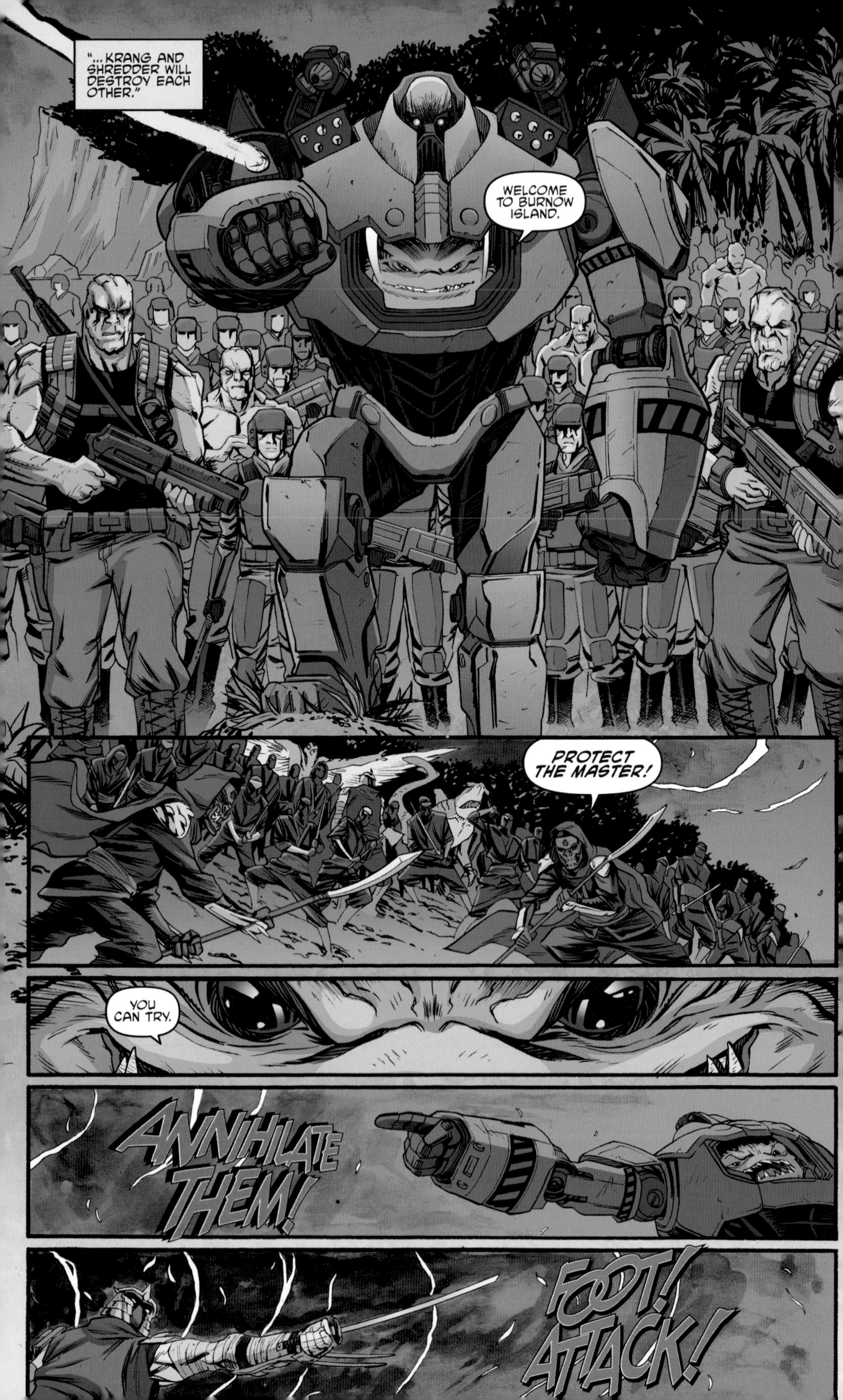
"...KRANG AND SHREDDER WILL DESTROY EACH OTHER."
WELCOME TO BURNOW ISLAND.
PROTECT THE MASTER!
YOU CAN TRY.
ANNIHILATE THEM!
FOOT! ATTACK!

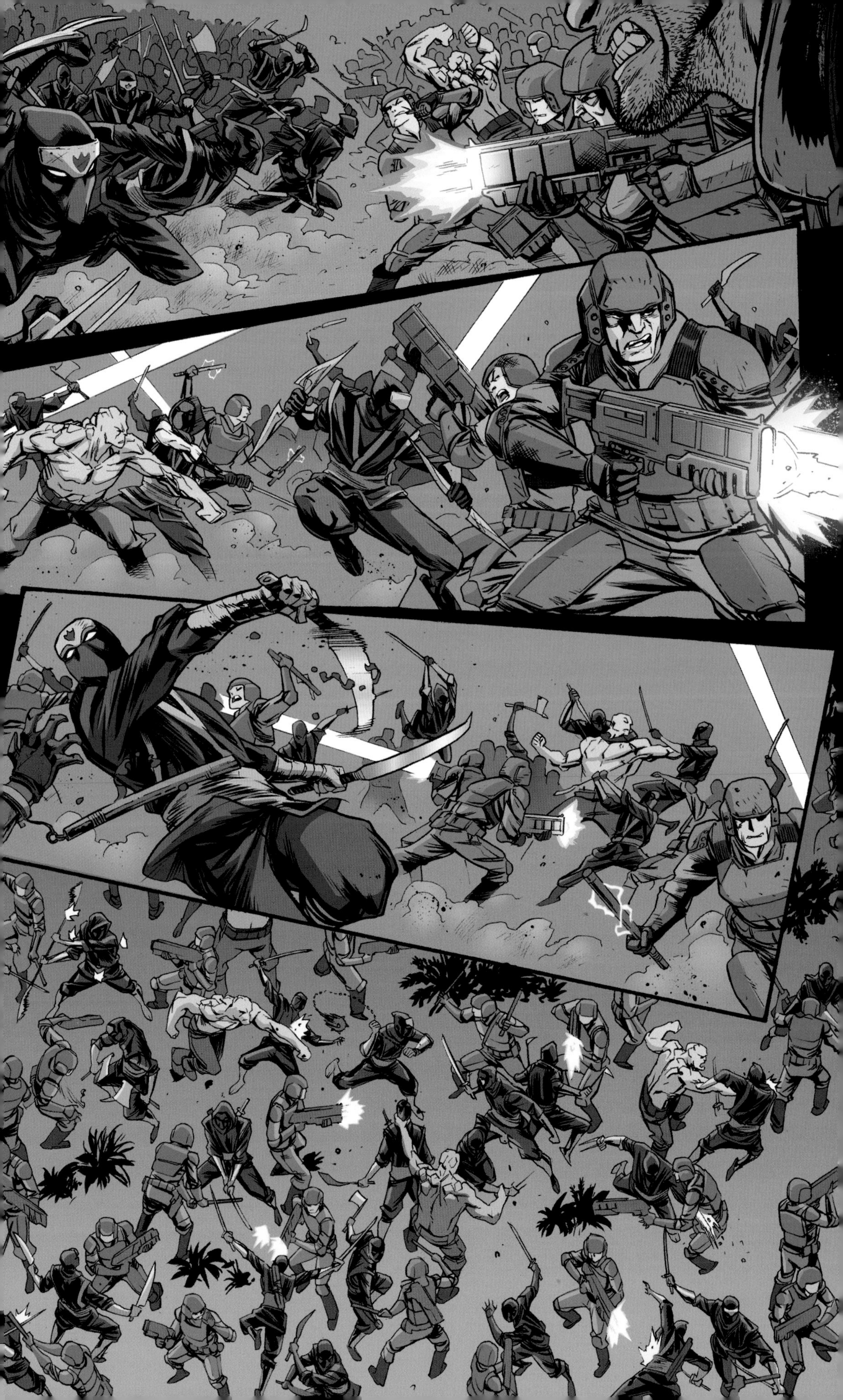

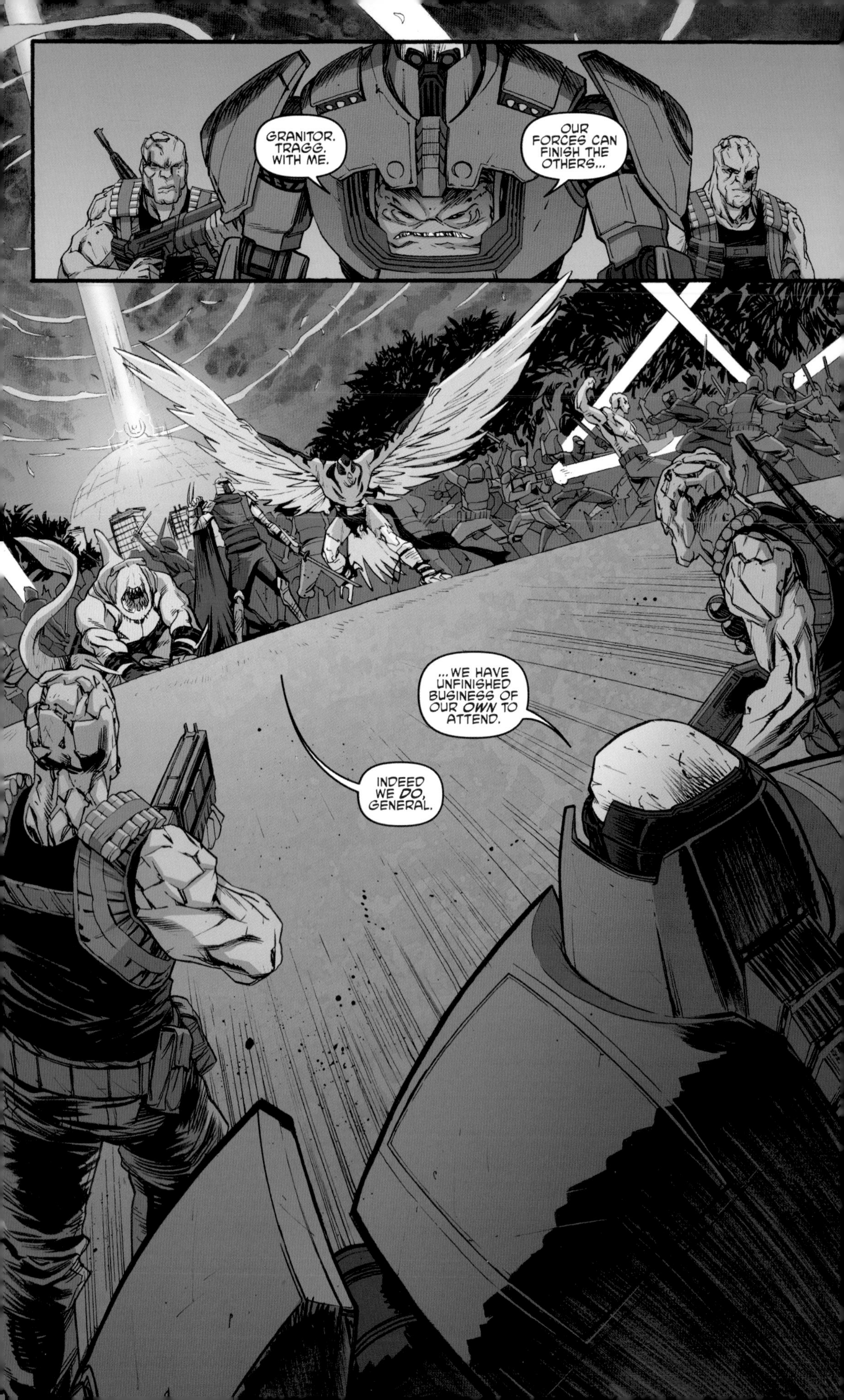
GRANITOR. TRAGG. WITH ME.
OUR FORCES CAN FINISH THE OTHERS...
...WE HAVE UNFINISHED BUSINESS OF OUR *OWN* TO ATTEND.
INDEED WE *DO*, GENERAL.

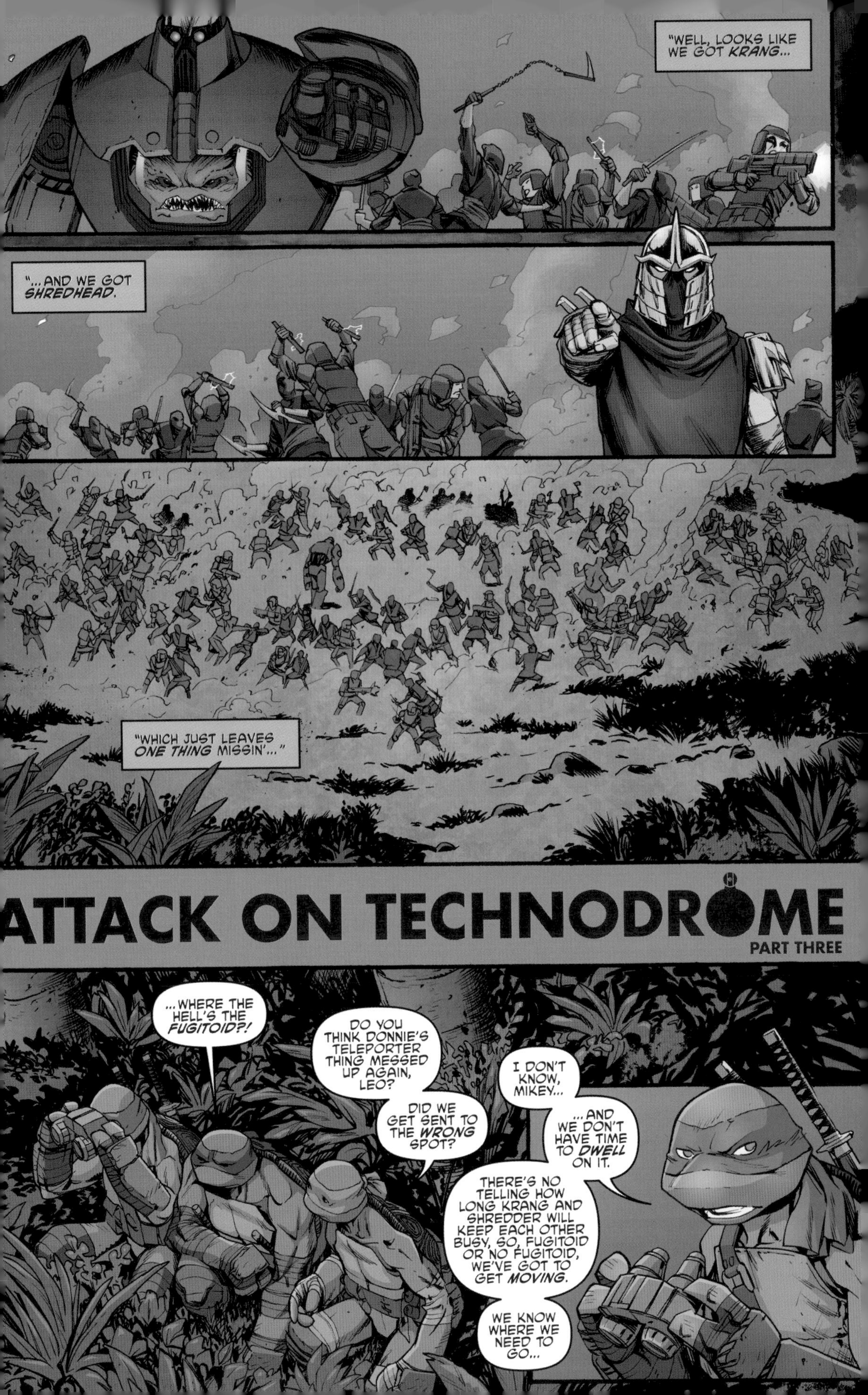
"WELL, LOOKS LIKE WE GOT *KRANG*...
"...AND WE GOT *SHREDHEAD*.
"WHICH JUST LEAVES *ONE THING* MISSIN'..."
ATTACK ON TECHNODROME
PART THREE
...WHERE THE HELL'S THE *FUGITOID?!*
DO YOU THINK DONNIE'S TELEPORTER THING MESSED UP AGAIN, LEO?
DID WE GET SENT TO THE *WRONG* SPOT?
I DON'T KNOW, MIKEY...
...AND WE DON'T HAVE TIME TO *DWELL* ON IT.
THERE'S NO TELLING HOW LONG KRANG AND SHREDDER WILL KEEP EACH OTHER BUSY, SO, FUGITOID OR NO FUGITOID, WE'VE GOT TO GET *MOVING*.
WE KNOW WHERE WE NEED TO GO...

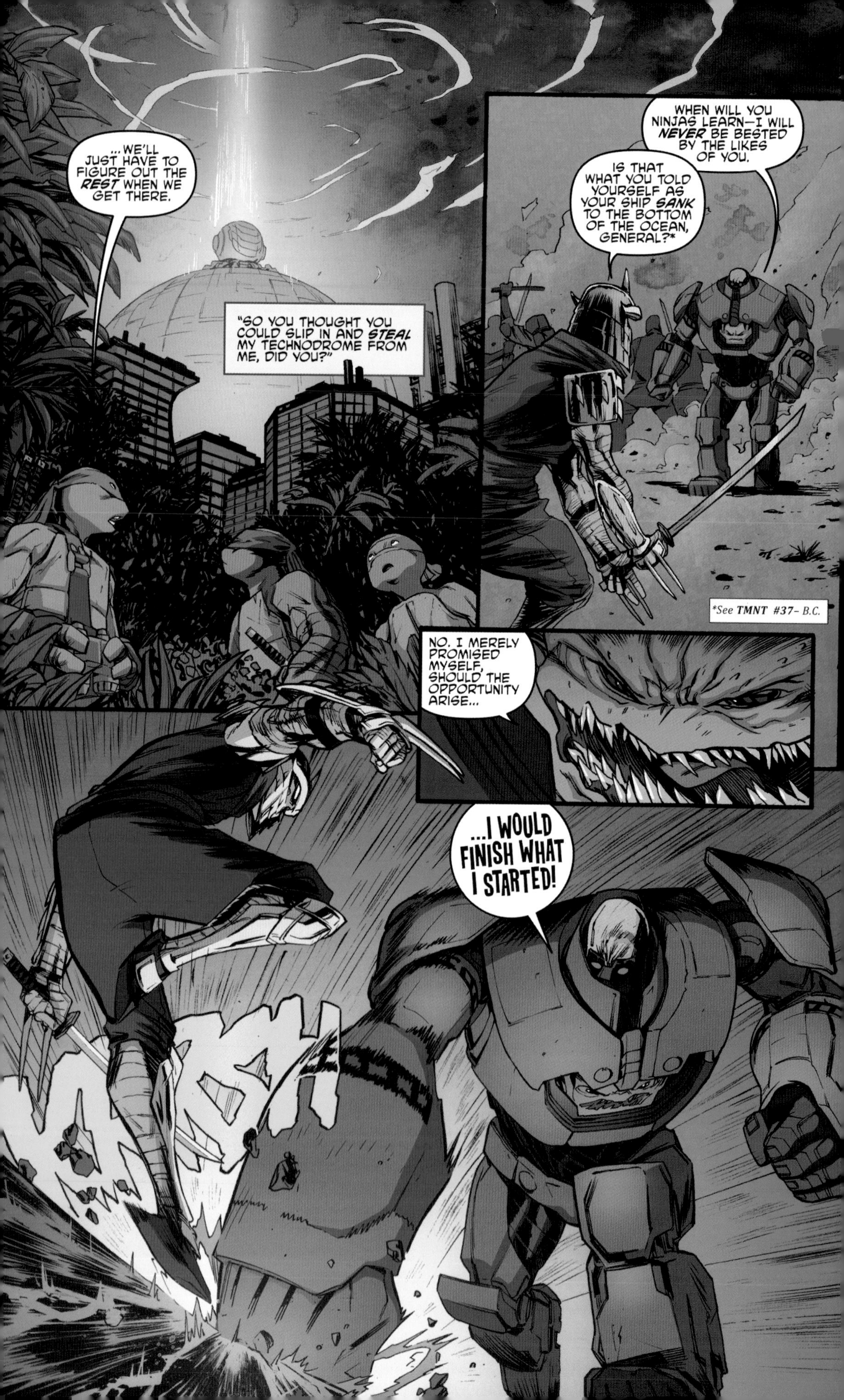

...WE'LL JUST HAVE TO FIGURE OUT THE REST WHEN WE GET THERE.
"SO YOU THOUGHT YOU COULD SLIP IN AND STEAL MY TECHNODROME FROM ME, DID YOU?"
WHEN WILL YOU NINJAS LEARN—I WILL NEVER BE BESTED BY THE LIKES OF YOU.
IS THAT WHAT YOU TOLD YOURSELF AS YOUR SHIP SANK TO THE BOTTOM OF THE OCEAN, GENERAL?*
*See TMNT #37– B.C.
NO. I MERELY PROMISED MYSELF, SHOULD THE OPPORTUNITY ARISE...
...I WOULD FINISH WHAT I STARTED!

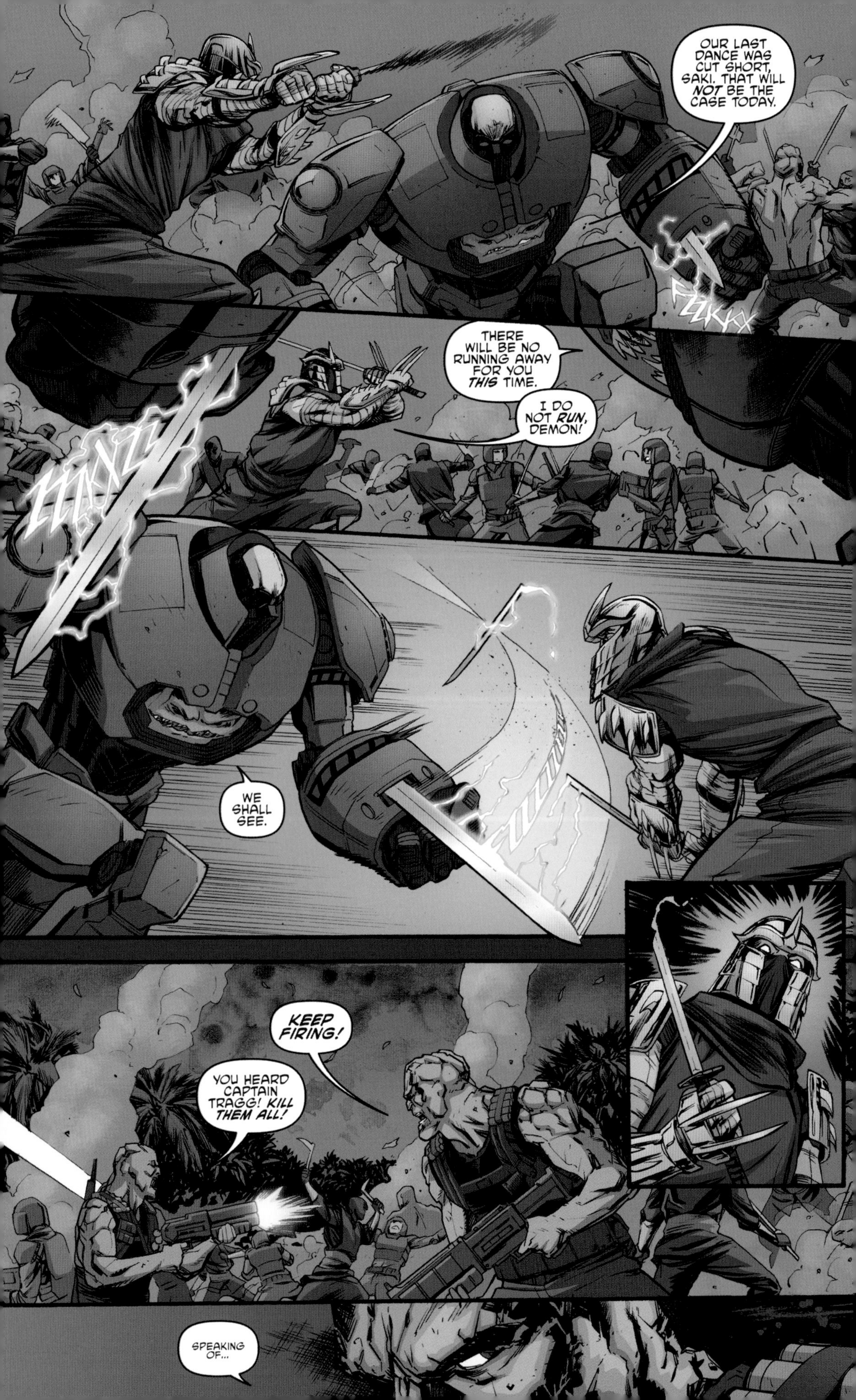
OUR LAST DANCE WAS CUT SHORT, SAKI. THAT WILL NOT BE THE CASE TODAY.
FZZKKX
THERE WILL BE NO RUNNING AWAY FOR YOU THIS TIME.
I DO NOT RUN, DEMON!
ZZZKZZ
WE SHALL SEE.
KEEP FIRING!
YOU HEARD CAPTAIN TRAGG! KILL THEM ALL!
SPEAKING OF...

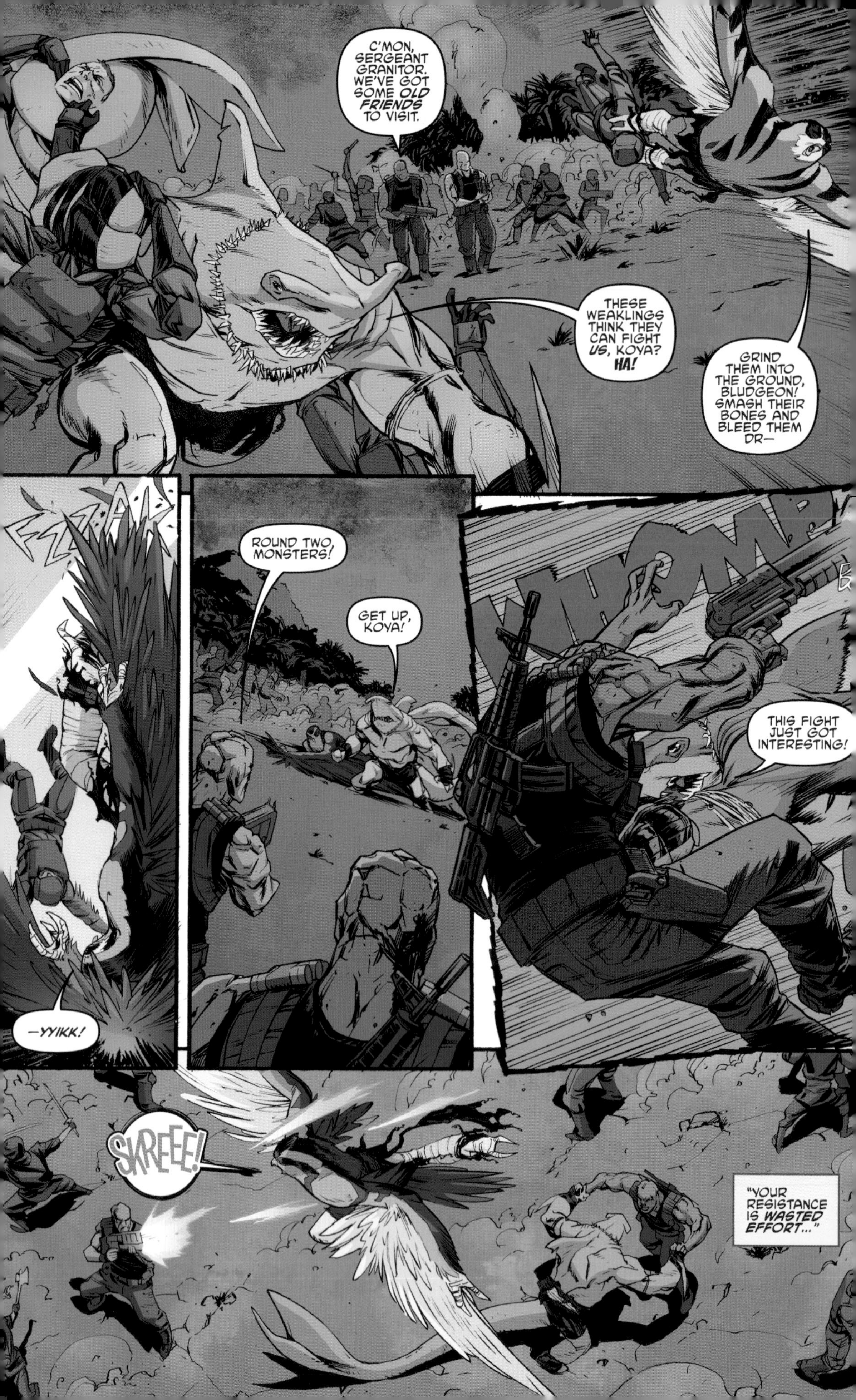
C'MON, SERGEANT GRANITOR. WE'VE GOT SOME *OLD FRIENDS* TO VISIT.
THESE WEAKLINGS THINK THEY CAN FIGHT *US*, KOYA? *HA!*
GRIND THEM INTO THE GROUND, BLUDGEON! SMASH THEIR BONES AND BLEED THEM DR—
—YYIKK!
ROUND TWO, MONSTERS!
GET UP, KOYA!
THIS FIGHT JUST GOT INTERESTING!
SKREEE!
"YOUR RESISTANCE IS *WASTED EFFORT...*"

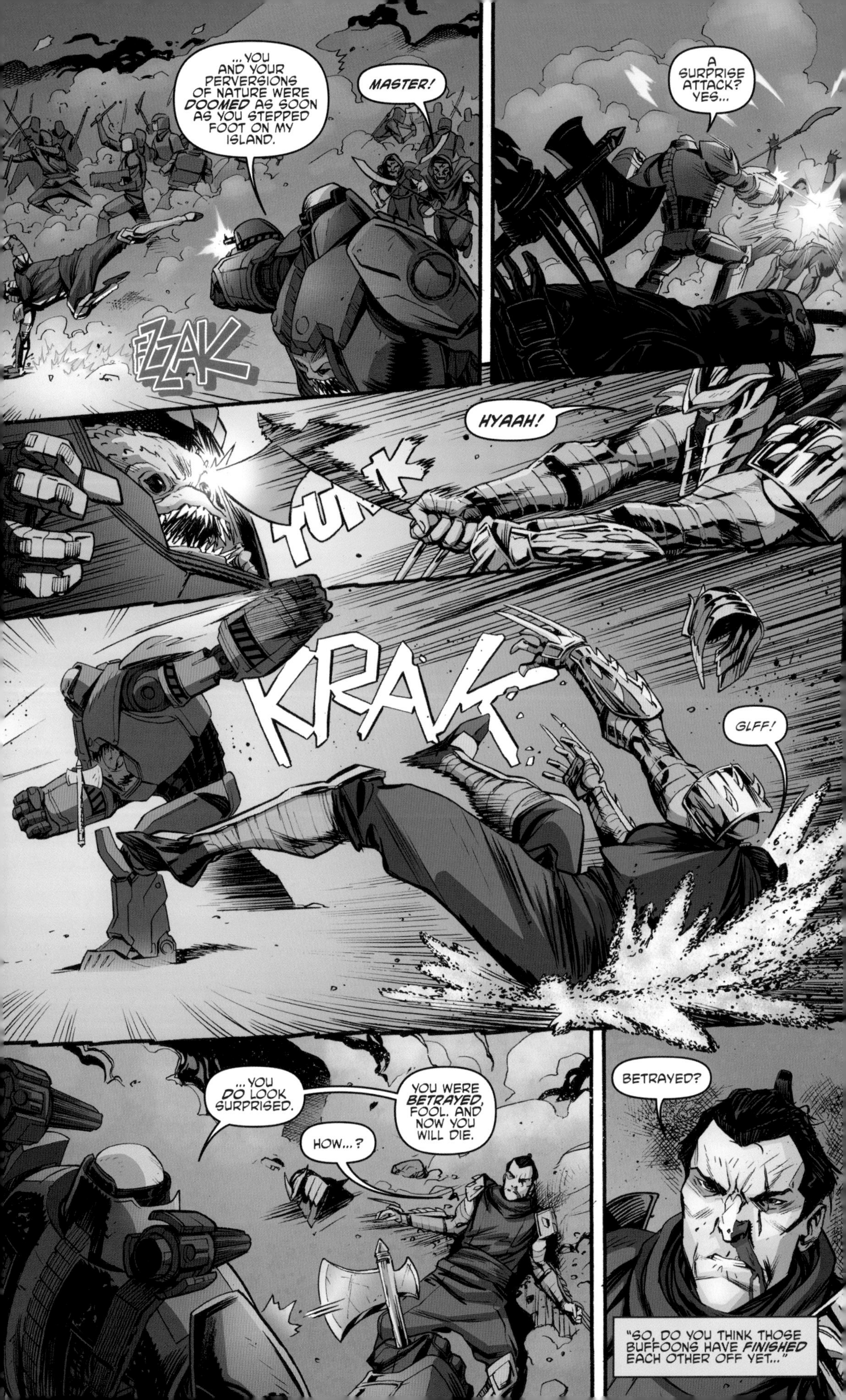
...YOU AND YOUR PERVERSIONS OF NATURE WERE DOOMED AS SOON AS YOU STEPPED FOOT ON MY ISLAND.
MASTER!
FZZAK
A SURPRISE ATTACK? YES...
HYAAH!
YUNK
KRAK
GLFF!
...YOU DO LOOK SURPRISED.
YOU WERE BETRAYED, FOOL, AND NOW YOU WILL DIE.
HOW...?
BETRAYED?
"SO, DO YOU THINK THOSE BUFFOONS HAVE FINISHED EACH OTHER OFF YET..."

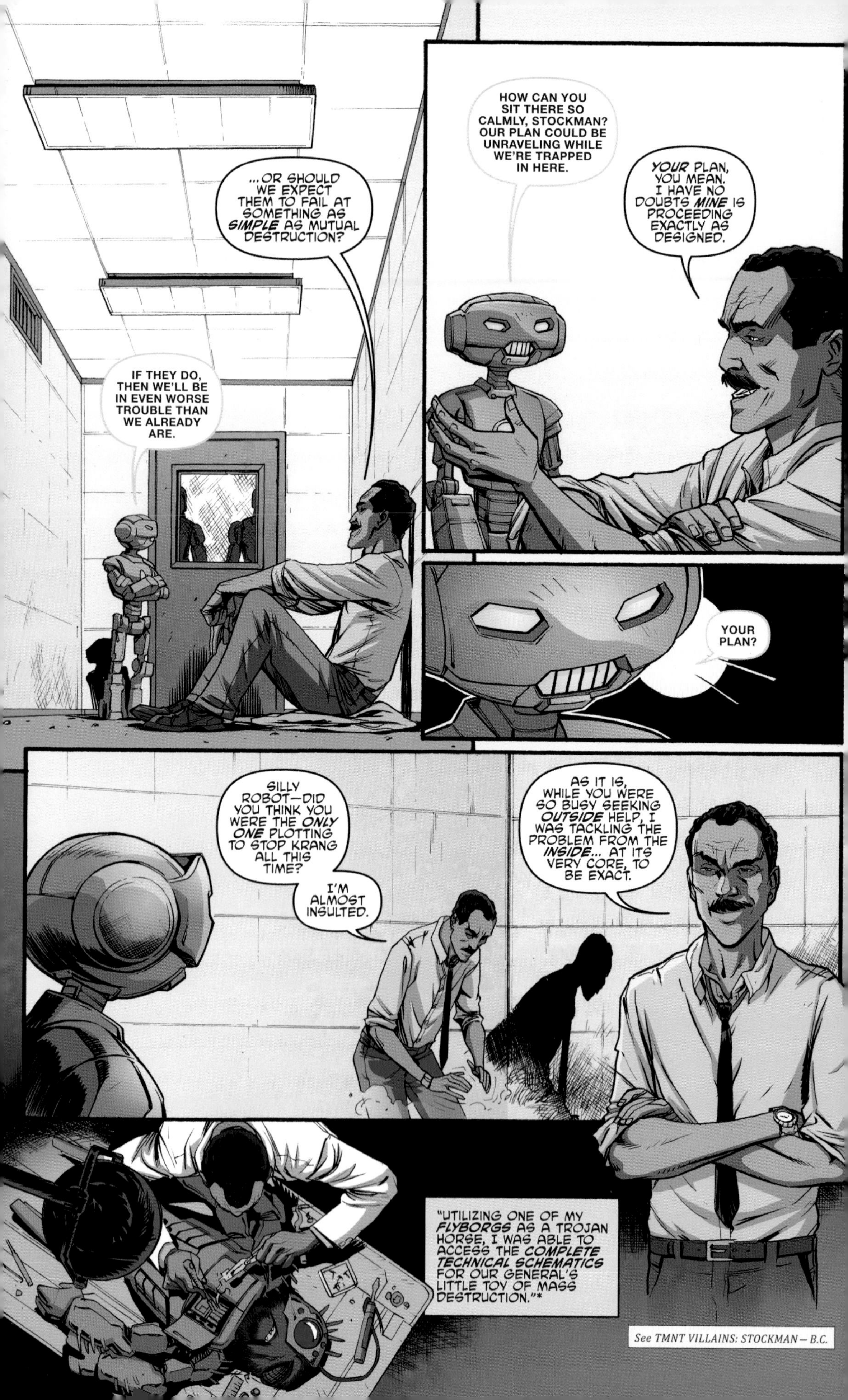
...OR SHOULD WE EXPECT THEM TO FAIL AT SOMETHING AS SIMPLE AS MUTUAL DESTRUCTION?
IF THEY DO, THEN WE'LL BE IN EVEN WORSE TROUBLE THAN WE ALREADY ARE.
HOW CAN YOU SIT THERE SO CALMLY, STOCKMAN? OUR PLAN COULD BE UNRAVELING WHILE WE'RE TRAPPED IN HERE.
YOUR PLAN, YOU MEAN. I HAVE NO DOUBTS MINE IS PROCEEDING EXACTLY AS DESIGNED.
YOUR PLAN?
SILLY ROBOT—DID YOU THINK YOU WERE THE ONLY ONE PLOTTING TO STOP KRANG ALL THIS TIME?
I'M ALMOST INSULTED.
AS IT IS, WHILE YOU WERE SO BUSY SEEKING OUTSIDE HELP, I WAS TACKLING THE PROBLEM FROM THE INSIDE... AT ITS VERY CORE, TO BE EXACT.
"UTILIZING ONE OF MY FLYBORGS AS A TROJAN HORSE, I WAS ABLE TO ACCESS THE COMPLETE TECHNICAL SCHEMATICS FOR OUR GENERAL'S LITTLE TOY OF MASS DESTRUCTION."*
*See TMNT VILLAINS: STOCKMAN — B.C.

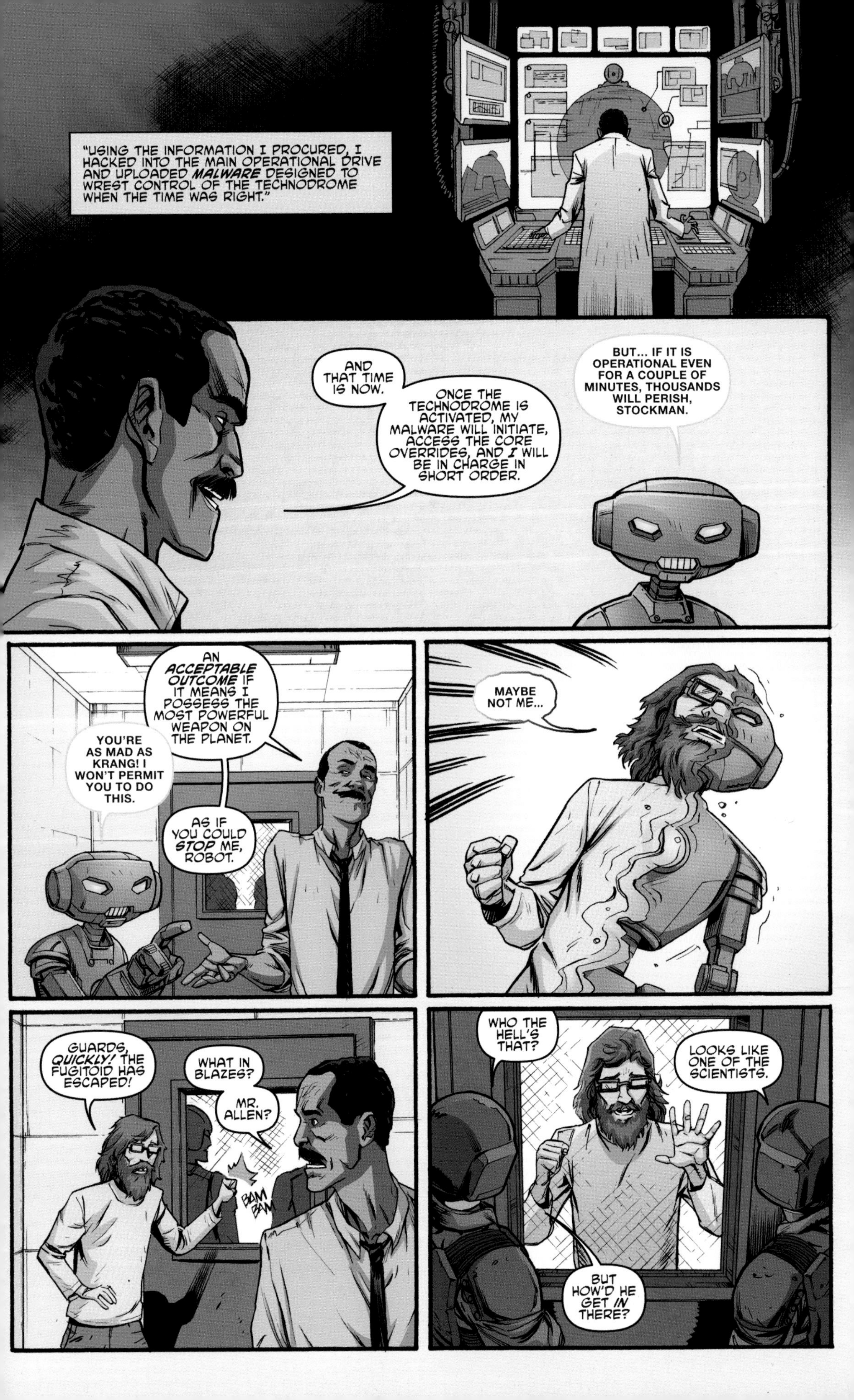
"USING THE INFORMATION I PROCURED, I HACKED INTO THE MAIN OPERATIONAL DRIVE AND UPLOADED *MALWARE* DESIGNED TO WREST CONTROL OF THE TECHNODROME WHEN THE TIME WAS RIGHT."
AND THAT TIME IS NOW.
ONCE THE TECHNODROME IS ACTIVATED, MY MALWARE WILL INITIATE, ACCESS THE CORE OVERRIDES, AND *I* WILL BE IN CHARGE IN SHORT ORDER.
BUT... IF IT IS OPERATIONAL EVEN FOR A COUPLE OF MINUTES, THOUSANDS WILL PERISH, STOCKMAN.
AN *ACCEPTABLE OUTCOME* IF IT MEANS I POSSESS THE MOST POWERFUL WEAPON ON THE PLANET.
YOU'RE AS MAD AS KRANG! I WON'T PERMIT YOU TO DO THIS.
AS IF YOU COULD *STOP* ME, ROBOT.
MAYBE NOT ME...
GUARDS, *QUICKLY!* THE FUGITOID HAS ESCAPED!
WHAT IN BLAZES?
MR. ALLEN?
BAM BAM
WHO THE HELL'S THAT?
LOOKS LIKE ONE OF THE SCIENTISTS.
BUT HOW'D HE GET *IN* THERE?

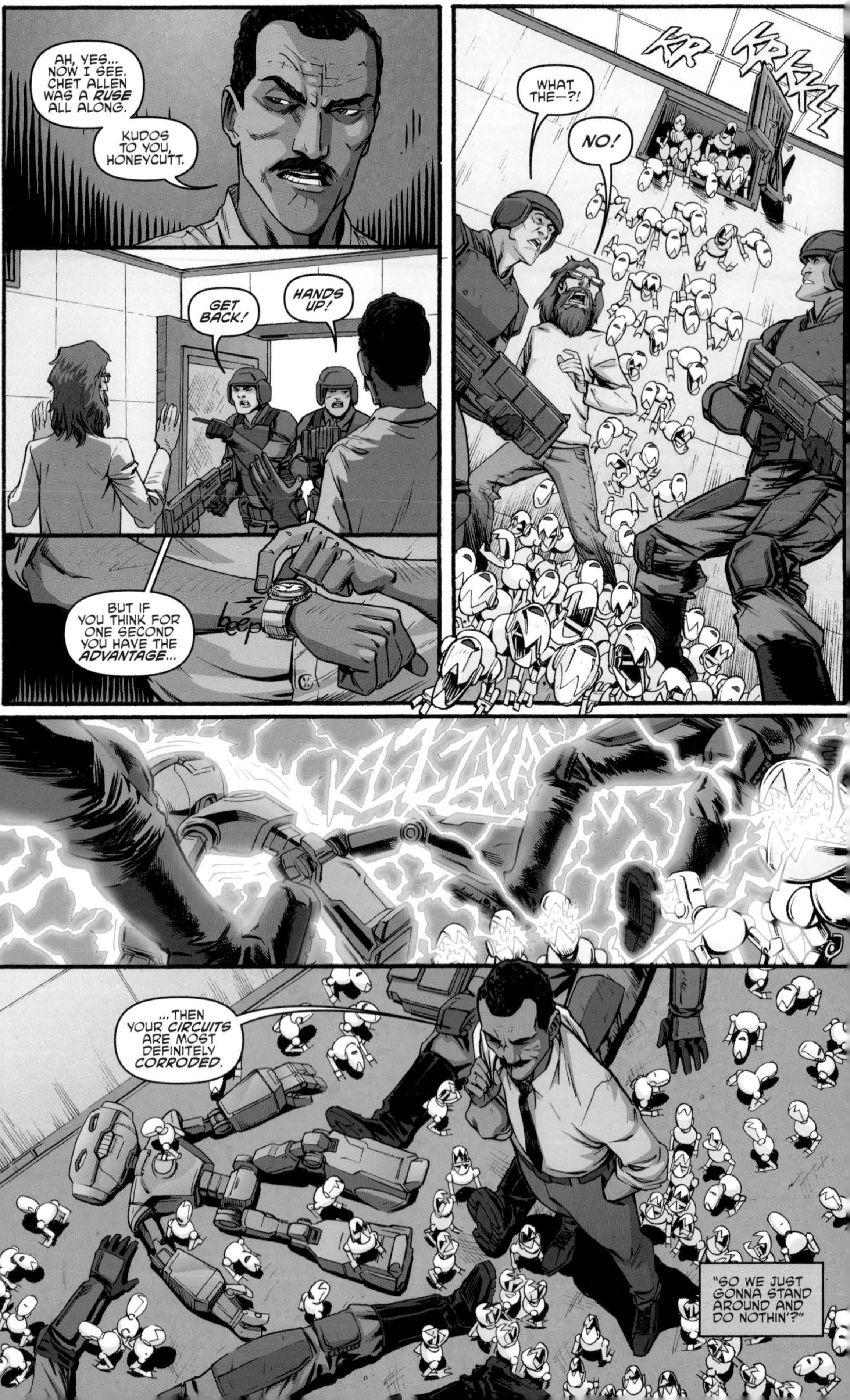

AH, YES... NOW I SEE. CHET ALLEN WAS A RUSE ALL ALONG.
KUDOS TO YOU, HONEYCUTT.
GET BACK!
HANDS UP!
BUT IF YOU THINK FOR ONE SECOND YOU HAVE THE ADVANTAGE...
beep
KR-KRKKL
WHAT THE—?!
NO!
...THEN YOUR CIRCUITS ARE MOST DEFINITELY CORRODED.
"SO WE JUST GONNA STAND AROUND AND DO NOTHIN'?"

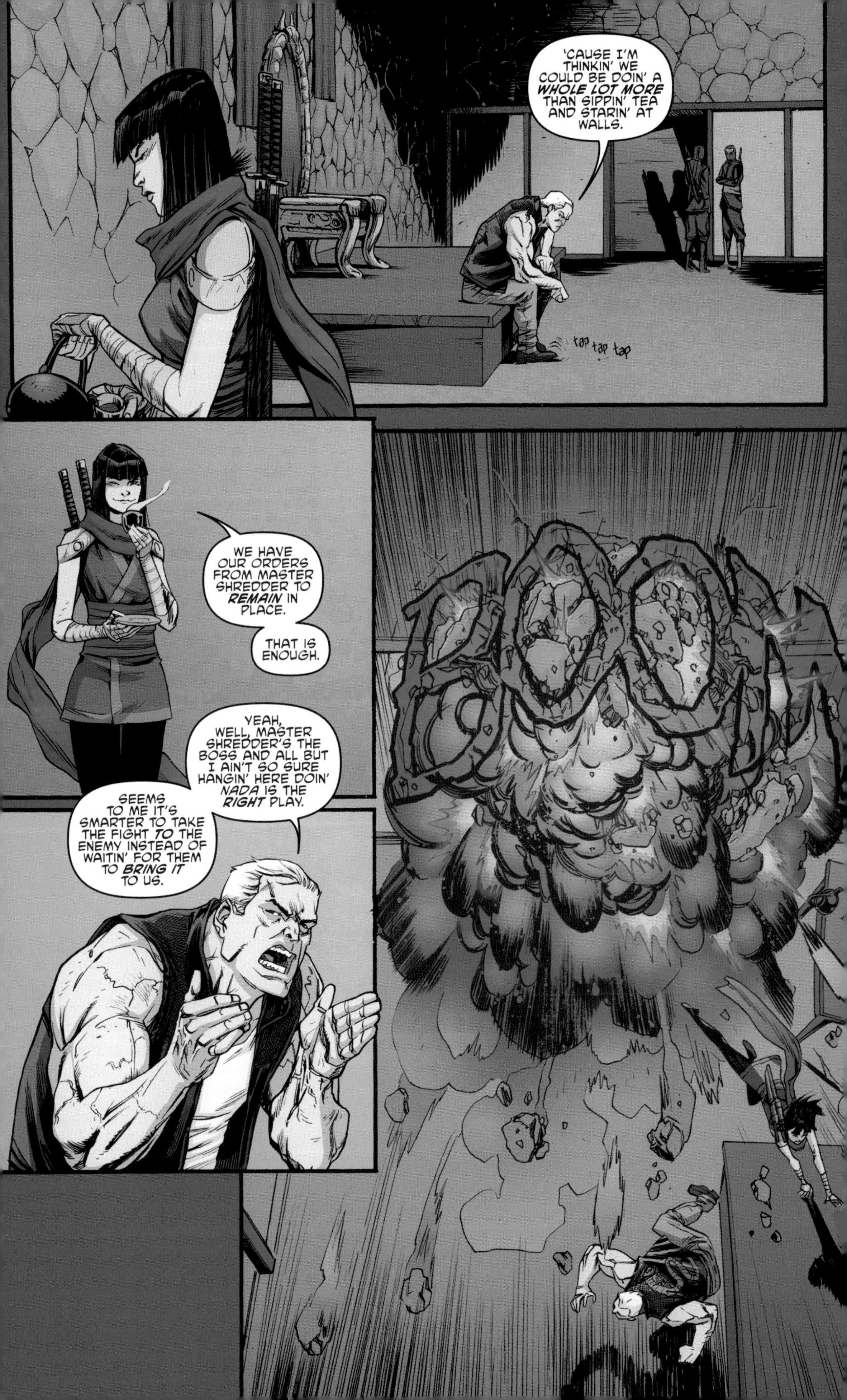
'CAUSE I'M THINKIN' WE COULD BE DOIN' A *WHOLE LOT MORE* THAN SIPPIN' TEA AND STARIN' AT WALLS.
tap tap tap
WE HAVE OUR ORDERS FROM MASTER SHREDDER TO *REMAIN* IN PLACE.
THAT IS ENOUGH.
YEAH, WELL, MASTER SHREDDER'S THE BOSS AND ALL BUT I AIN'T SO SURE HANGIN' HERE DOIN' *NADA* IS THE *RIGHT* PLAY.
SEEMS TO ME IT'S SMARTER TO TAKE THE FIGHT *TO* THE ENEMY INSTEAD OF WAITIN' FOR THEM TO *BRING IT* TO US.

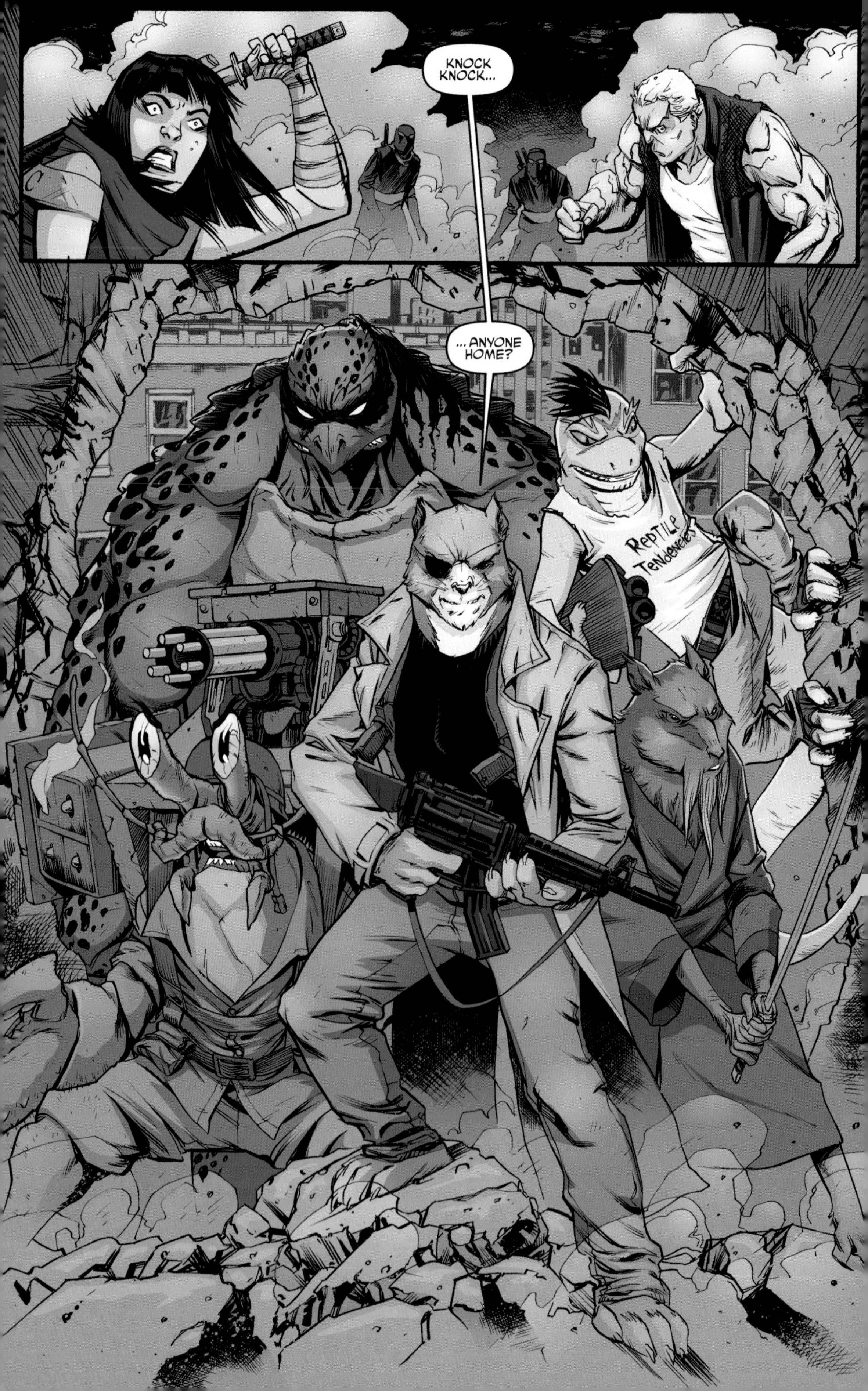
KNOCK KNOCK...
...ANYONE HOME?

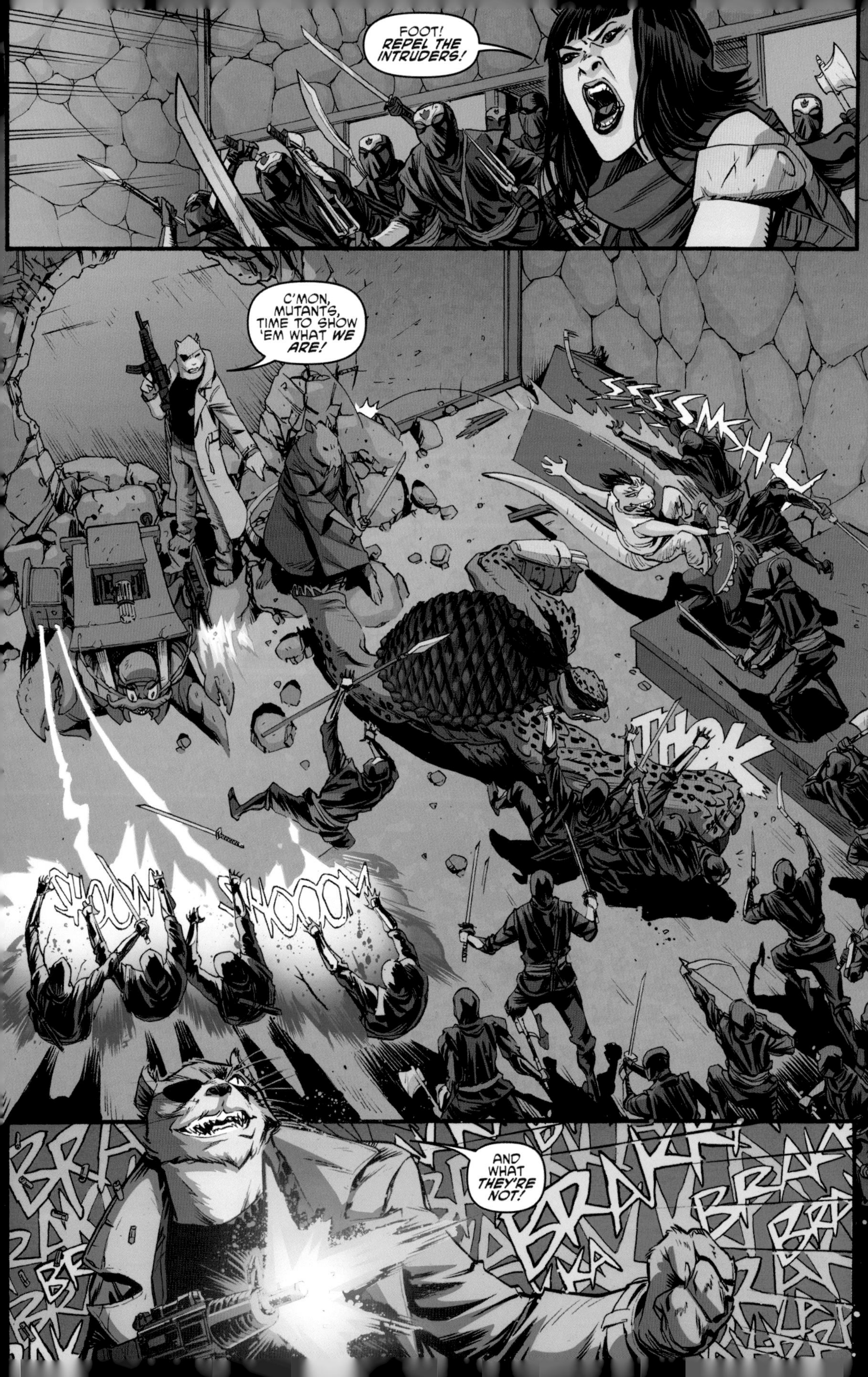
FOOT! REPEL THE INTRUDERS!
C'MON, MUTANTS, TIME TO SHOW 'EM WHAT WE ARE!
THOK
SHOOM
SHOOOOM
AND WHAT THEY'RE NOT!

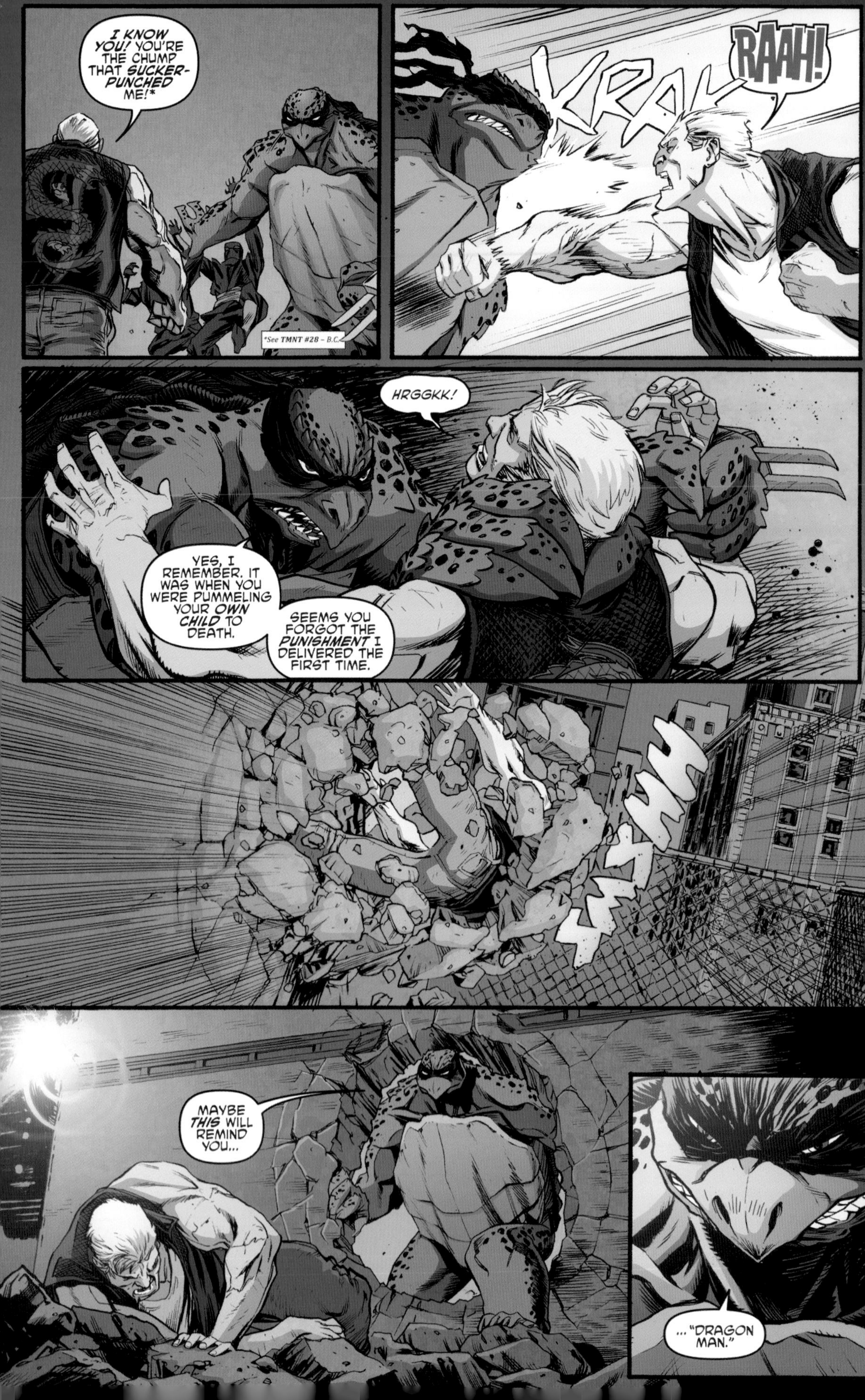
I KNOW YOU! YOU'RE THE CHUMP THAT SUCKER-PUNCHED ME!*
*See TMNT #28 – B.C.
KRAK
RAAH!
HRGGKK!
YES, I REMEMBER. IT WAS WHEN YOU WERE PUMMELING YOUR OWN CHILD TO DEATH.
SEEMS YOU FORGOT THE PUNISHMENT I DELIVERED THE FIRST TIME.
MAYBE THIS WILL REMIND YOU...
..."DRAGON MAN."

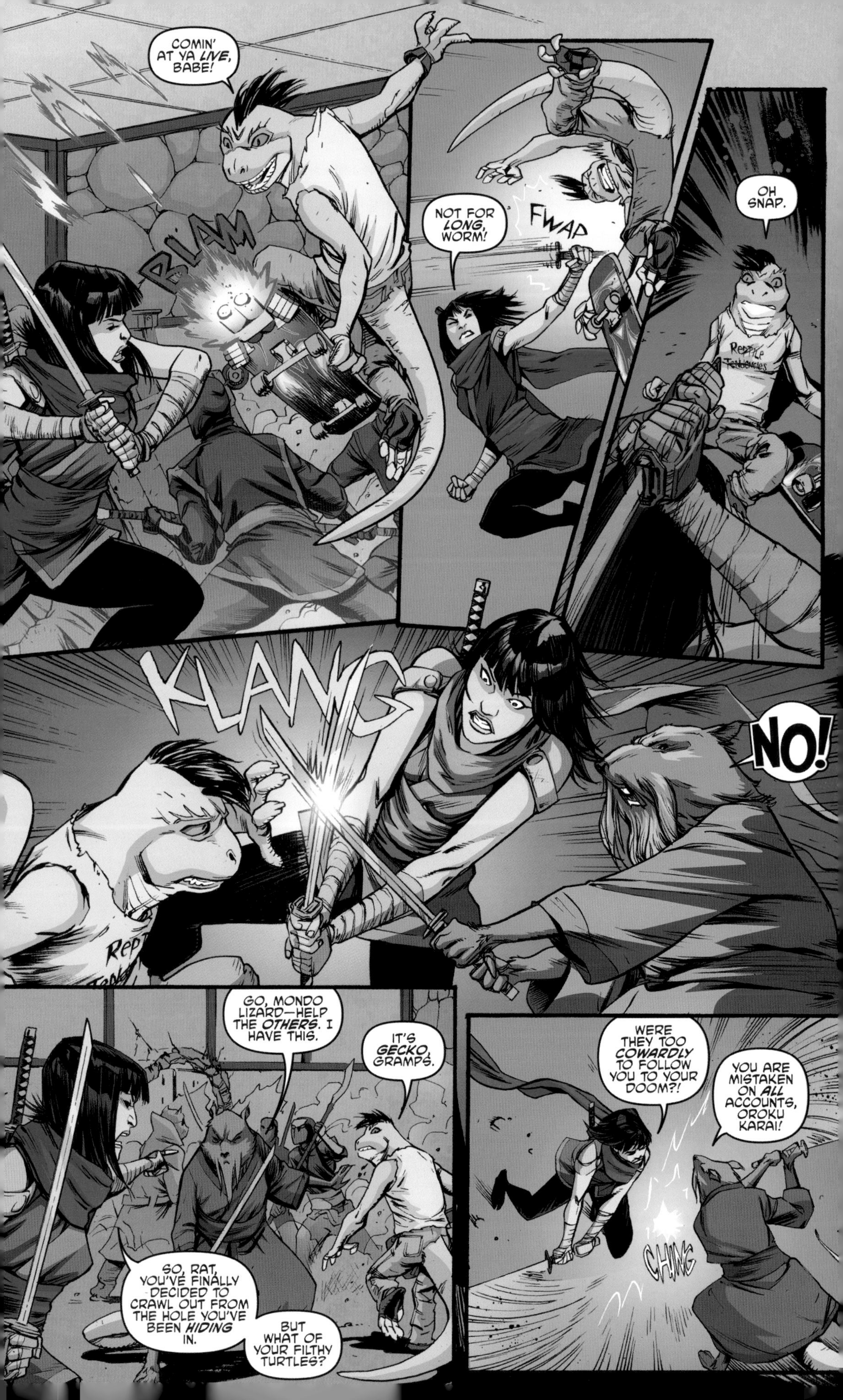

COMIN' AT YA LIVE, BABE!
BLAM
NOT FOR LONG, WORM!
FWAP
OH SNAP.
KLANG
NO!
GO, MONDO LIZARD—HELP THE OTHERS. I HAVE THIS.
IT'S GECKO, GRAMPS.
SO, RAT, YOU'VE FINALLY DECIDED TO CRAWL OUT FROM THE HOLE YOU'VE BEEN HIDING IN.
BUT WHAT OF YOUR FILTHY TURTLES?
WERE THEY TOO COWARDLY TO FOLLOW YOU TO YOUR DOOM?!
YOU ARE MISTAKEN ON ALL ACCOUNTS, OROKU KARAI!
CHING

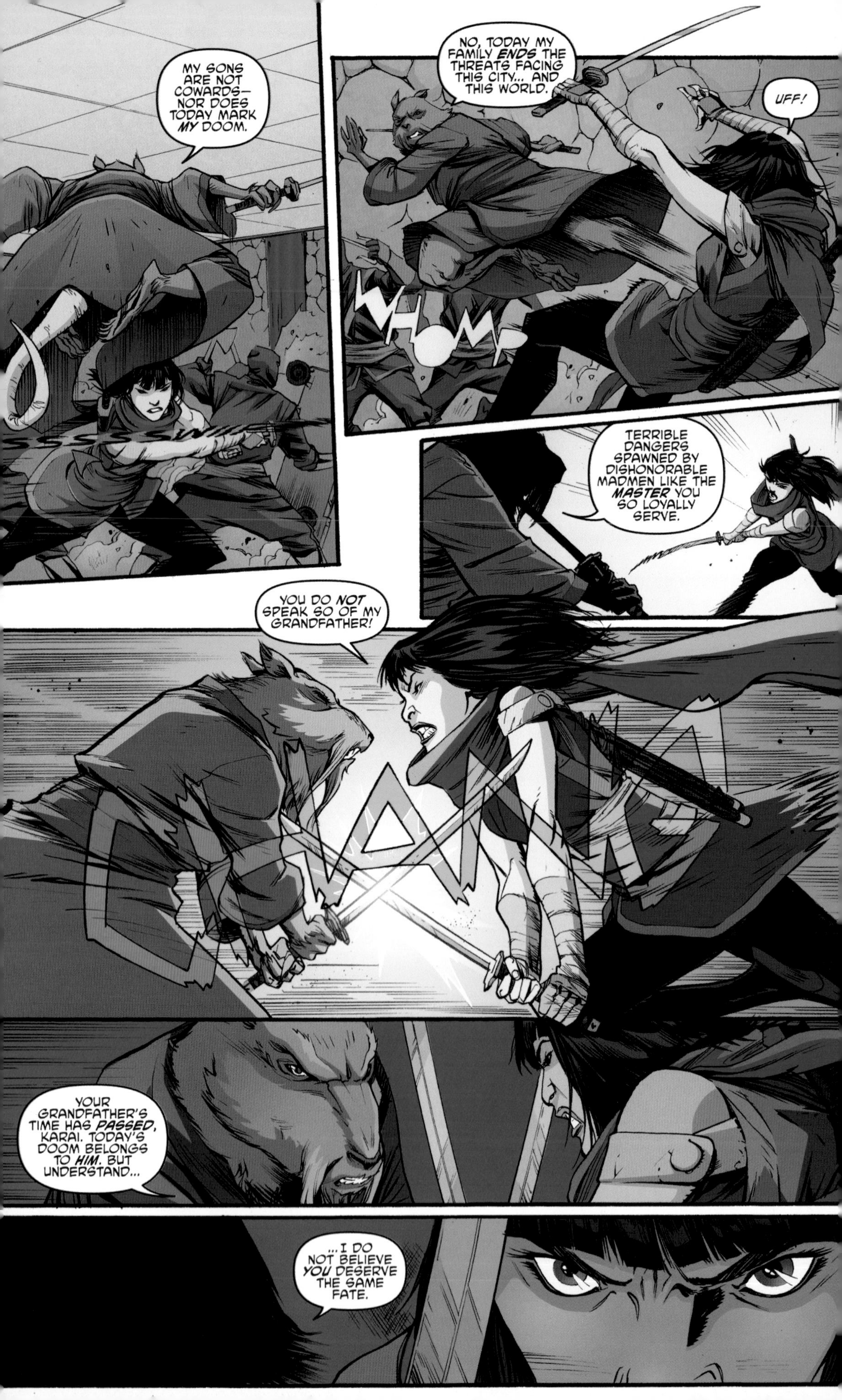
MY SONS ARE NOT COWARDS— NOR DOES TODAY MARK *MY* DOOM.
NO, TODAY MY FAMILY *ENDS* THE THREATS FACING THIS CITY... AND THIS WORLD.
UFF!
WHOMP
TERRIBLE DANGERS SPAWNED BY DISHONORABLE MADMEN LIKE THE *MASTER* YOU SO LOYALLY SERVE.
YOU DO *NOT* SPEAK SO OF MY GRANDFATHER!
YOUR GRANDFATHER'S TIME HAS *PASSED*, KARAI. TODAY'S DOOM BELONGS TO *HIM*. BUT UNDERSTAND...
...I DO NOT BELIEVE *YOU* DESERVE THE SAME FATE.

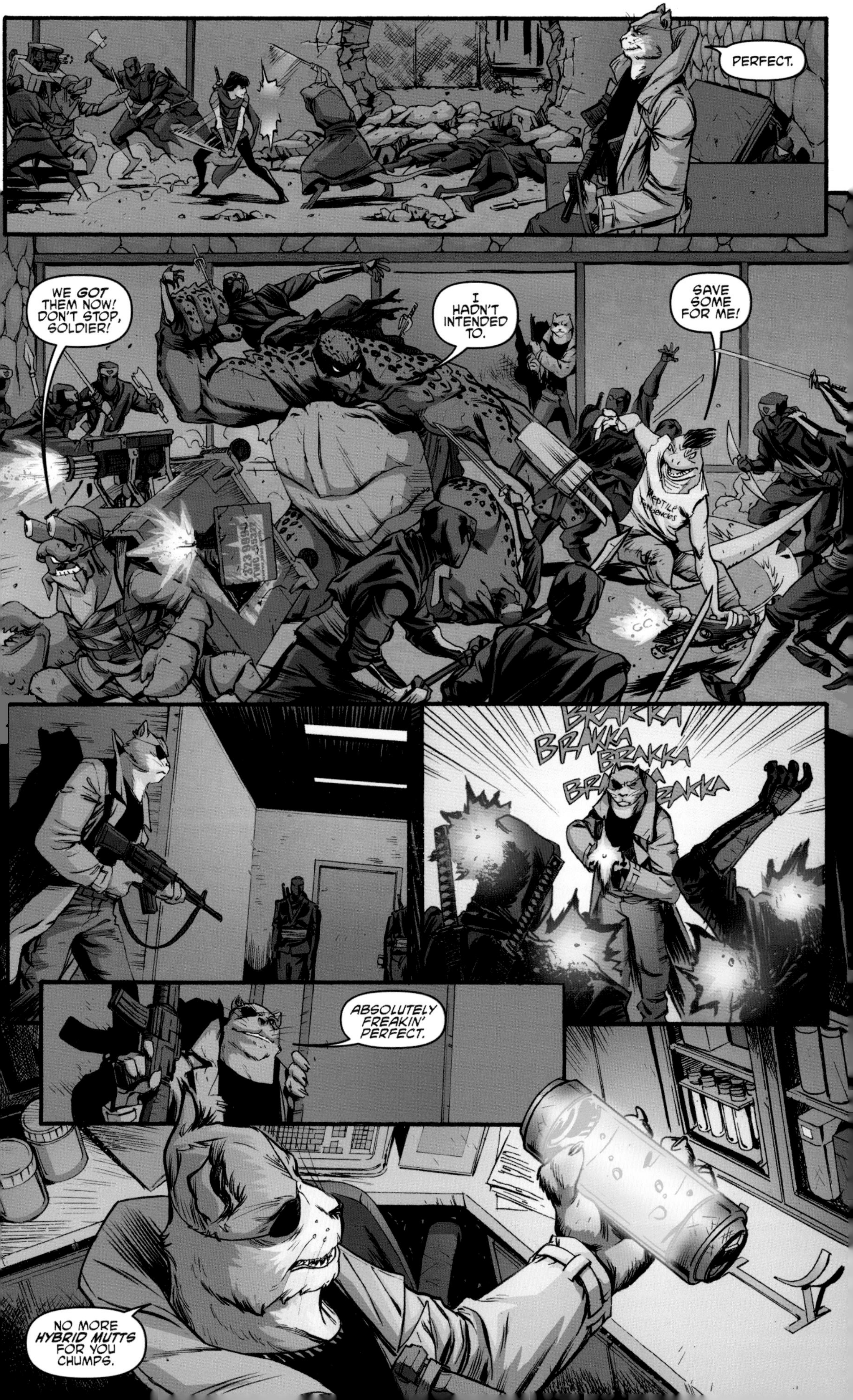

PERFECT.
WE *GOT* THEM NOW! DON'T STOP, SOLDIER!
I HADN'T INTENDED TO.
SAVE SOME FOR ME!
REPTILE Tendencies
BRAKKA
BRAKKA
ABSOLUTELY FREAKIN' PERFECT.
NO MORE ***HYBRID MUTTS*** FOR YOU CHUMPS.

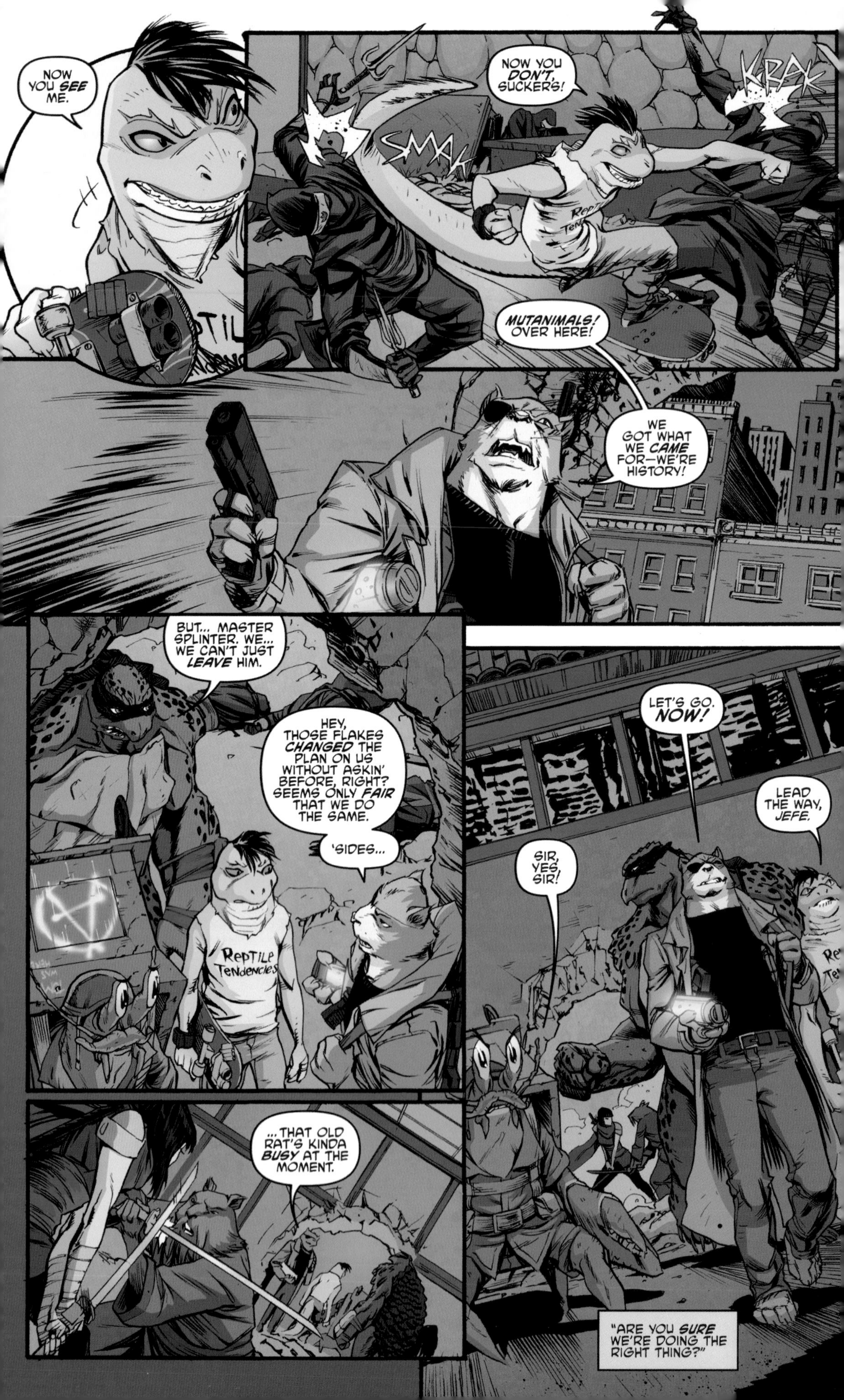
NOW YOU SEE ME.
NOW YOU DON'T, SUCKERS!
SMAK
KRAK
MUTANIMALS! OVER HERE!
WE GOT WHAT WE CAME FOR—WE'RE HISTORY!
BUT... MASTER SPLINTER. WE... WE CAN'T JUST LEAVE HIM.
HEY, THOSE FLAKES CHANGED THE PLAN ON US WITHOUT ASKIN' BEFORE, RIGHT? SEEMS ONLY FAIR THAT WE DO THE SAME.
'SIDES...
REPTILE TENDENCIES
...THAT OLD RAT'S KINDA BUSY AT THE MOMENT.
LET'S GO. NOW!
LEAD THE WAY, JEFE.
SIR, YES, SIR!
"ARE YOU SURE WE'RE DOING THE RIGHT THING?"

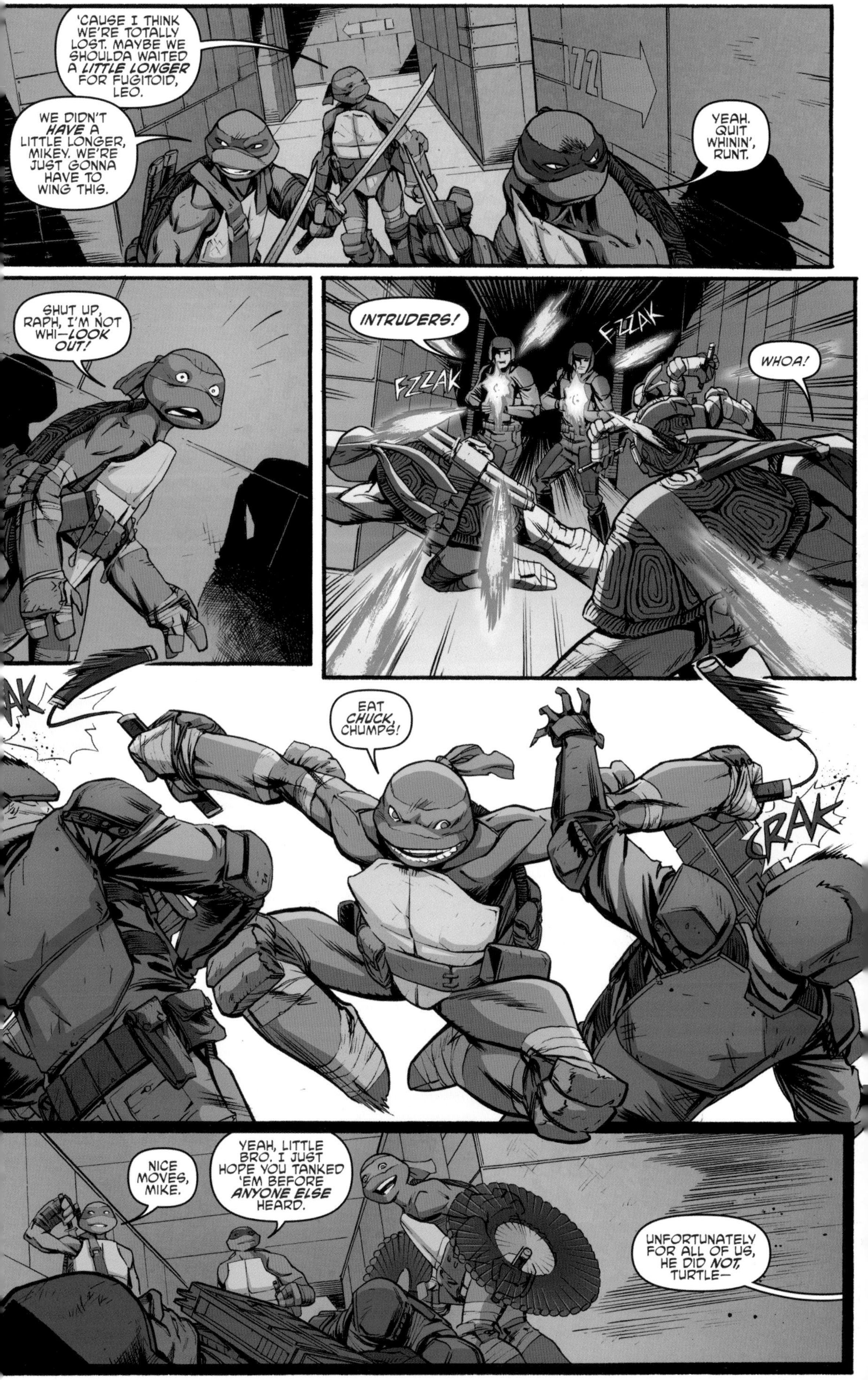

'CAUSE I THINK WE'RE TOTALLY LOST. MAYBE WE SHOULDA WAITED A LITTLE LONGER FOR FUGITOID, LEO.
WE DIDN'T HAVE A LITTLE LONGER, MIKEY. WE'RE JUST GONNA HAVE TO WING THIS.
YEAH. QUIT WHININ', RUNT.
172
SHUT UP, RAPH, I'M NOT WHI—LOOK OUT!
INTRUDERS!
FZZAK
FZZAK
WHOA!
EAT CHUCK, CHUMPS!
CRAK
NICE MOVES, MIKE.
YEAH, LITTLE BRO. I JUST HOPE YOU TANKED 'EM BEFORE ANYONE ELSE HEARD.
UNFORTUNATELY FOR ALL OF US, HE DID NOT, TURTLE—

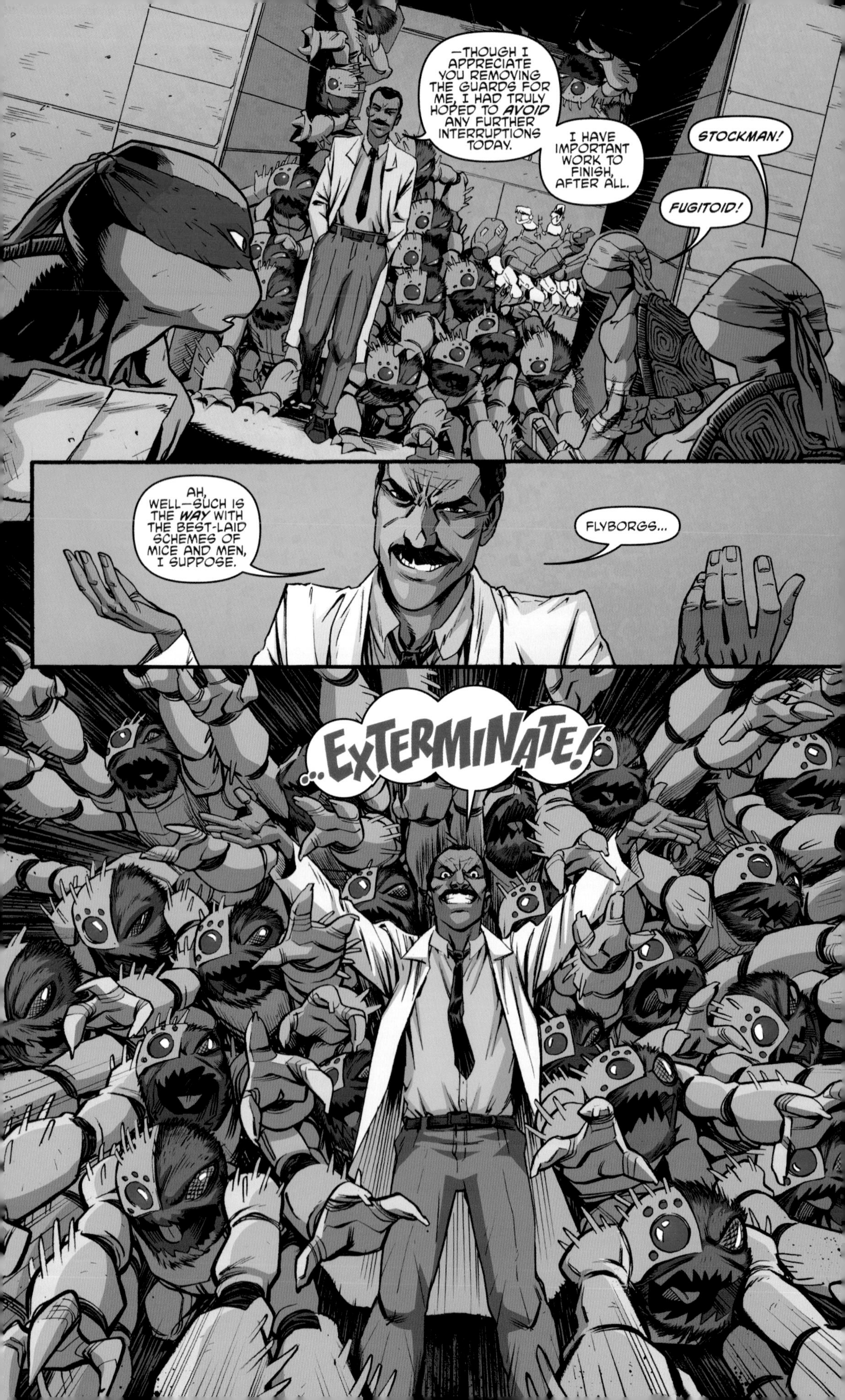
—THOUGH I APPRECIATE YOU REMOVING THE GUARDS FOR ME, I HAD TRULY HOPED TO AVOID ANY FURTHER INTERRUPTIONS TODAY.
I HAVE IMPORTANT WORK TO FINISH, AFTER ALL.
STOCKMAN!
FUGITOID!
AH, WELL—SUCH IS THE WAY WITH THE BEST-LAID SCHEMES OF MICE AND MEN, I SUPPOSE.
FLYBORGS...
...EXTERMINATE!

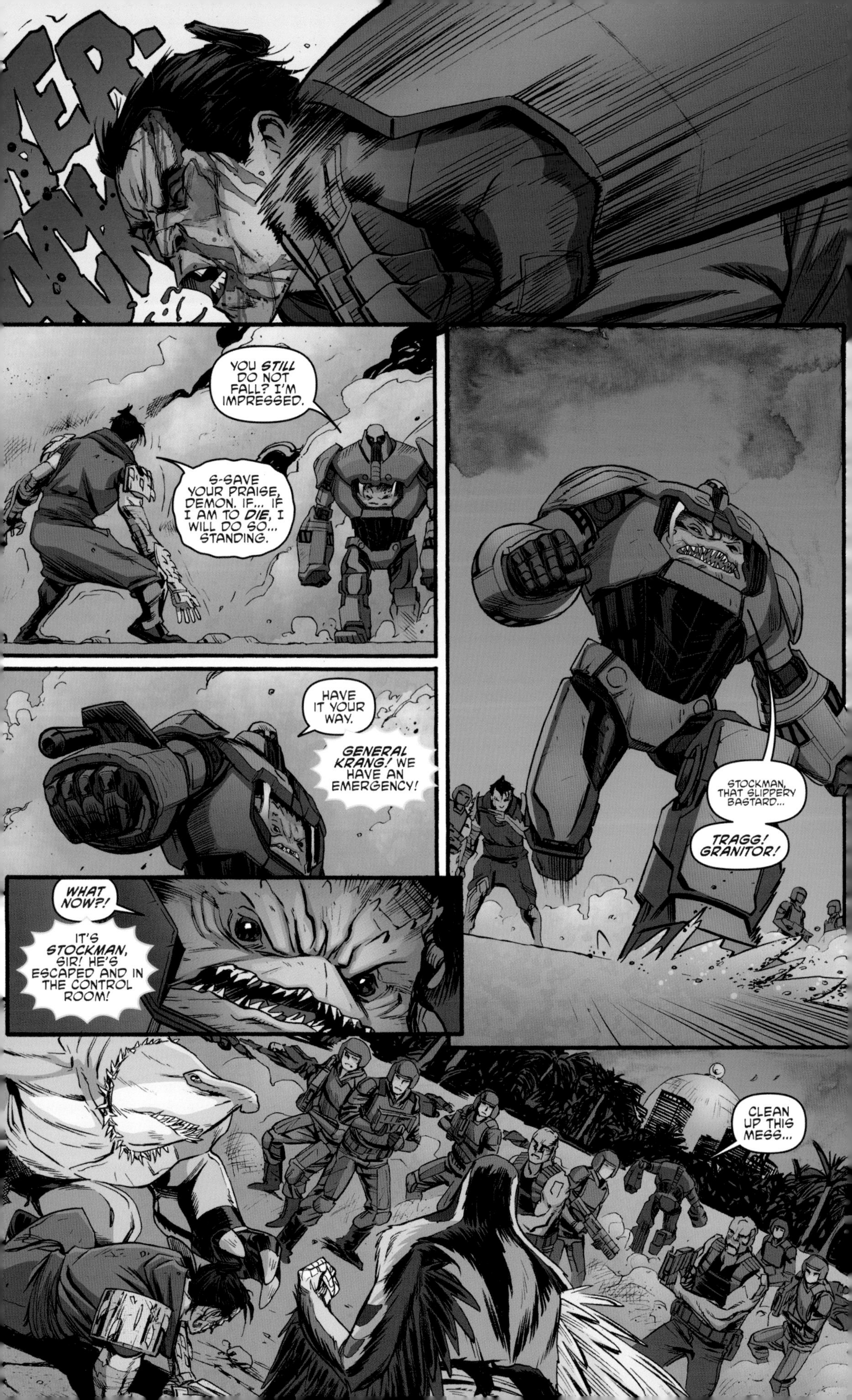
YOU STILL DO NOT FALL? I'M IMPRESSED.
S-SAVE YOUR PRAISE, DEMON. IF... IF I AM TO DIE, I WILL DO SO... STANDING.
HAVE IT YOUR WAY.
GENERAL KRANG! WE HAVE AN EMERGENCY!
WHAT NOW?!
IT'S STOCKMAN, SIR! HE'S ESCAPED AND IN THE CONTROL ROOM!
STOCKMAN, THAT SLIPPERY BASTARD...
TRAGG! GRANITOR!
CLEAN UP THIS MESS...

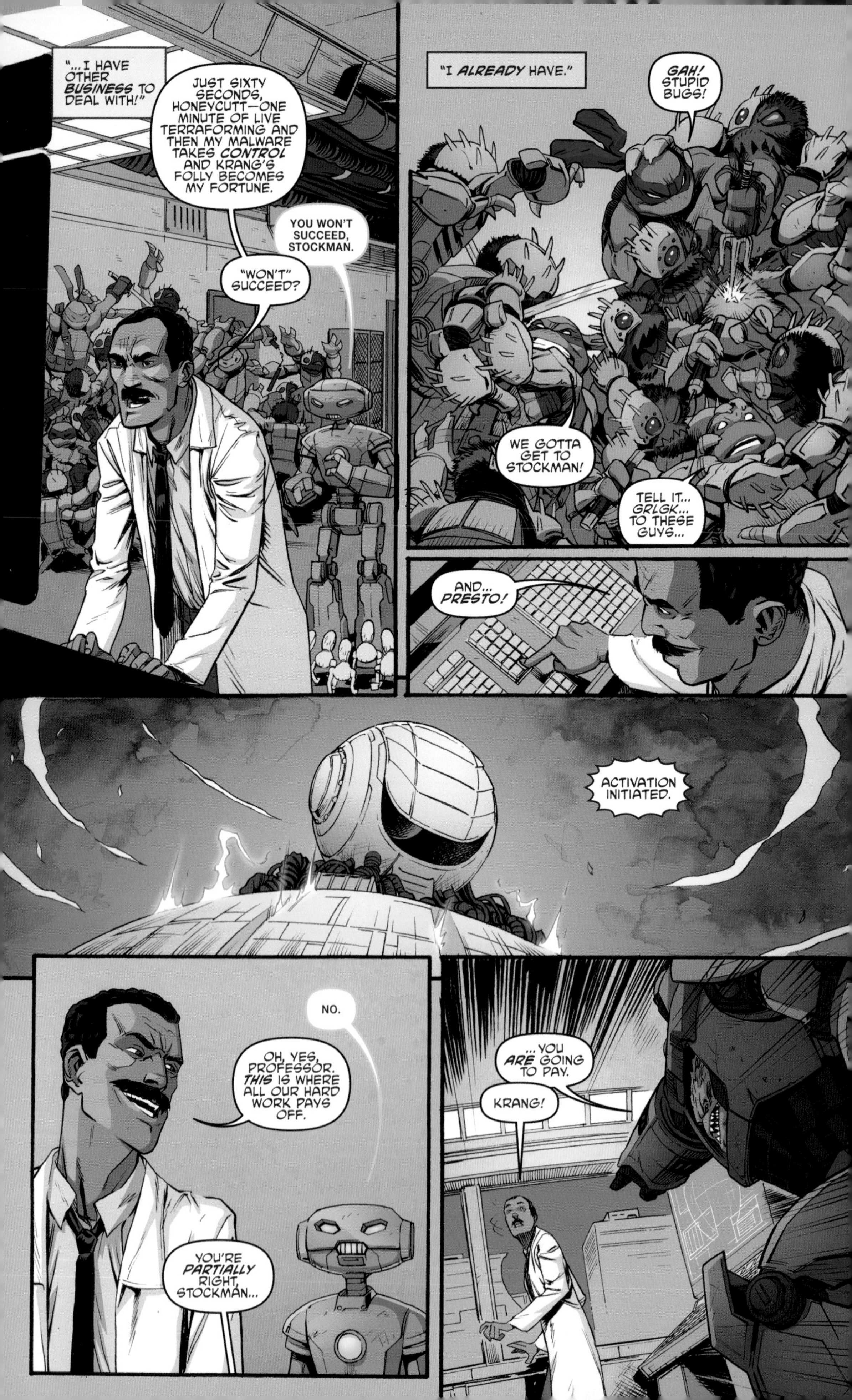
"...I HAVE OTHER BUSINESS TO DEAL WITH!"
JUST SIXTY SECONDS, HONEYCUTT—ONE MINUTE OF LIVE TERRAFORMING AND THEN MY MALWARE TAKES CONTROL AND KRANG'S FOLLY BECOMES MY FORTUNE.
YOU WON'T SUCCEED, STOCKMAN.
"WON'T" SUCCEED?
"I ALREADY HAVE."
GAH! STUPID BUGS!
WE GOTTA GET TO STOCKMAN!
TELL IT... GRLGK... TO THESE GUYS...
AND... PRESTO!
ACTIVATION INITIATED.
OH, YES, PROFESSOR. THIS IS WHERE ALL OUR HARD WORK PAYS OFF.
NO.
YOU'RE PARTIALLY RIGHT, STOCKMAN...
... YOU ARE GOING TO PAY.
KRANG!

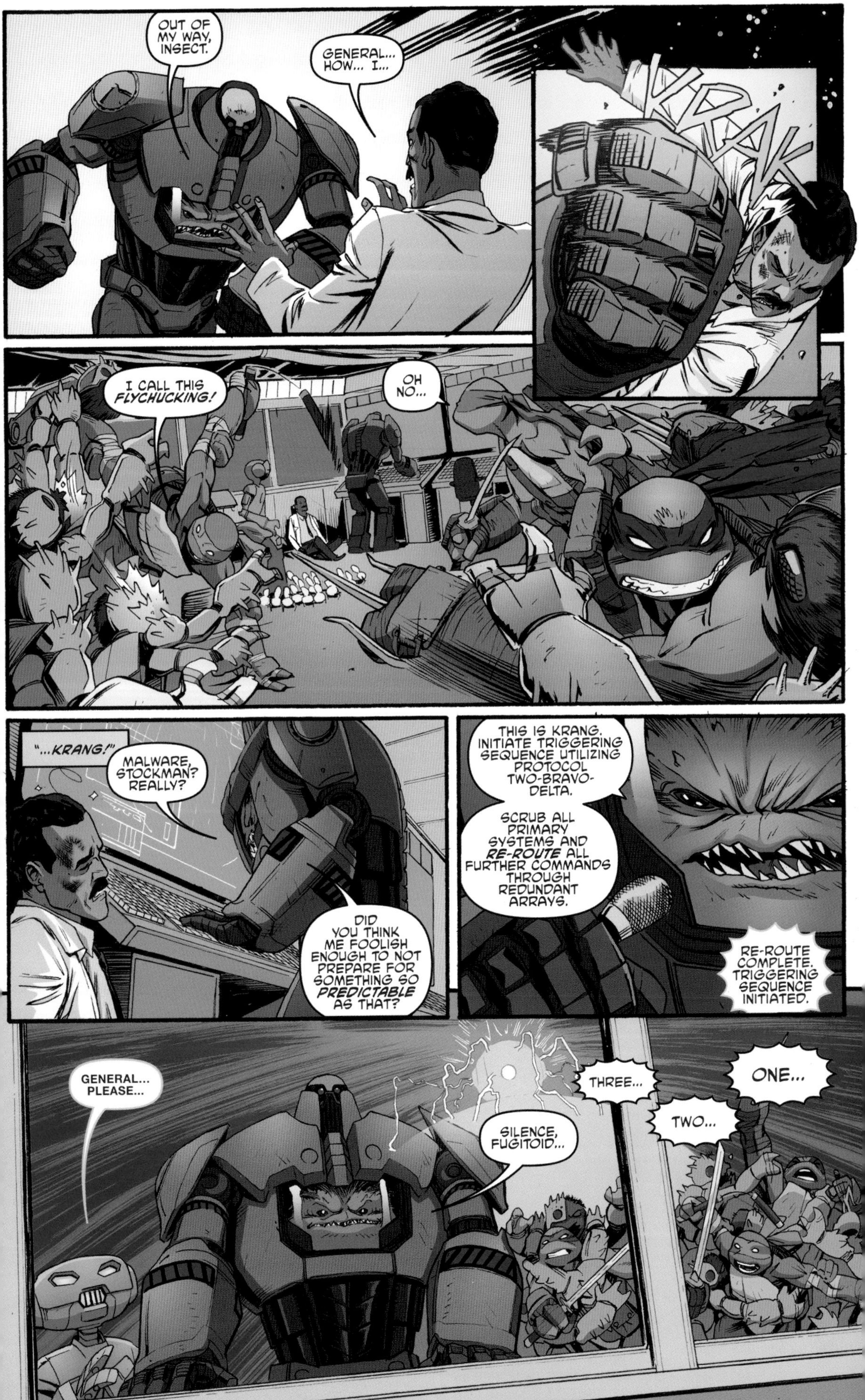
OUT OF MY WAY, INSECT.
GENERAL... HOW... I...
KRAK
I CALL THIS FLYCHUCKING!
OH NO...
"...KRANG!"
MALWARE, STOCKMAN? REALLY?
DID YOU THINK ME FOOLISH ENOUGH TO NOT PREPARE FOR SOMETHING SO PREDICTABLE AS THAT?
THIS IS KRANG. INITIATE TRIGGERING SEQUENCE UTILIZING PROTOCOL TWO-BRAVO-DELTA.
SCRUB ALL PRIMARY SYSTEMS AND RE-ROUTE ALL FURTHER COMMANDS THROUGH REDUNDANT ARRAYS.
RE-ROUTE COMPLETE. TRIGGERING SEQUENCE INITIATED.
GENERAL... PLEASE...
SILENCE, FUGITOID...
THREE...
TWO...
ONE...

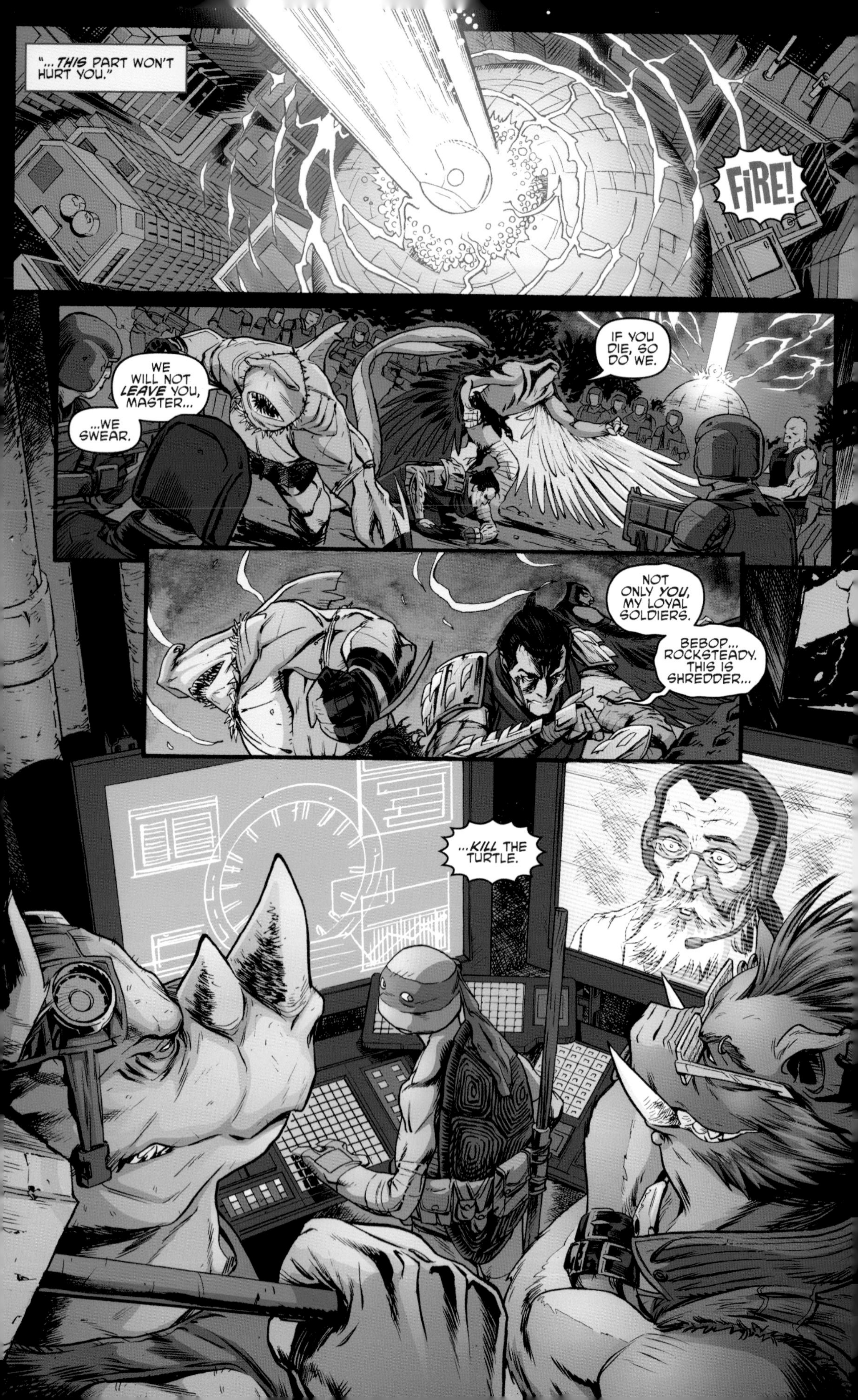
"...THIS PART WON'T HURT YOU."
FIRE!
WE WILL NOT LEAVE YOU, MASTER...
...WE SWEAR.
IF YOU DIE, SO DO WE.
NOT ONLY YOU, MY LOYAL SOLDIERS.
BEBOP... ROCKSTEADY. THIS IS SHREDDER...
...KILL THE TURTLE.

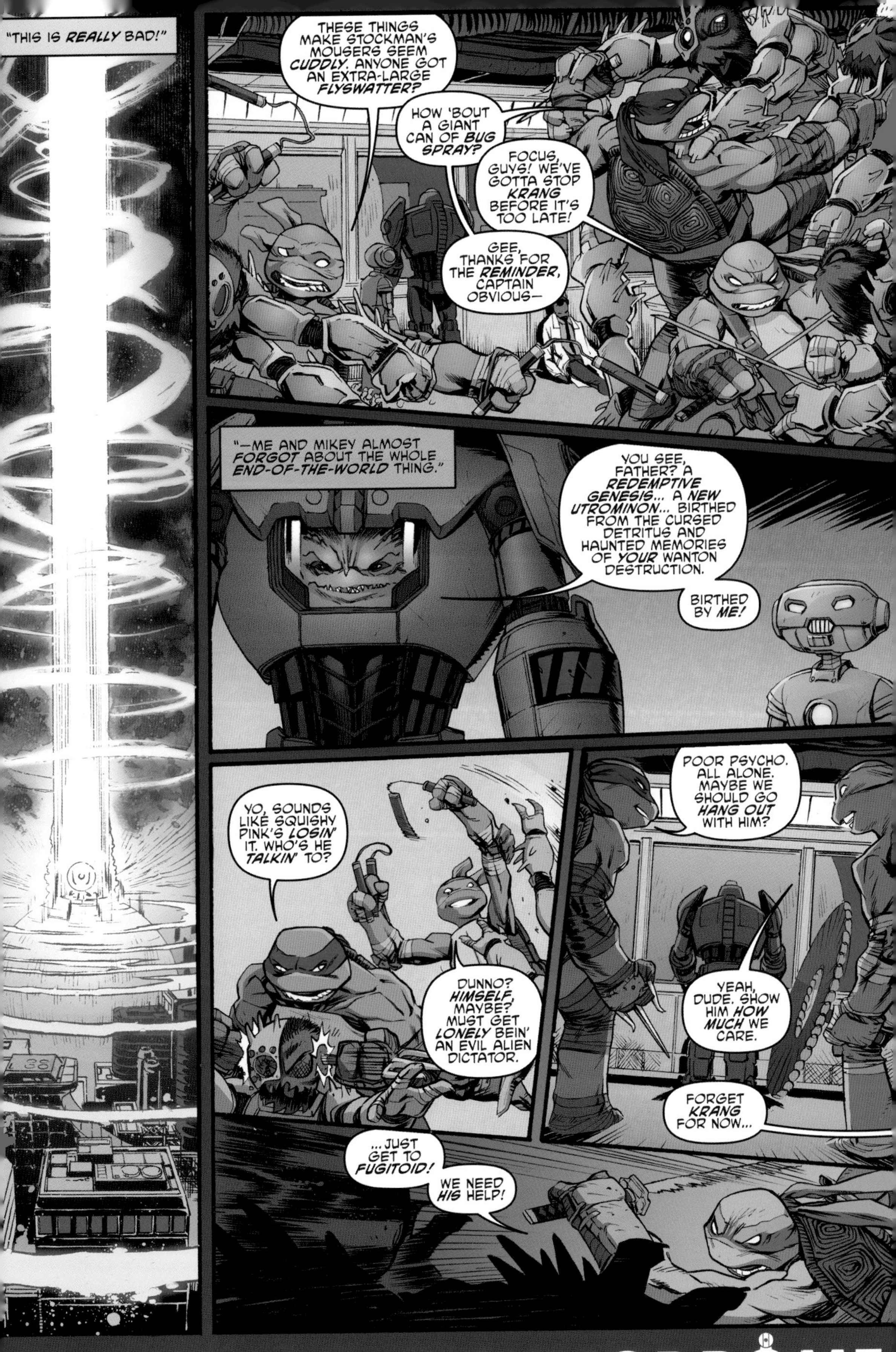
"THIS IS REALLY BAD!"
THESE THINGS MAKE STOCKMAN'S MOUSERS SEEM CUDDLY. ANYONE GOT AN EXTRA-LARGE FLYSWATTER?
HOW 'BOUT A GIANT CAN OF BUG SPRAY?
FOCUS, GUYS! WE'VE GOTTA STOP KRANG BEFORE IT'S TOO LATE!
GEE, THANKS FOR THE REMINDER, CAPTAIN OBVIOUS—
"—ME AND MIKEY ALMOST FORGOT ABOUT THE WHOLE END-OF-THE-WORLD THING."
YOU SEE, FATHER? A REDEMPTIVE GENESIS... A NEW UTROMINON... BIRTHED FROM THE CURSED DETRITUS AND HAUNTED MEMORIES OF YOUR WANTON DESTRUCTION.
BIRTHED BY ME!
YO, SOUNDS LIKE SQUISHY PINK'S LOSIN' IT. WHO'S HE TALKIN' TO?
DUNNO? HIMSELF, MAYBE? MUST GET LONELY BEIN' AN EVIL ALIEN DICTATOR.
POOR PSYCHO. ALL ALONE. MAYBE WE SHOULD GO HANG OUT WITH HIM?
YEAH, DUDE. SHOW HIM HOW MUCH WE CARE.
FORGET KRANG FOR NOW...
...JUST GET TO FUGITOID!
WE NEED HIS HELP!

ATTACK ON TECHNODROME

PART FOUR

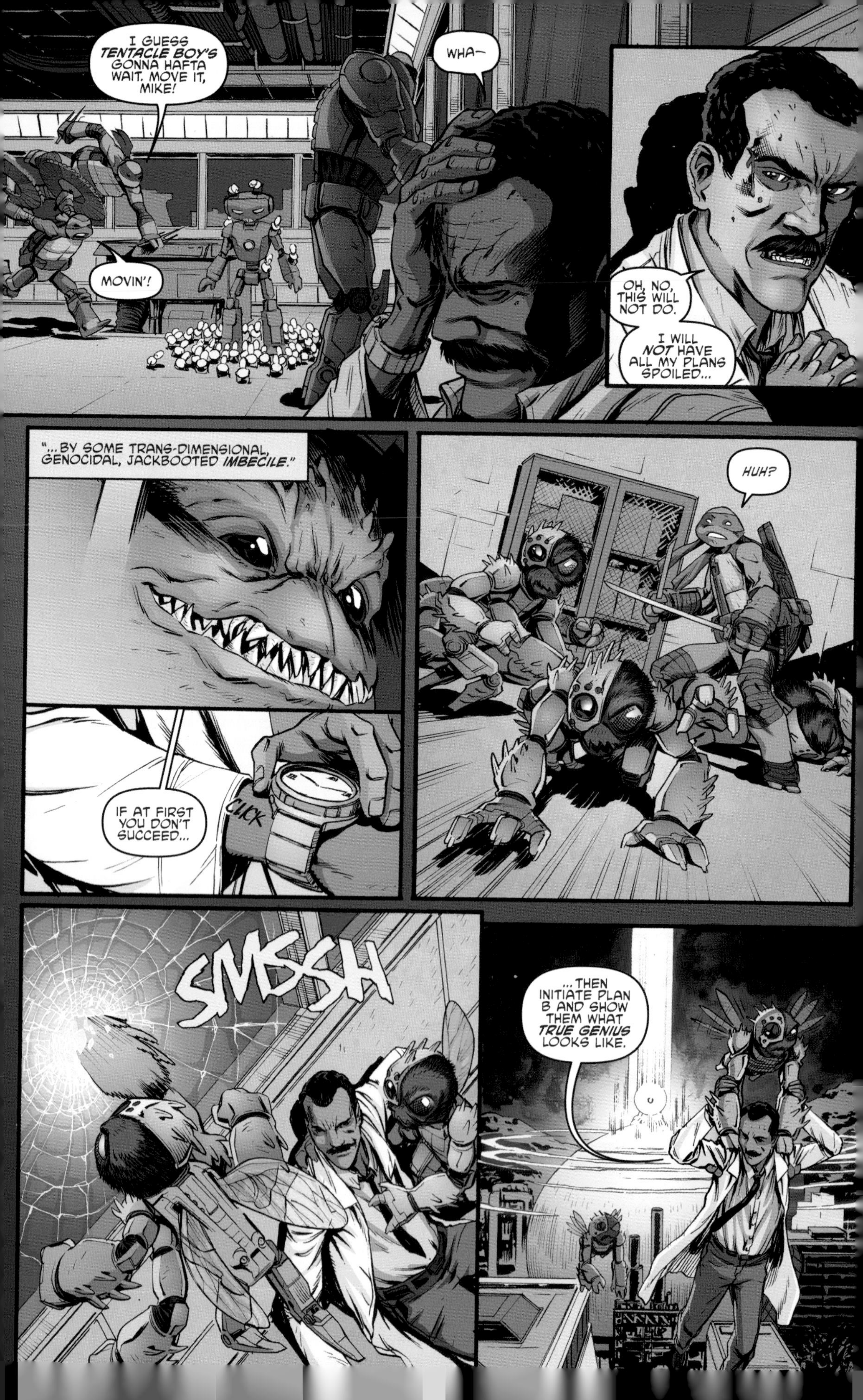
I GUESS TENTACLE BOY'S GONNA HAFTA WAIT. MOVE IT, MIKE!
MOVIN'!
WHA—
OH, NO, THIS WILL NOT DO.
I WILL NOT HAVE ALL MY PLANS SPOILED...
"...BY SOME TRANS-DIMENSIONAL, GENOCIDAL, JACKBOOTED IMBECILE."
HUH?
CLICK
IF AT FIRST YOU DON'T SUCCEED...
SMSSH
...THEN INITIATE PLAN B AND SHOW THEM WHAT TRUE GENIUS LOOKS LIKE.

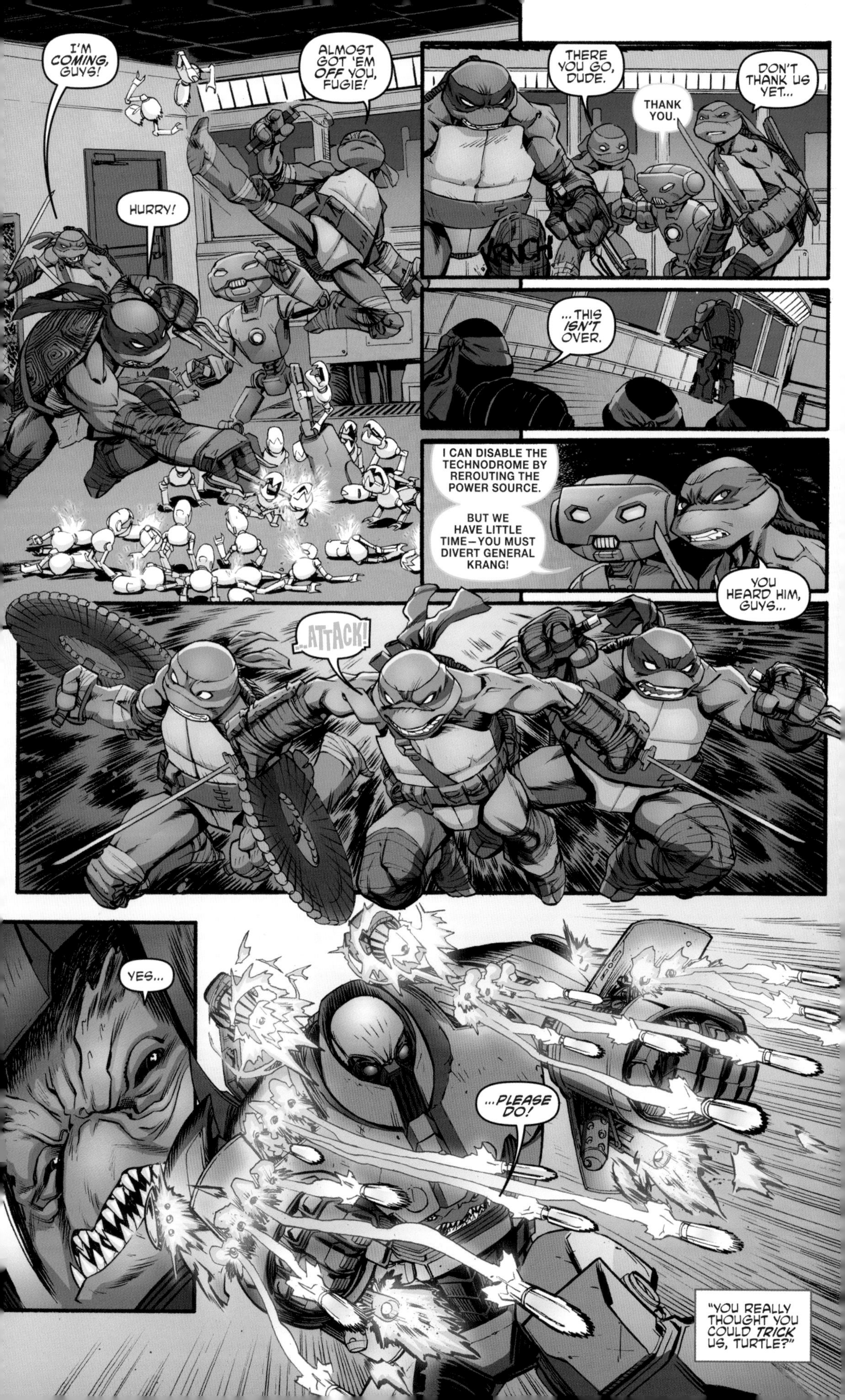

I'M COMING, GUYS!
ALMOST GOT 'EM OFF YOU, FUGIE!
HURRY!
THERE YOU GO, DUDE.
THANK YOU.
DON'T THANK US YET...
...THIS ISN'T OVER.
I CAN DISABLE THE TECHNODROME BY REROUTING THE POWER SOURCE.
BUT WE HAVE LITTLE TIME—YOU MUST DIVERT GENERAL KRANG!
YOU HEARD HIM, GUYS...
...ATTACK!
YES...
...PLEASE DO!
"YOU REALLY THOUGHT YOU COULD TRICK US, TURTLE?"

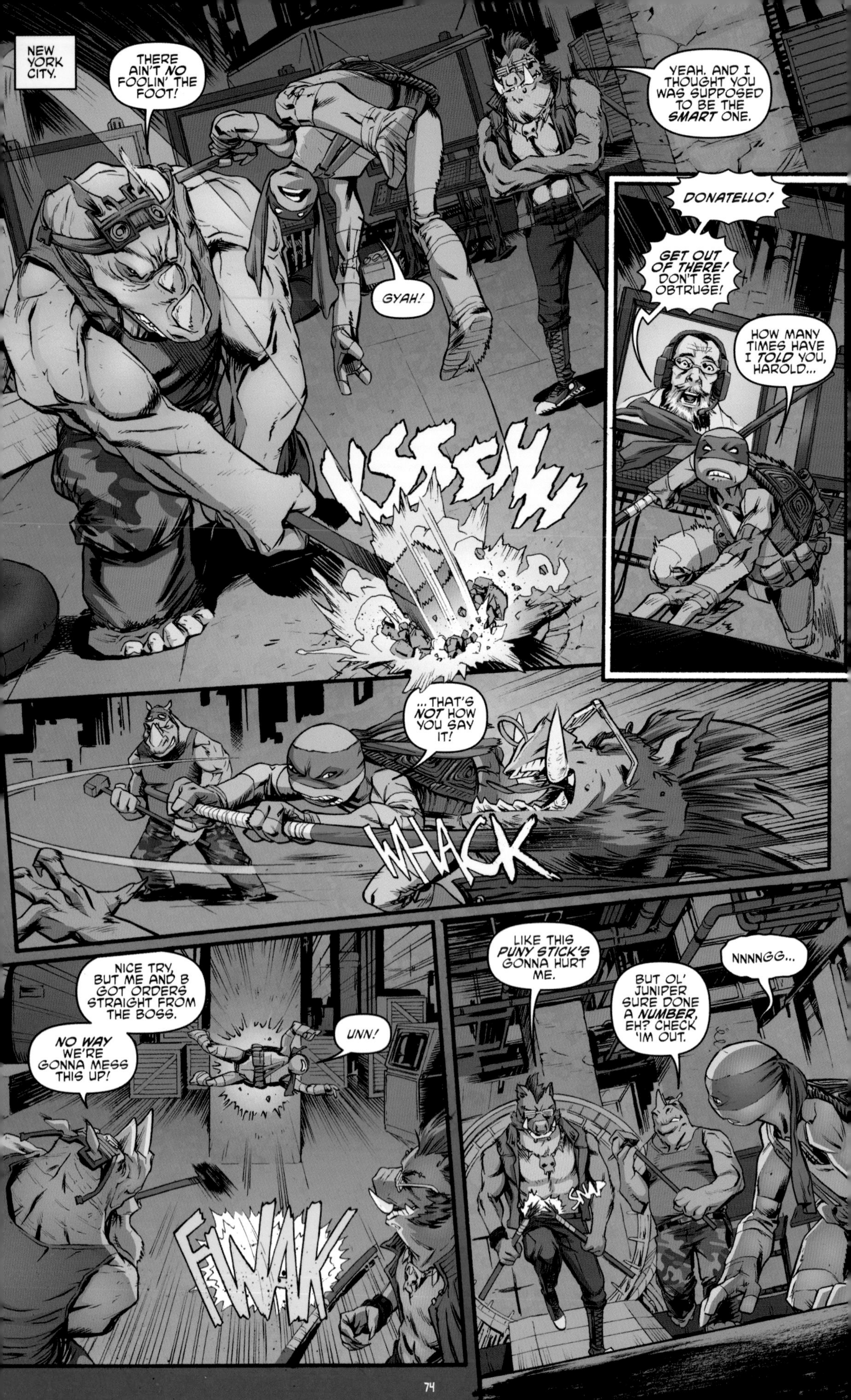

NEW YORK CITY.
THERE AIN'T NO FOOLIN' THE FOOT!
YEAH. AND I THOUGHT YOU WAS SUPPOSED TO BE THE SMART ONE.
GYAH!
DONATELLO!
GET OUT OF THERE! DON'T BE OBTRUSE!
HOW MANY TIMES HAVE I TOLD YOU, HAROLD...
...THAT'S NOT HOW YOU SAY IT!
WHACK
NICE TRY, BUT ME AND B GOT ORDERS STRAIGHT FROM THE BOSS.
NO WAY WE'RE GONNA MESS THIS UP!
UNN!
LIKE THIS PUNY STICK'S GONNA HURT ME.
BUT OL' JUNIPER SURE DONE A NUMBER, EH? CHECK 'IM OUT.
NNNNGG...
SNAP

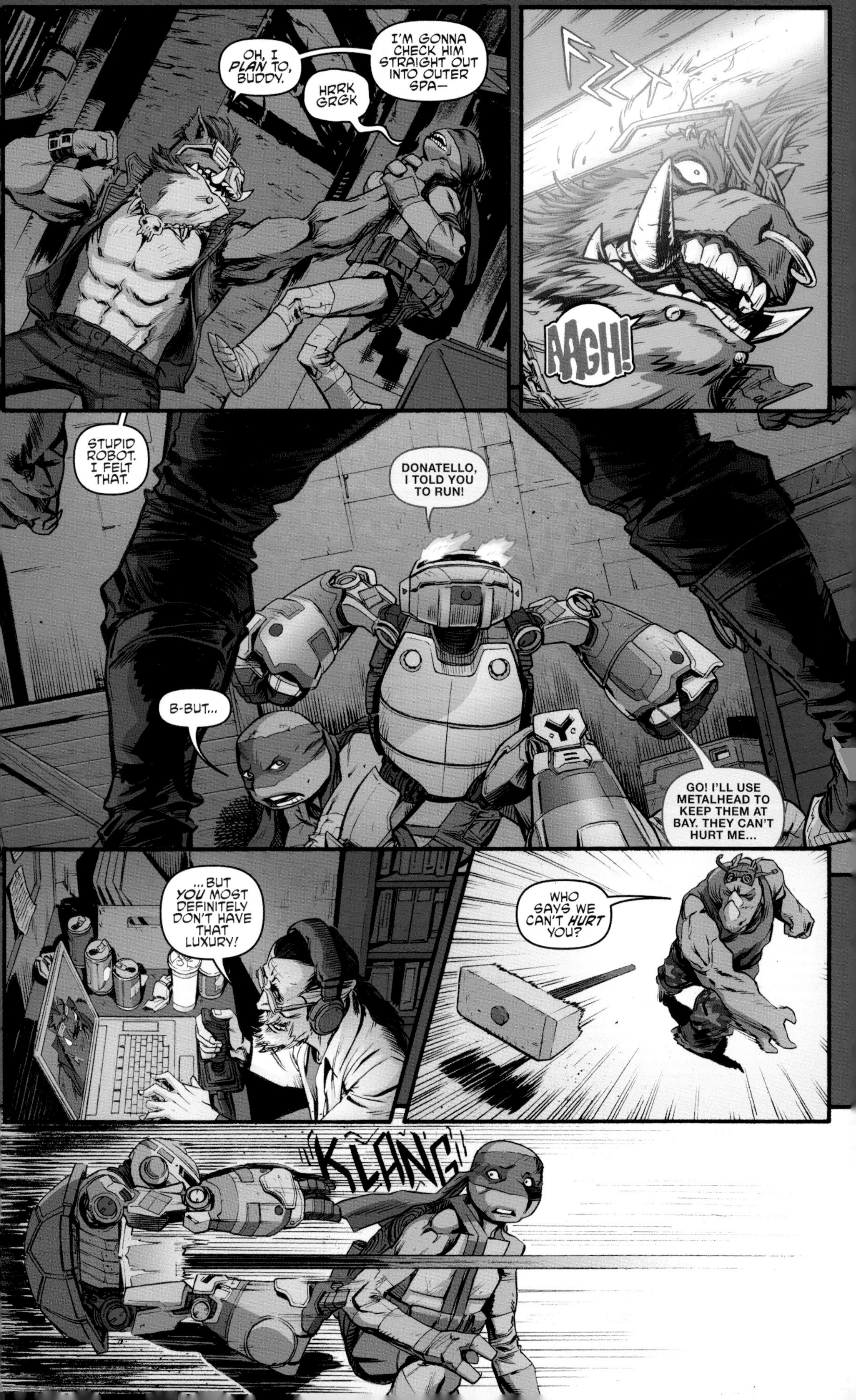
I'M GONNA CHECK HIM STRAIGHT OUT INTO OUTER SPA—
OH, I PLAN TO, BUDDY.
HRRK GRGK
FZZX
AAGH!
STUPID ROBOT. I FELT THAT.
DONATELLO, I TOLD YOU TO RUN!
B-BUT...
GO! I'LL USE METALHEAD TO KEEP THEM AT BAY. THEY CAN'T HURT ME...
...BUT YOU MOST DEFINITELY DON'T HAVE THAT LUXURY!
WHO SAYS WE CAN'T HURT YOU?
KLANG

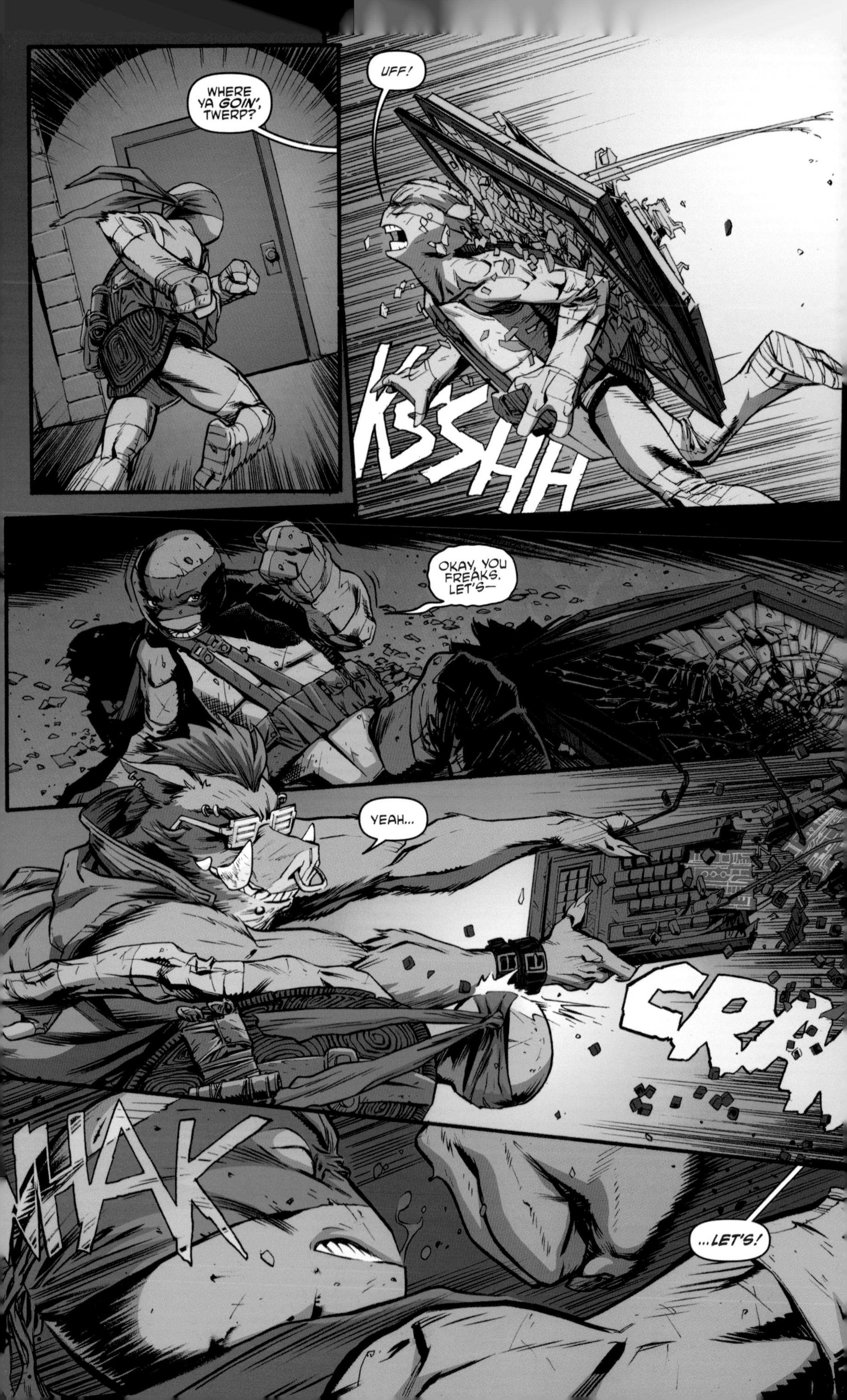
WHERE YA GOIN', TWERP?
UFF!
KSSHH
OKAY, YOU FREAKS. LET'S—
YEAH...
CRK
WHAK
...LET'S!

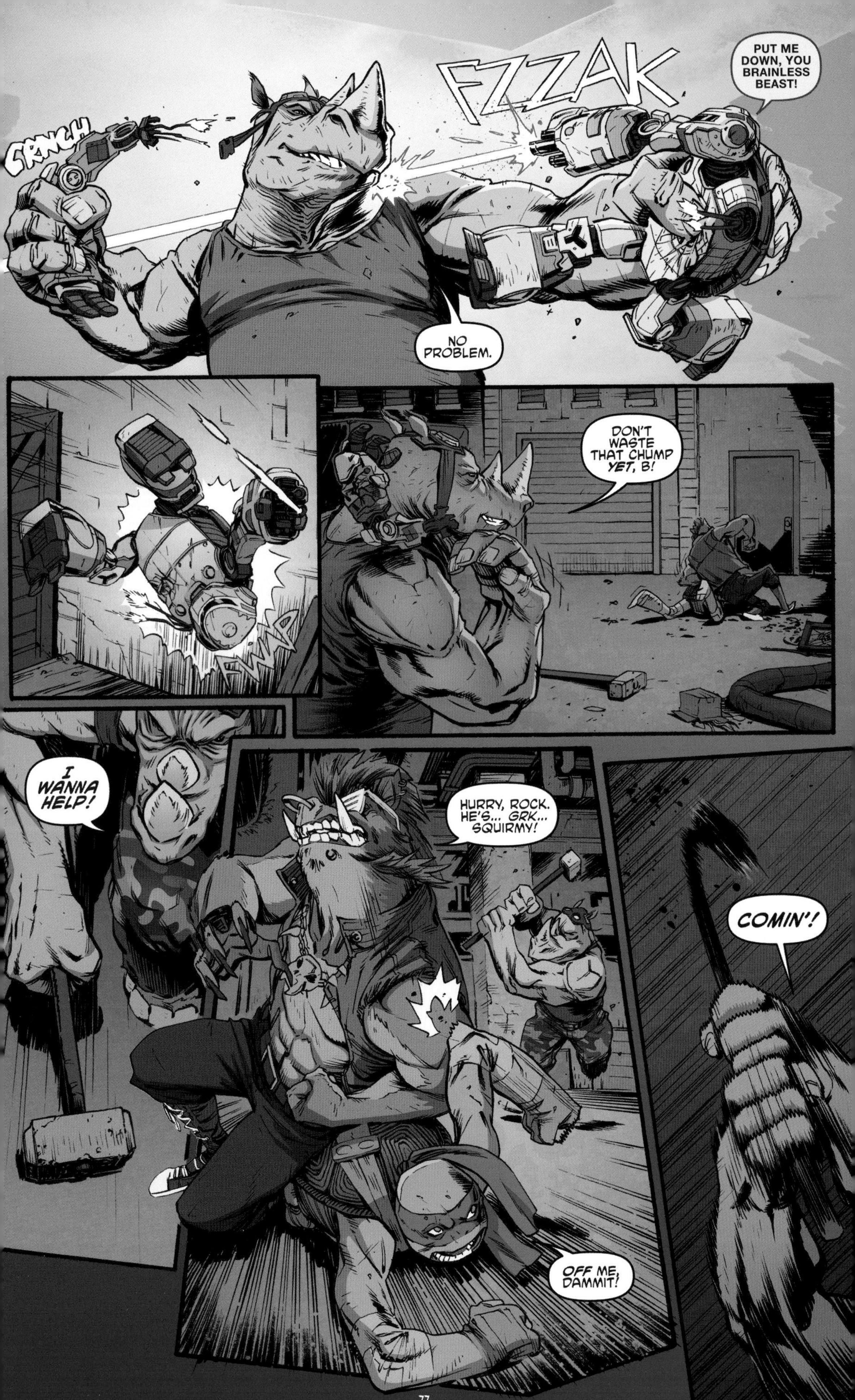
CRNCH
FZZAK
PUT ME DOWN, YOU BRAINLESS BEAST!
NO PROBLEM.
DON'T WASTE THAT CHUMP YET, B!
I WANNA HELP!
HURRY, ROCK. HE'S... GRK... SQUIRMY!
COMIN'!
OFF ME, DAMMIT!

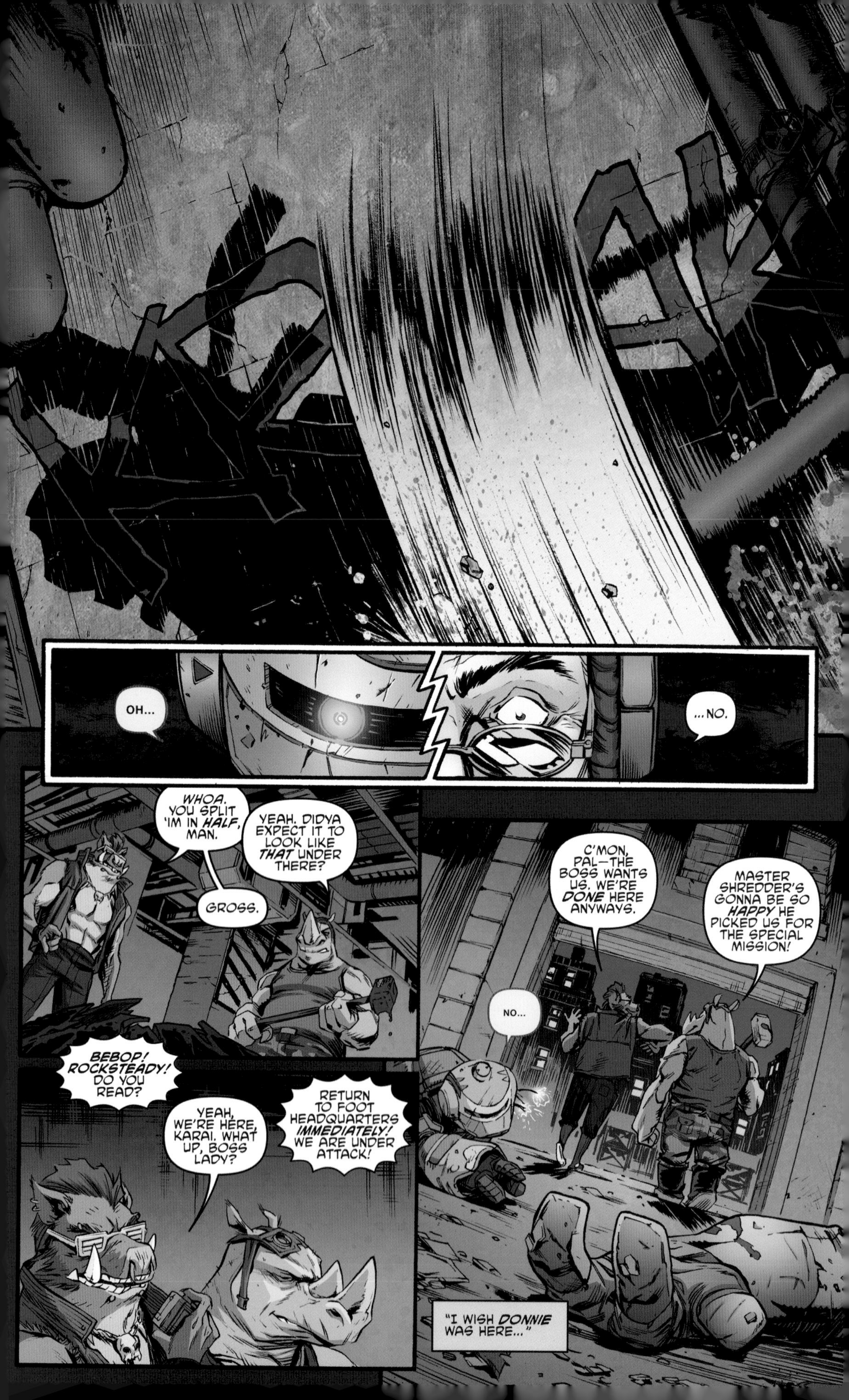
OH...
...NO.
WHOA. YOU SPLIT 'IM IN HALF, MAN.
YEAH. DIDYA EXPECT IT TO LOOK LIKE THAT UNDER THERE?
GROSS.
BEBOP! ROCKSTEADY! DO YOU READ?
YEAH, WE'RE HERE, KARAI. WHAT UP, BOSS LADY?
RETURN TO FOOT HEADQUARTERS IMMEDIATELY! WE ARE UNDER ATTACK!
C'MON, PAL—THE BOSS WANTS US. WE'RE DONE HERE ANYWAYS.
MASTER SHREDDER'S GONNA BE SO HAPPY HE PICKED US FOR THE SPECIAL MISSION!
NO...
"I WISH DONNIE WAS HERE..."

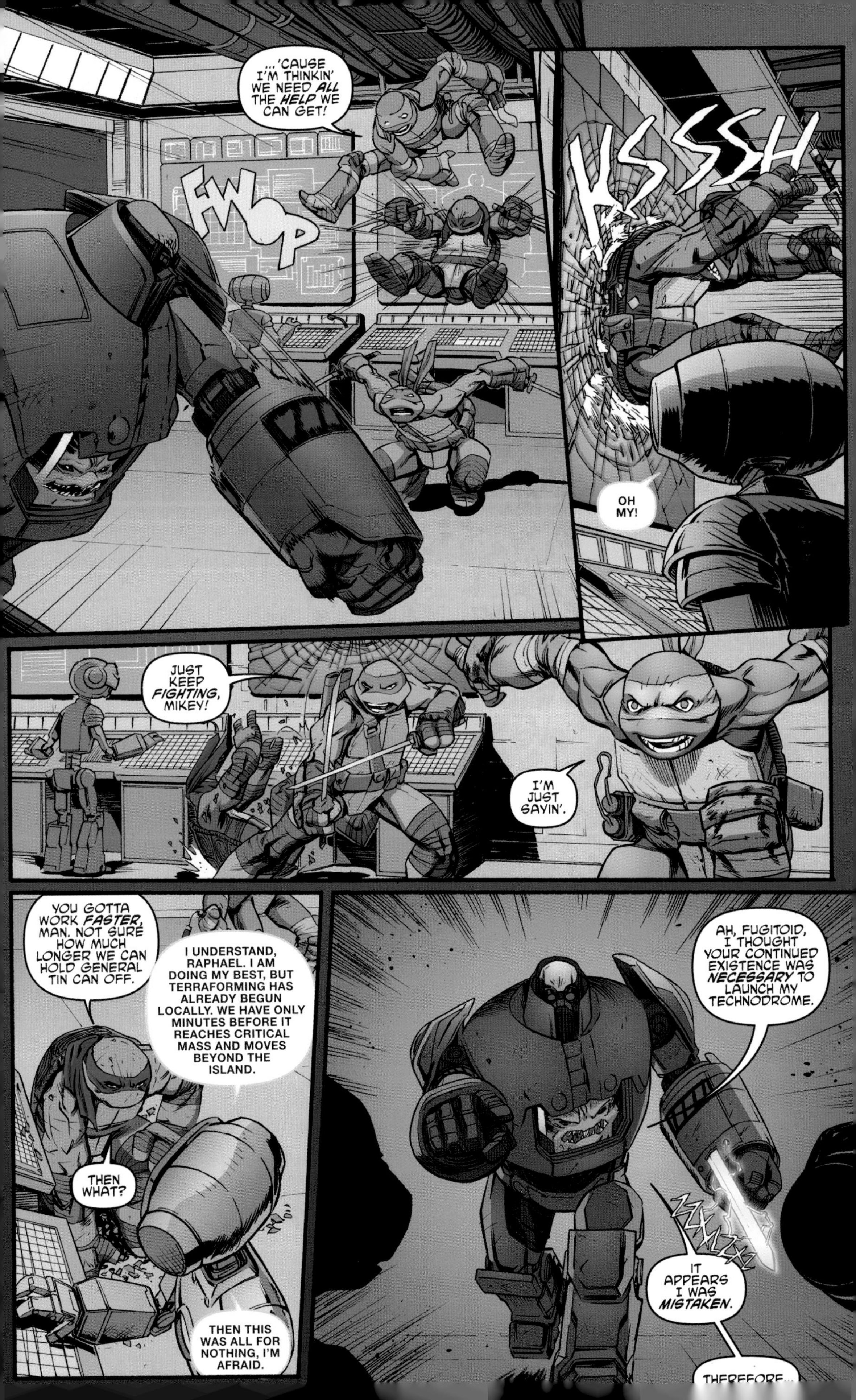
...'CAUSE I'M THINKIN' WE NEED *ALL* THE *HELP* WE CAN GET!
FWOP
KSSSH
OH MY!
JUST KEEP *FIGHTING*, MIKEY!
I'M JUST SAYIN'.
YOU GOTTA WORK *FASTER*, MAN. NOT SURE HOW MUCH LONGER WE CAN HOLD GENERAL TIN CAN OFF.
I UNDERSTAND, RAPHAEL. I AM DOING MY BEST, BUT TERRAFORMING HAS ALREADY BEGUN LOCALLY. WE HAVE ONLY MINUTES BEFORE IT REACHES CRITICAL MASS AND MOVES BEYOND THE ISLAND.
THEN WHAT?
THEN THIS WAS ALL FOR NOTHING, I'M AFRAID.
AH, FUGITOID, I THOUGHT YOUR CONTINUED EXISTENCE WAS *NECESSARY* TO LAUNCH MY TECHNODROME.
IT APPEARS I WAS *MISTAKEN*.
THEREFORE...

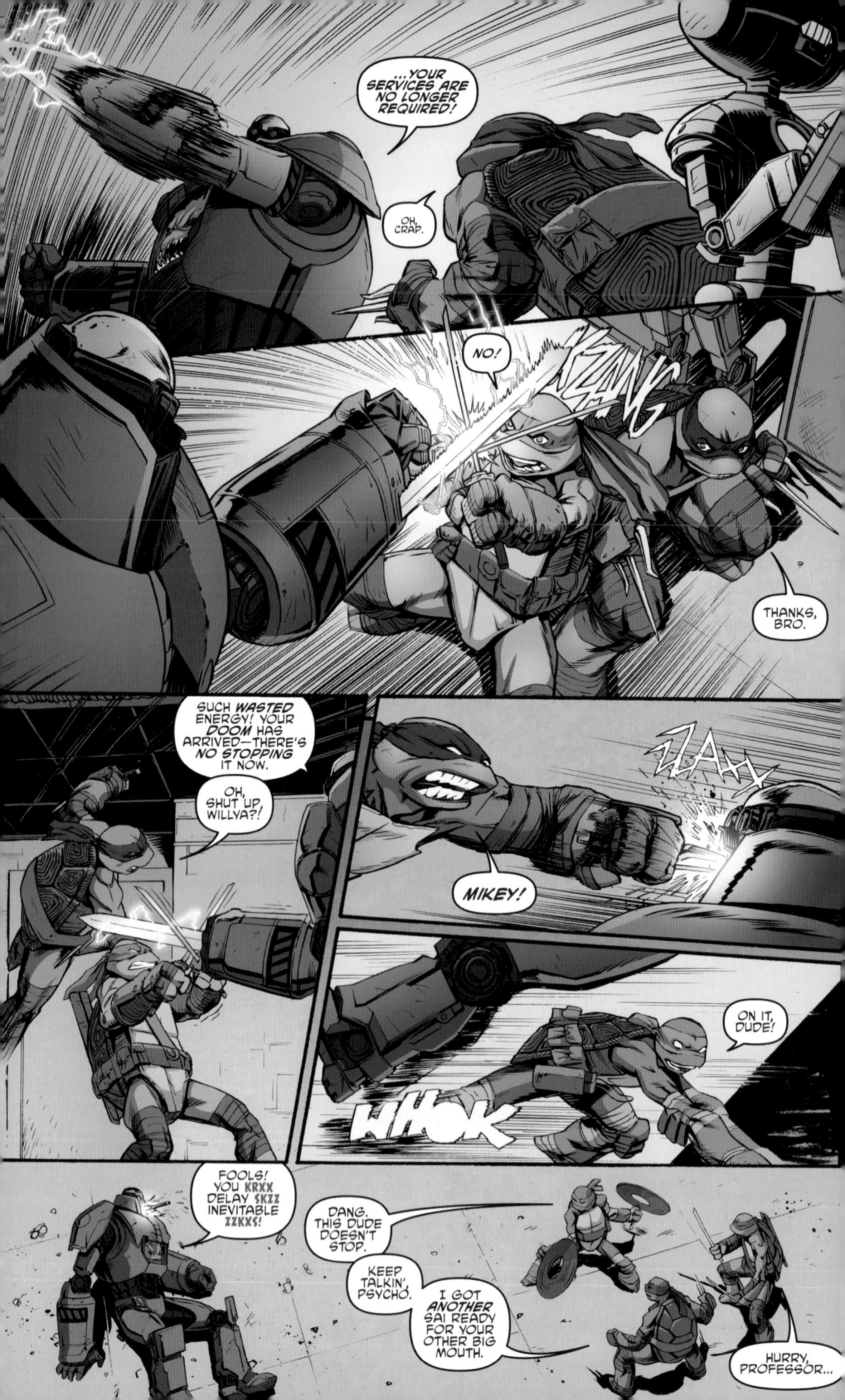
...YOUR SERVICES ARE NO LONGER REQUIRED!
OH, CRAP.
NO!
THANKS, BRO.
SUCH WASTED ENERGY! YOUR DOOM HAS ARRIVED—THERE'S NO STOPPING IT NOW.
OH, SHUT UP WILLYA?!
MIKEY!
ON IT, DUDE!
WHOK
FOOLS! YOU KRXX DELAY SKZZ INEVITABLE ZZKXS!
DANG. THIS DUDE DOESN'T STOP.
KEEP TALKIN', PSYCHO.
I GOT ANOTHER SAI READY FOR YOUR OTHER BIG MOUTH.
HURRY, PROFESSOR...

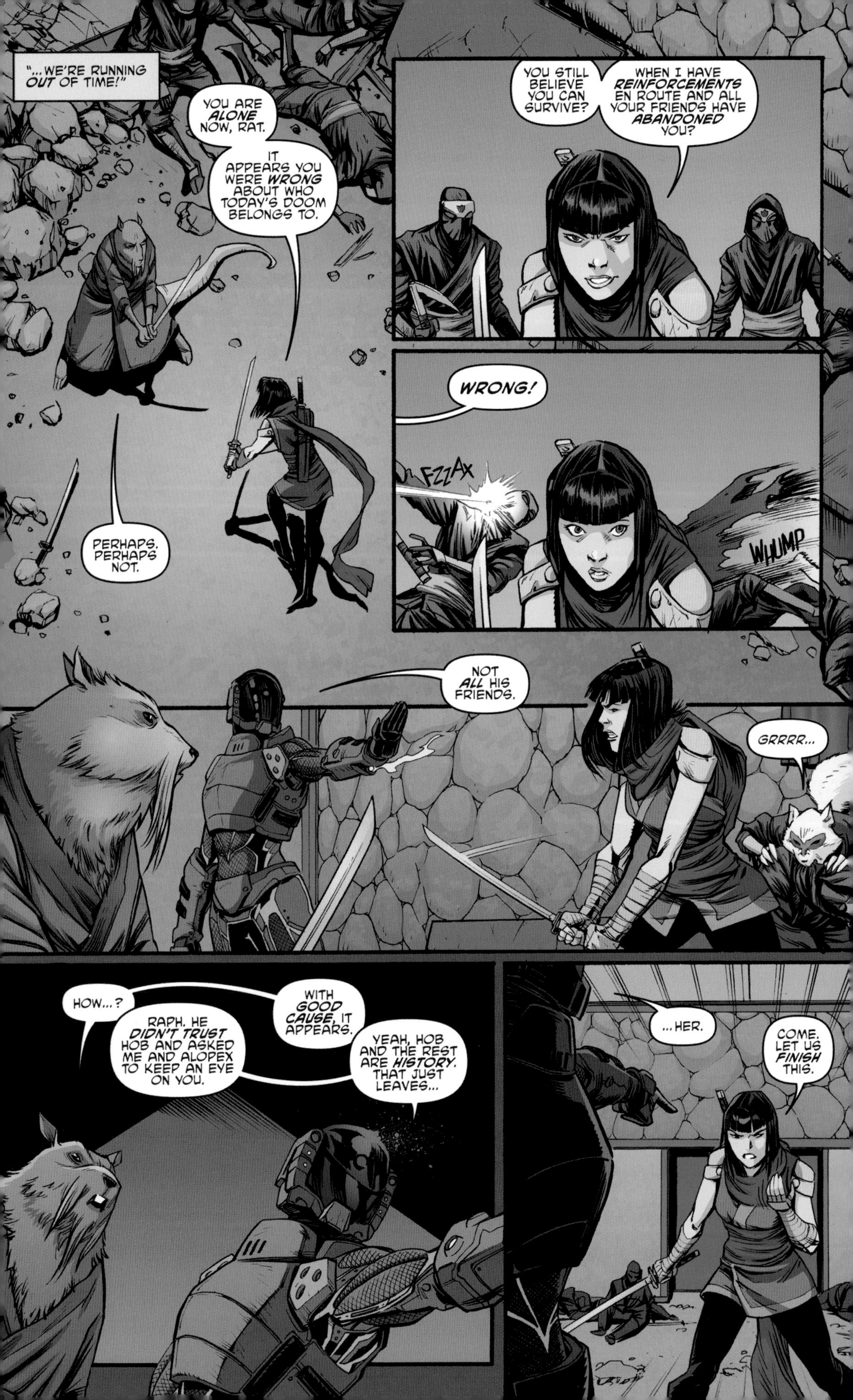
"...WE'RE RUNNING OUT OF TIME!"
YOU ARE ALONE NOW, RAT.
IT APPEARS YOU WERE WRONG ABOUT WHO TODAY'S DOOM BELONGS TO.
YOU STILL BELIEVE YOU CAN SURVIVE?
WHEN I HAVE REINFORCEMENTS EN ROUTE AND ALL YOUR FRIENDS HAVE ABANDONED YOU?
PERHAPS. PERHAPS NOT.
WRONG!
FZZAX
WHUMP
NOT ALL HIS FRIENDS.
GRRRR...
HOW...?
RAPH. HE DIDN'T TRUST HOB AND ASKED ME AND ALOPEX TO KEEP AN EYE ON YOU.
WITH GOOD CAUSE, IT APPEARS.
YEAH, HOB AND THE REST ARE HISTORY. THAT JUST LEAVES...
...HER.
COME. LET US FINISH THIS.

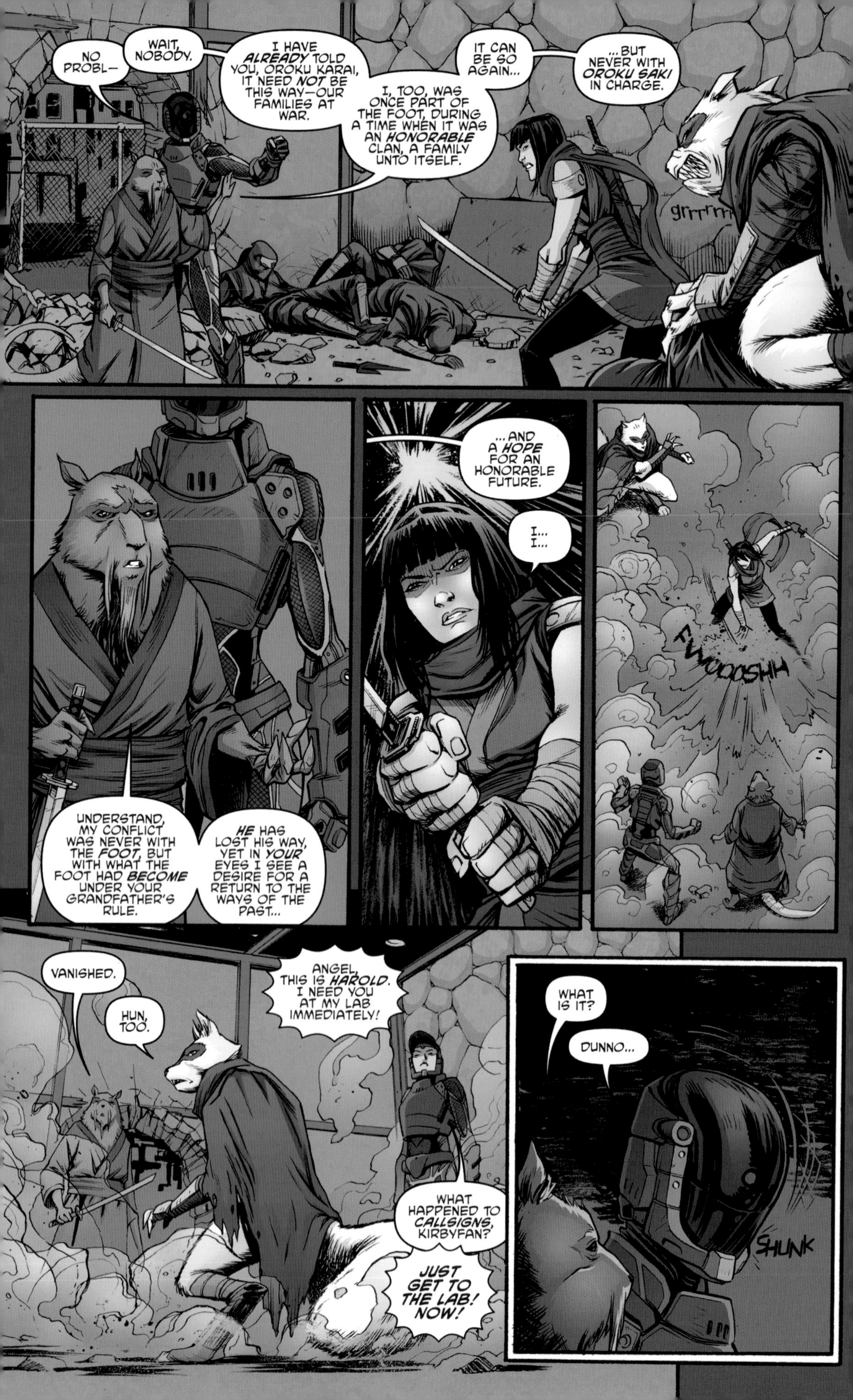
NO PROBL—
WAIT, NOBODY.
I HAVE ALREADY TOLD YOU, OROKU KARAI, IT NEED NOT BE THIS WAY—OUR FAMILIES AT WAR.
I, TOO, WAS ONCE PART OF THE FOOT, DURING A TIME WHEN IT WAS AN HONORABLE CLAN, A FAMILY UNTO ITSELF.
IT CAN BE SO AGAIN...
...BUT NEVER WITH OROKU SAKI IN CHARGE.
grrrrrr
UNDERSTAND, MY CONFLICT WAS NEVER WITH THE FOOT, BUT WITH WHAT THE FOOT HAD BECOME UNDER YOUR GRANDFATHER'S RULE.
HE HAS LOST HIS WAY, YET IN YOUR EYES I SEE A DESIRE FOR A RETURN TO THE WAYS OF THE PAST...
...AND A HOPE FOR AN HONORABLE FUTURE.
I... I...
FWOOOSHH
VANISHED.
HUN, TOO.
ANGEL, THIS IS HAROLD. I NEED YOU AT MY LAB IMMEDIATELY!
WHAT HAPPENED TO CALLSIGNS, KIRBYFAN?
JUST GET TO THE LAB! NOW!
WHAT IS IT?
DUNNO...
SHUNK

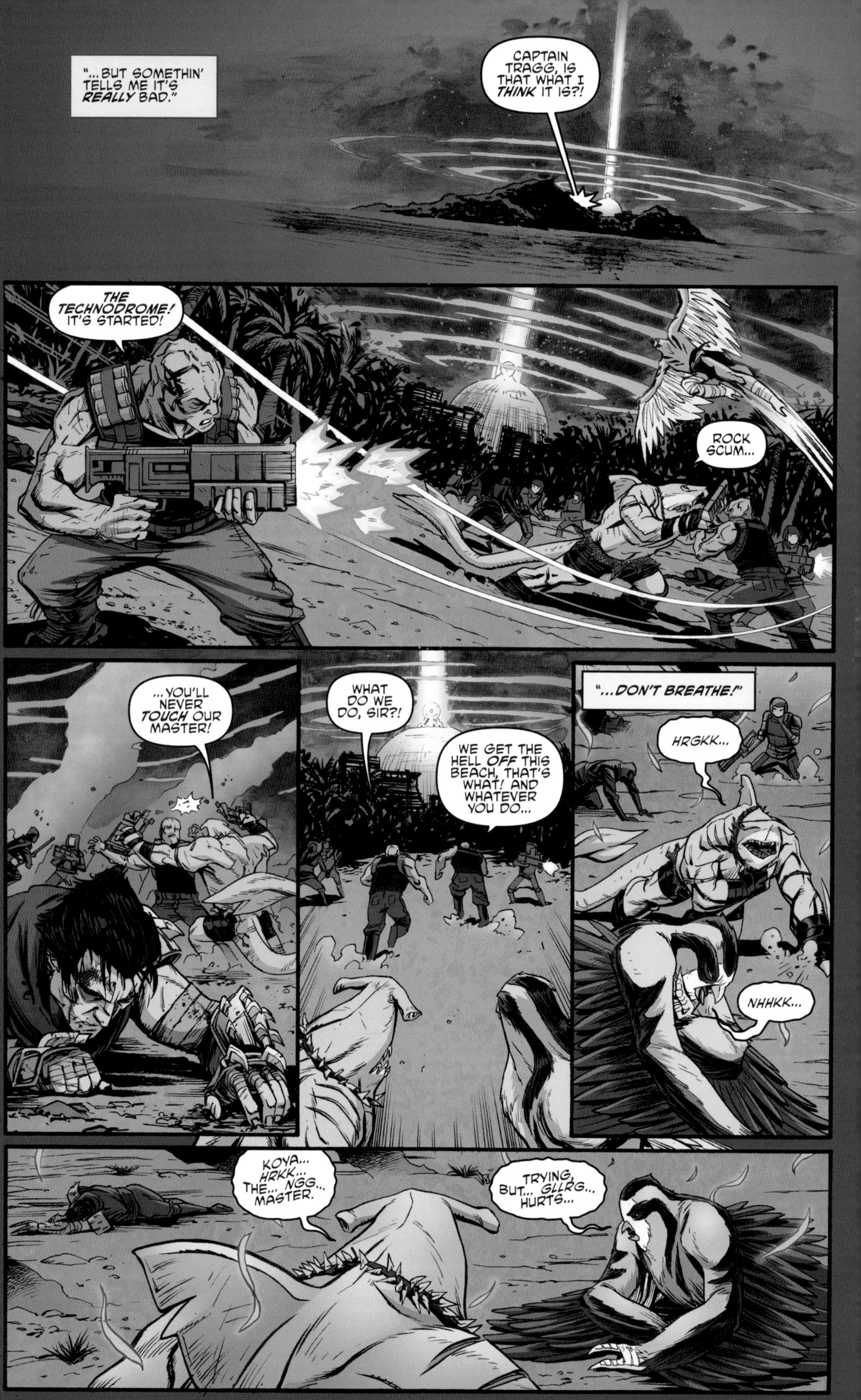
"...BUT SOMETHIN' TELLS ME IT'S REALLY BAD."
CAPTAIN TRAGG, IS THAT WHAT I THINK IT IS?!
THE TECHNODROME! IT'S STARTED!
ROCK SCUM...
...YOU'LL NEVER TOUCH OUR MASTER!
WHAT DO WE DO, SIR?!
WE GET THE HELL OFF THIS BEACH, THAT'S WHAT! AND WHATEVER YOU DO...
"...DON'T BREATHE!"
HRGKK...
NHHKK...
KOYA... HRKK... THE... NGG... MASTER.
TRYING, BUT... GLLRG... HURTS...

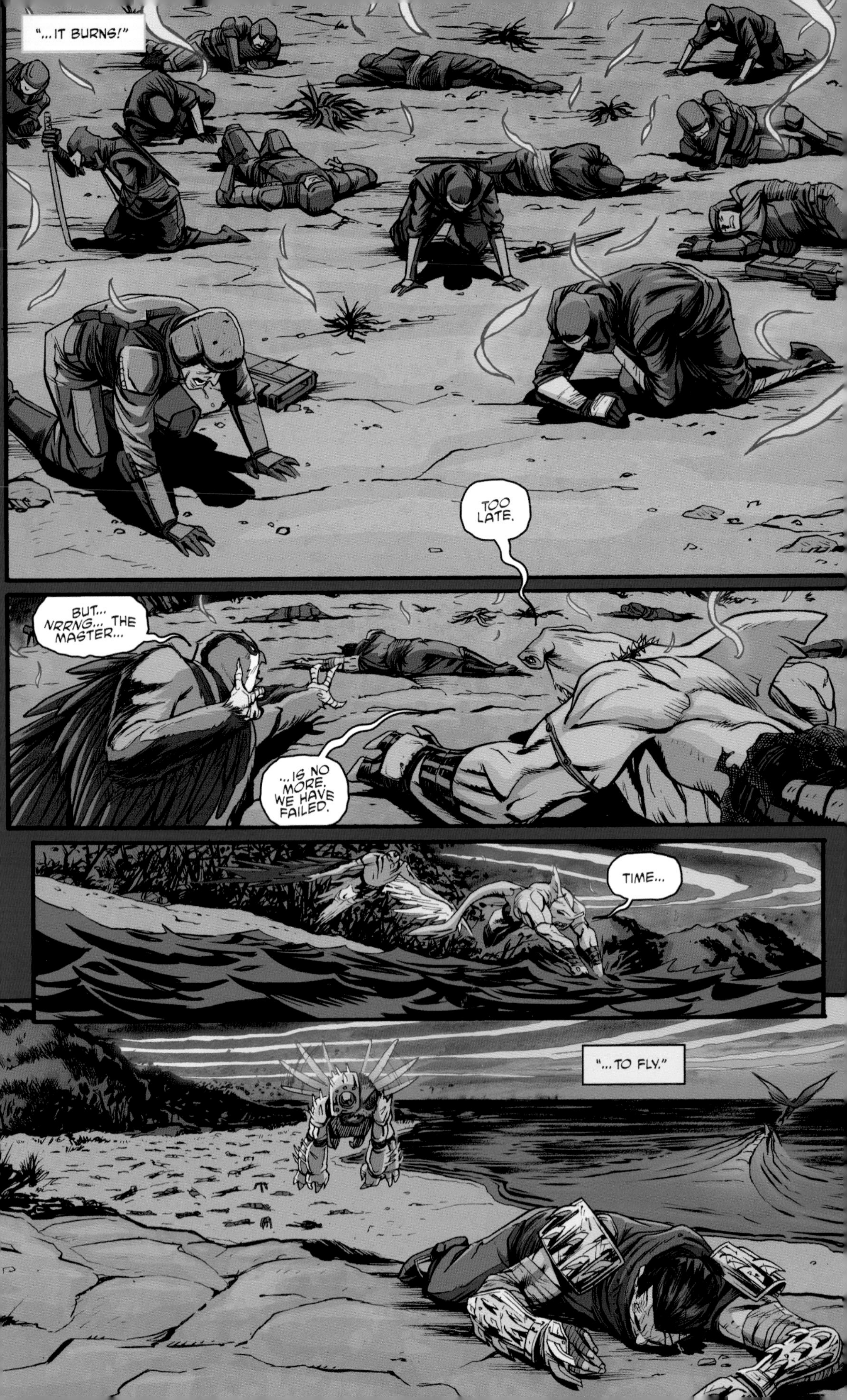
"... IT BURNS!"
TOO LATE.
BUT... NRRNG... THE MASTER...
...IS NO MORE. WE HAVE FAILED.
TIME...
"... TO FLY."

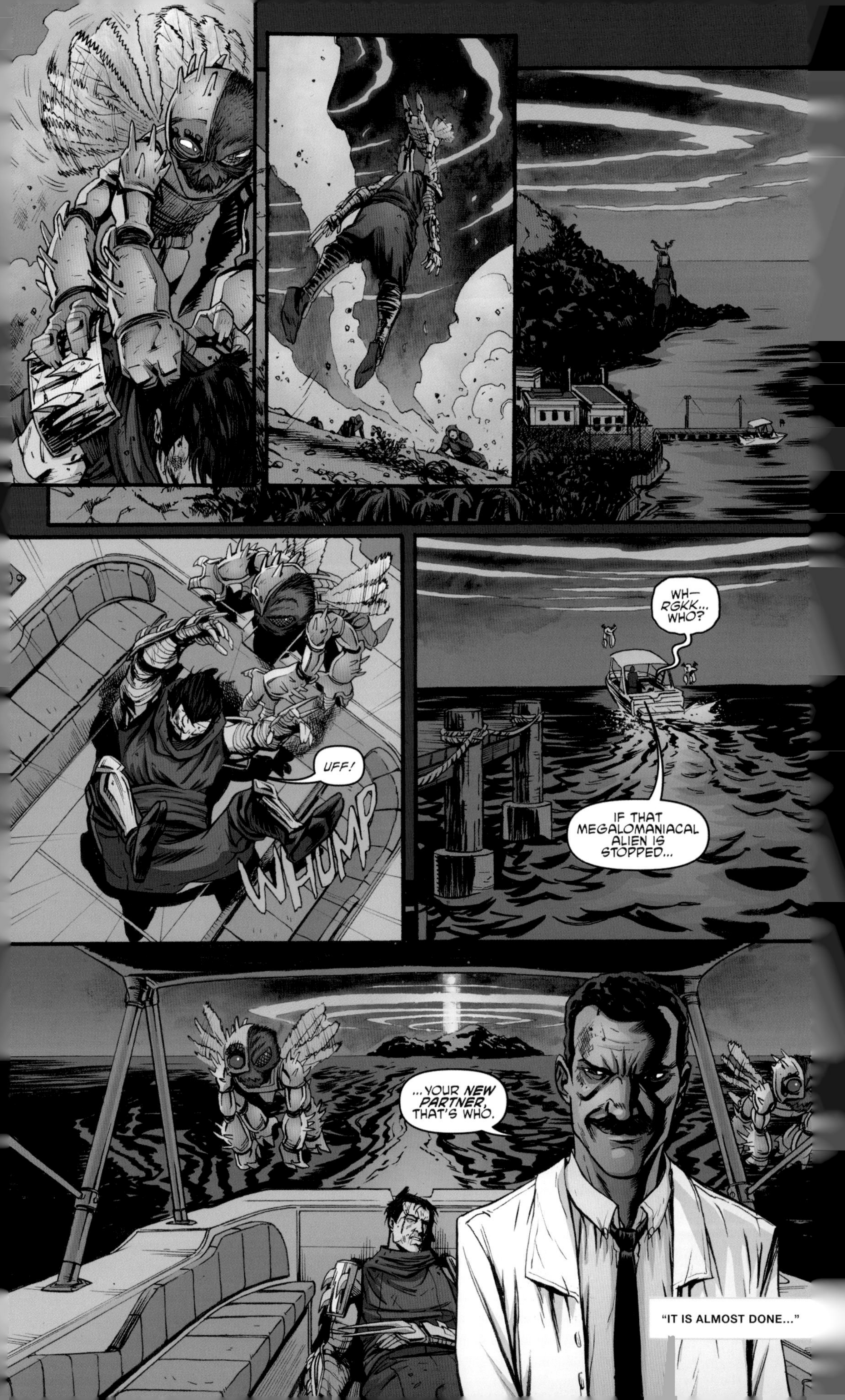
UFF!
WHUMP
WH—
RGKK...
WHO?
IF THAT
MEGALOMANIACAL
ALIEN IS
STOPPED...
...YOUR NEW
PARTNER,
THAT'S WHO.
"IT IS ALMOST DONE..."

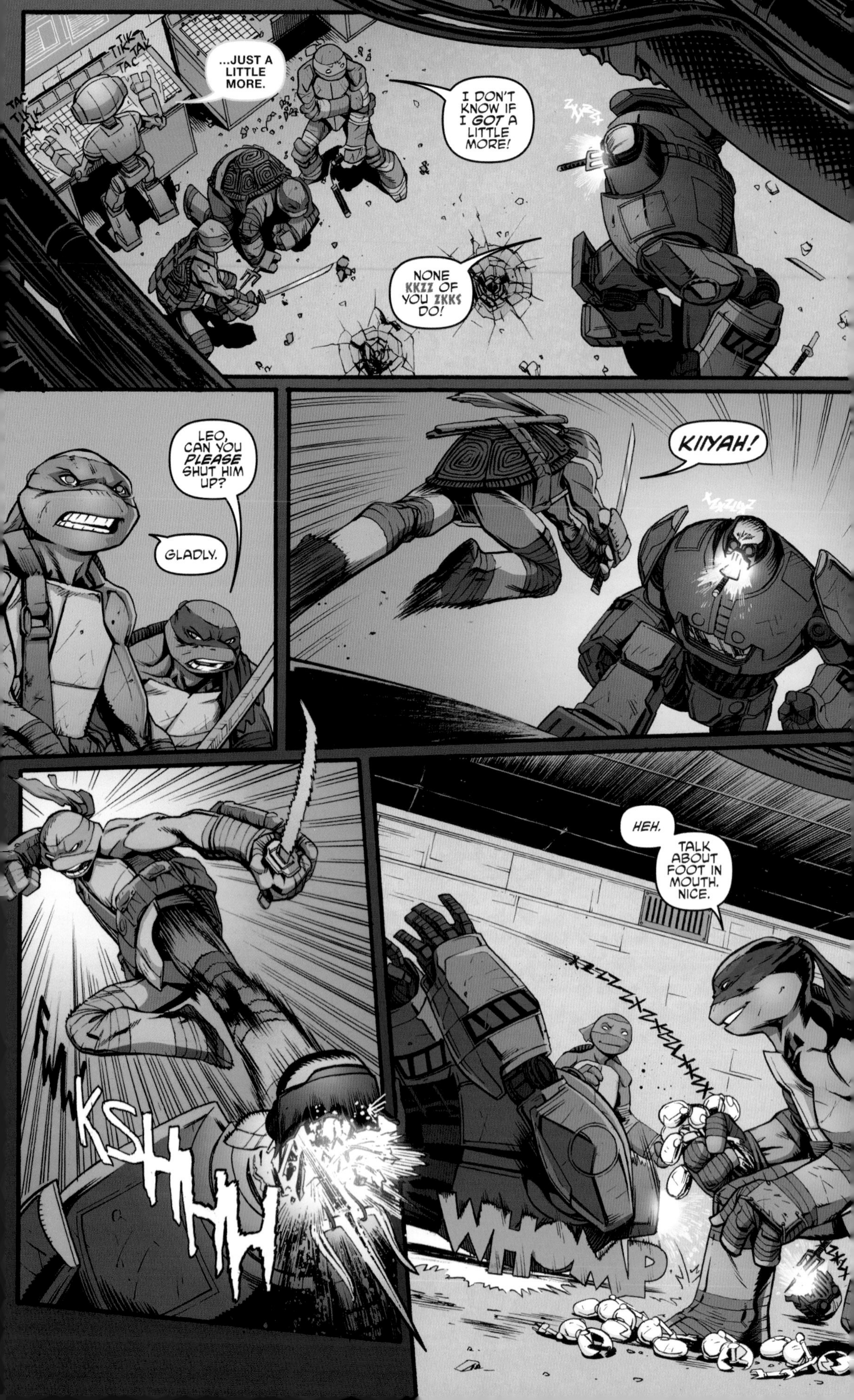
TIK TAK TAC
TAC TIK TAK
...JUST A LITTLE MORE.
I DON'T KNOW IF I GOT A LITTLE MORE!
NONE KKZZ OF YOU ZKKS DO!
LEO, CAN YOU PLEASE SHUT HIM UP?
GLADLY.
KIIYAH!
FWKSHHH
HEH.
TALK ABOUT FOOT IN MOUTH. NICE.
WHOMP

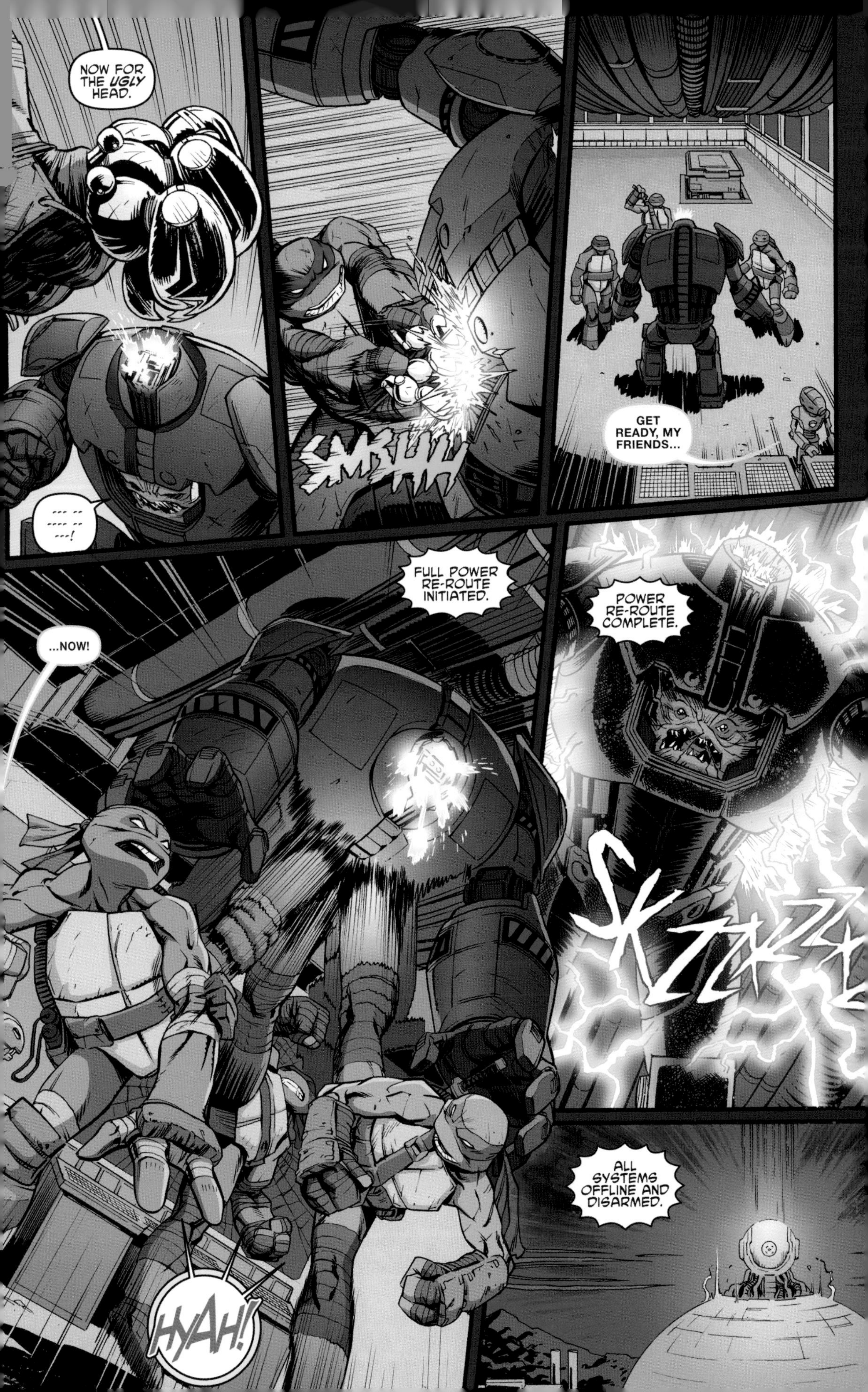
NOW FOR THE UGLY HEAD.
--- --
---- --
---!
SMRHHH
GET READY, MY FRIENDS...
FULL POWER RE-ROUTE INITIATED.
...NOW!
HYAH!
POWER RE-ROUTE COMPLETE.
ALL SYSTEMS OFFLINE AND DISARMED.

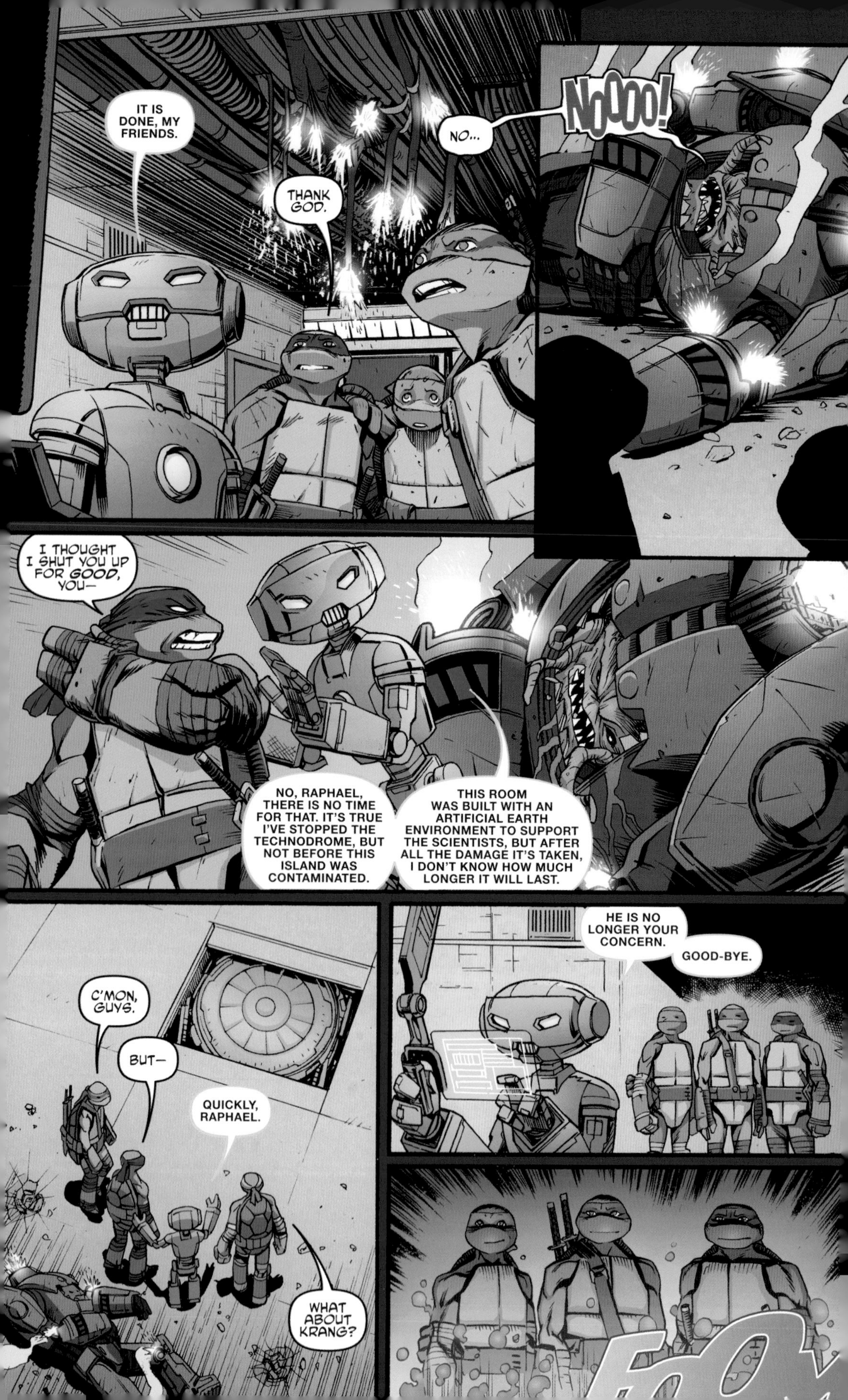
IT IS DONE, MY FRIENDS.
THANK GOD.
NO...
NOOOO!
I THOUGHT I SHUT YOU UP FOR GOOD, YOU—
NO, RAPHAEL, THERE IS NO TIME FOR THAT. IT'S TRUE I'VE STOPPED THE TECHNODROME, BUT NOT BEFORE THIS ISLAND WAS CONTAMINATED.
THIS ROOM WAS BUILT WITH AN ARTIFICIAL EARTH ENVIRONMENT TO SUPPORT THE SCIENTISTS, BUT AFTER ALL THE DAMAGE IT'S TAKEN, I DON'T KNOW HOW MUCH LONGER IT WILL LAST.
C'MON, GUYS.
BUT—
QUICKLY, RAPHAEL.
WHAT ABOUT KRANG?
HE IS NO LONGER YOUR CONCERN.
GOOD-BYE.

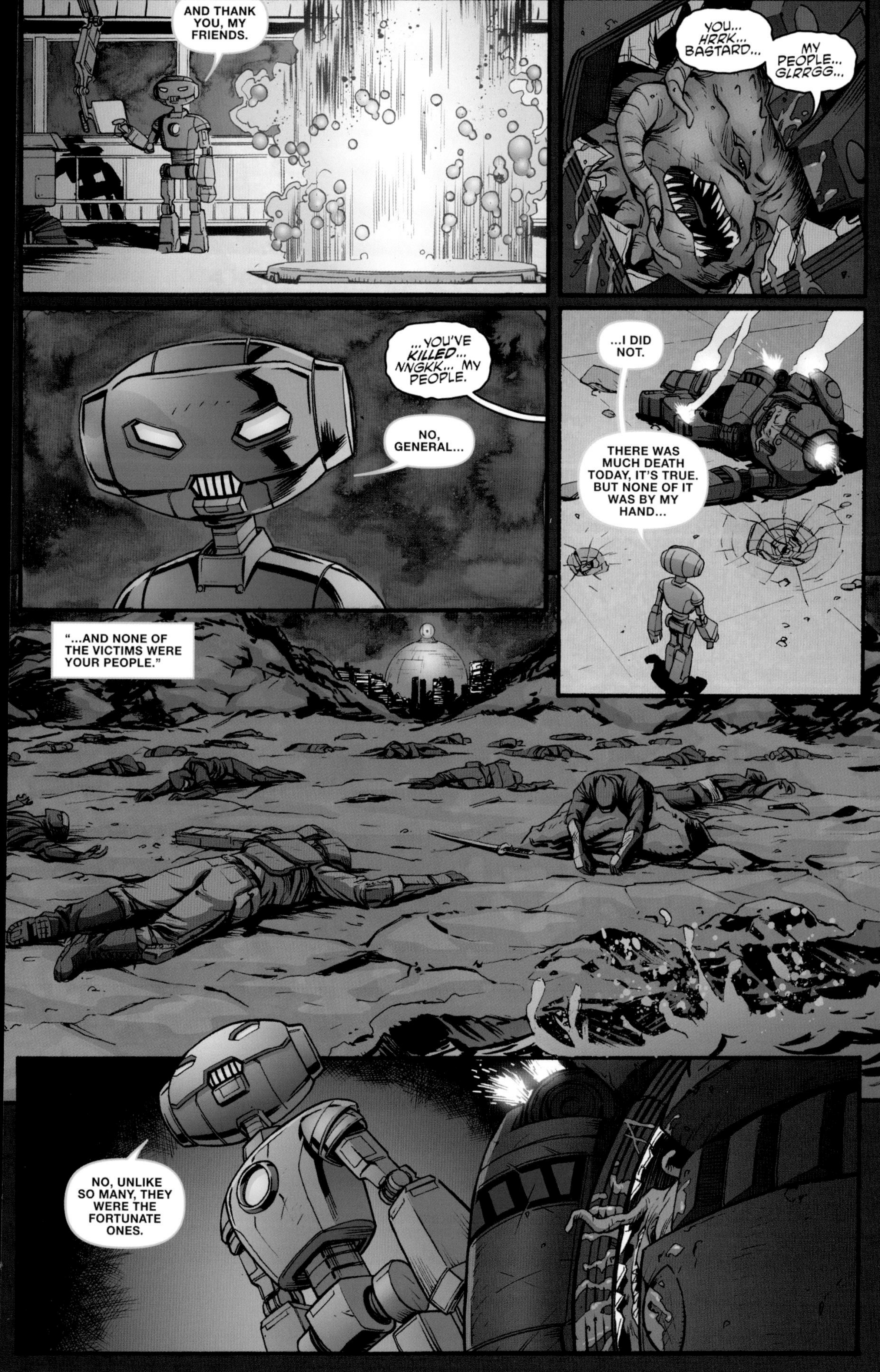
AND THANK YOU, MY FRIENDS.
YOU... HRRK... BASTARD...
MY PEOPLE... GLRRGG...
...YOU'VE KILLED... NNGKK... MY PEOPLE.
NO, GENERAL...
...I DID NOT.
THERE WAS MUCH DEATH TODAY, IT'S TRUE. BUT NONE OF IT WAS BY MY HAND...
"...AND NONE OF THE VICTIMS WERE YOUR PEOPLE."
NO, UNLIKE SO MANY, THEY WERE THE FORTUNATE ONES.

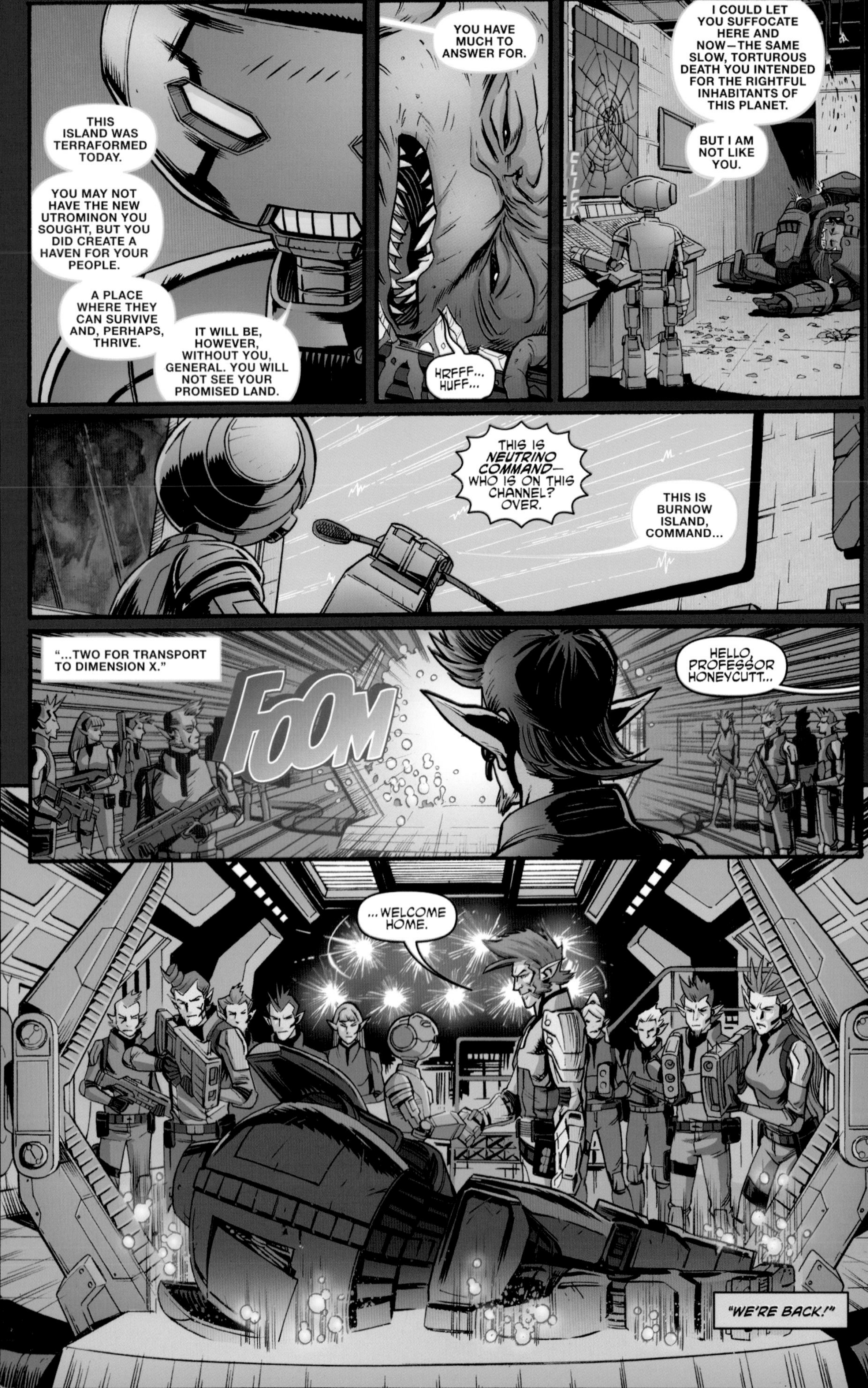
THIS ISLAND WAS TERRAFORMED TODAY.
YOU MAY NOT HAVE THE NEW UTROMINON YOU SOUGHT, BUT YOU DID CREATE A HAVEN FOR YOUR PEOPLE.
A PLACE WHERE THEY CAN SURVIVE AND, PERHAPS, THRIVE.
IT WILL BE, HOWEVER, WITHOUT YOU, GENERAL. YOU WILL NOT SEE YOUR PROMISED LAND.
YOU HAVE MUCH TO ANSWER FOR.
HRFFF... HUFF...
CLICK
I COULD LET YOU SUFFOCATE HERE AND NOW—THE SAME SLOW, TORTUROUS DEATH YOU INTENDED FOR THE RIGHTFUL INHABITANTS OF THIS PLANET.
BUT I AM NOT LIKE YOU.
THIS IS NEUTRINO COMMAND—WHO IS ON THIS CHANNEL? OVER.
THIS IS BURNOW ISLAND, COMMAND...
"...TWO FOR TRANSPORT TO DIMENSION X."
FOOM
HELLO, PROFESSOR HONEYCUTT...
...WELCOME HOME.
"WE'RE BACK!"

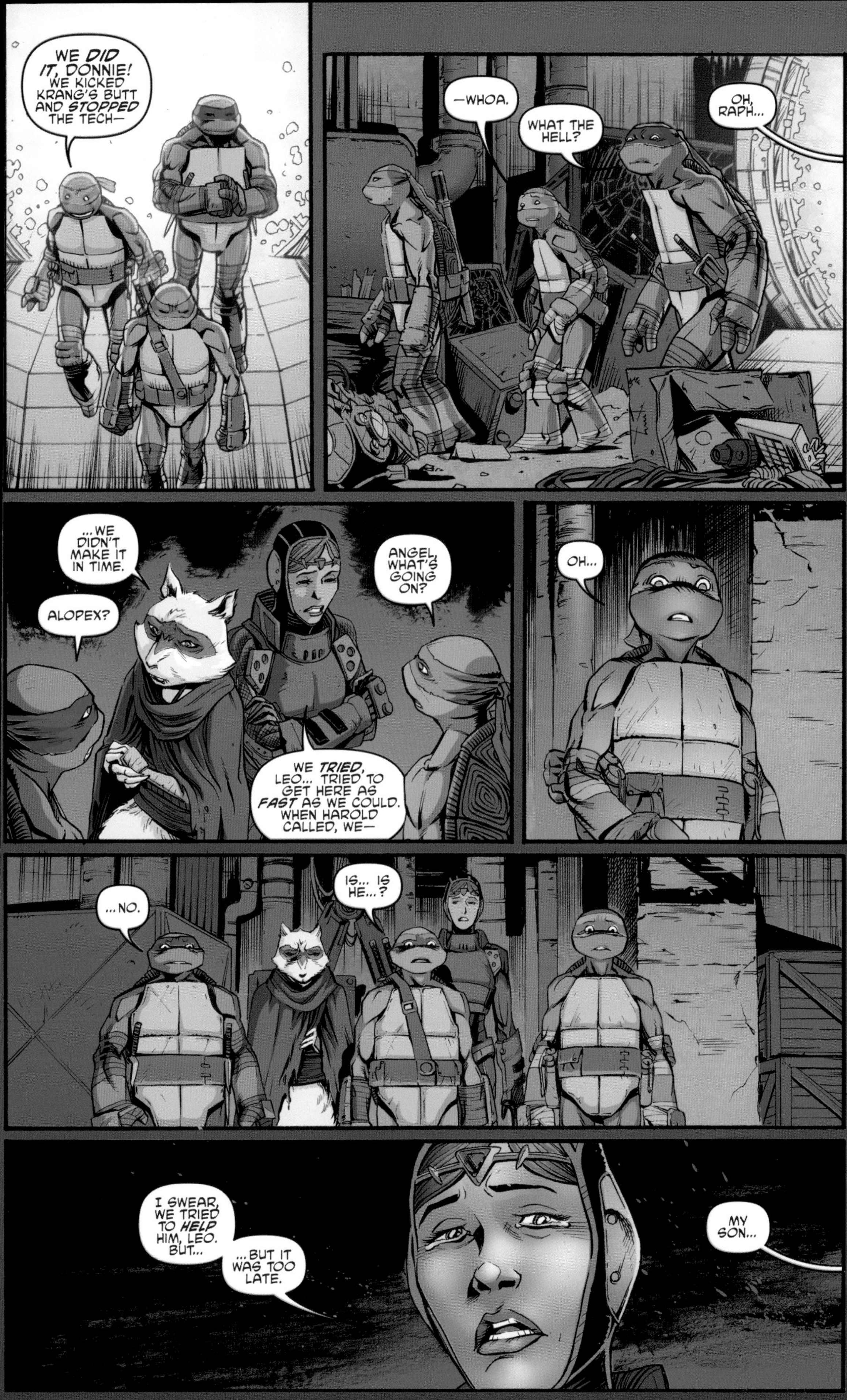
WE DID IT, DONNIE! WE KICKED KRANG'S BUTT AND STOPPED THE TECH—
—WHOA.
WHAT THE HELL?
OH, RAPH...
...WE DIDN'T MAKE IT IN TIME.
ALOPEX?
ANGEL, WHAT'S GOING ON?
WE TRIED, LEO... TRIED TO GET HERE AS FAST AS WE COULD. WHEN HAROLD CALLED, WE—
OH...
...NO.
IS... IS HE...?
I SWEAR, WE TRIED TO HELP HIM, LEO. BUT...
...BUT IT WAS TOO LATE.
MY SON...

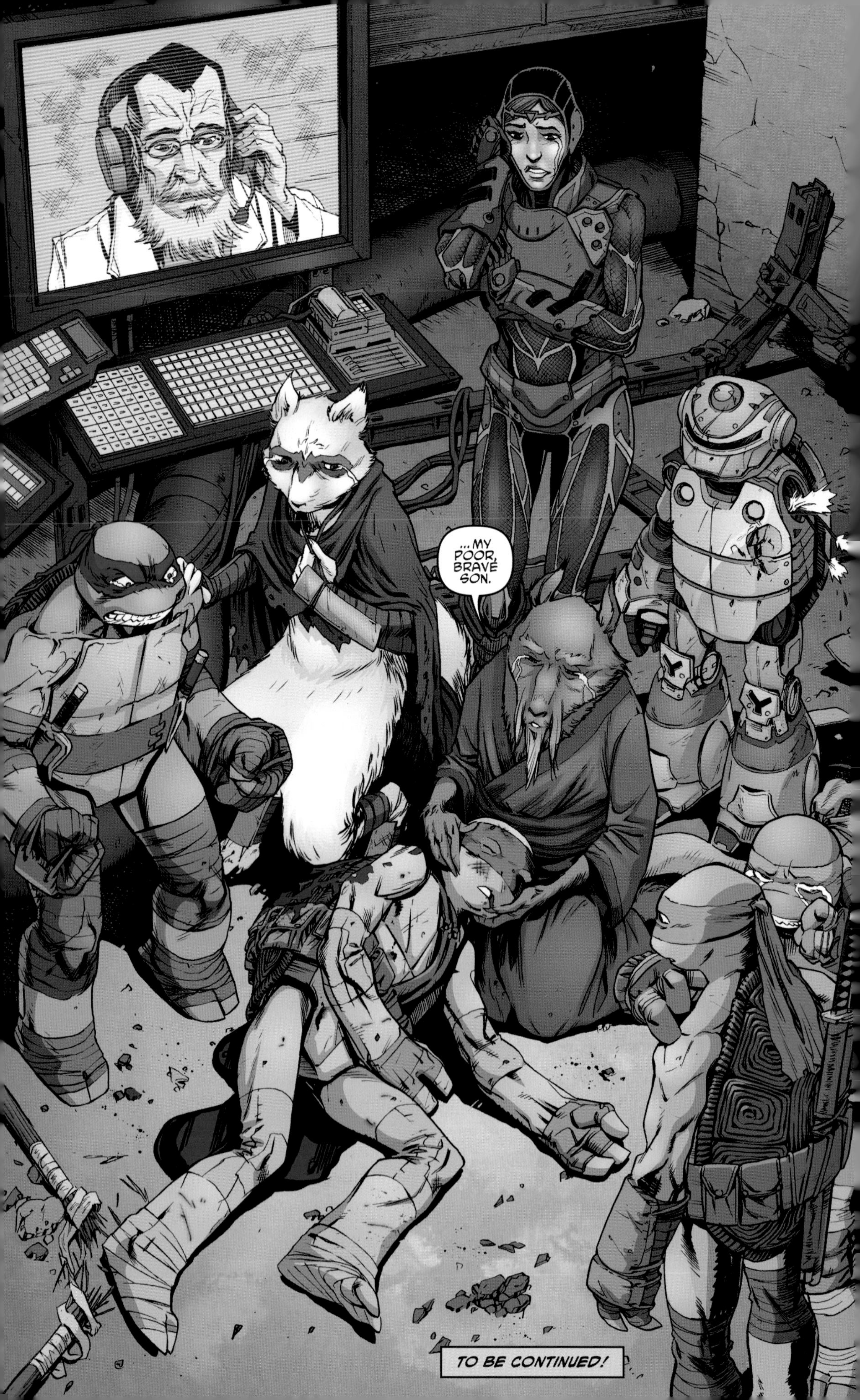
...MY POOR, BRAVE SON.
TO BE CONTINUED!

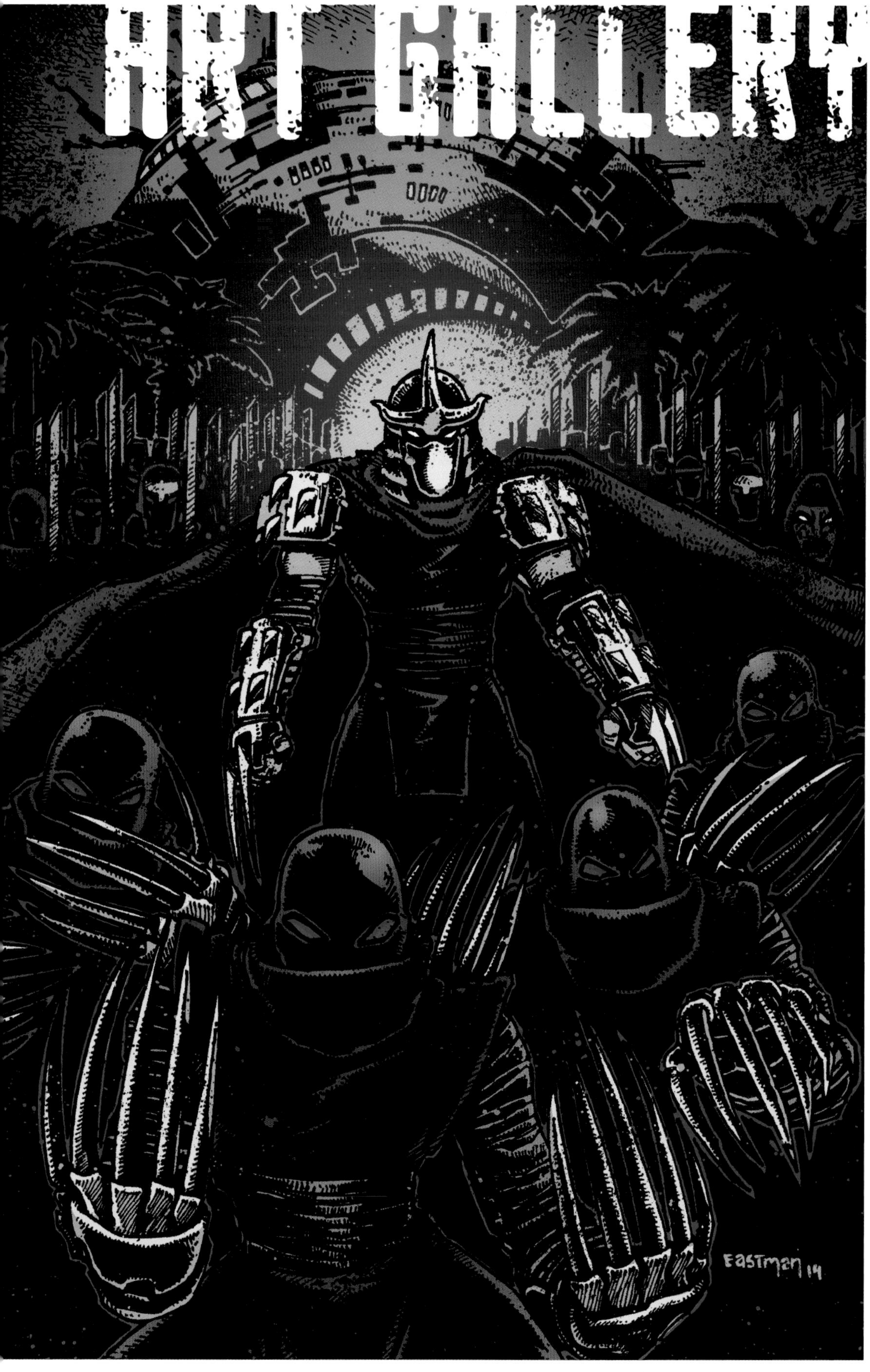
ART GALLERY
EASTMAN '14

ART BY KEVIN EASTMAN · COLORS BY RONDA PATTISON

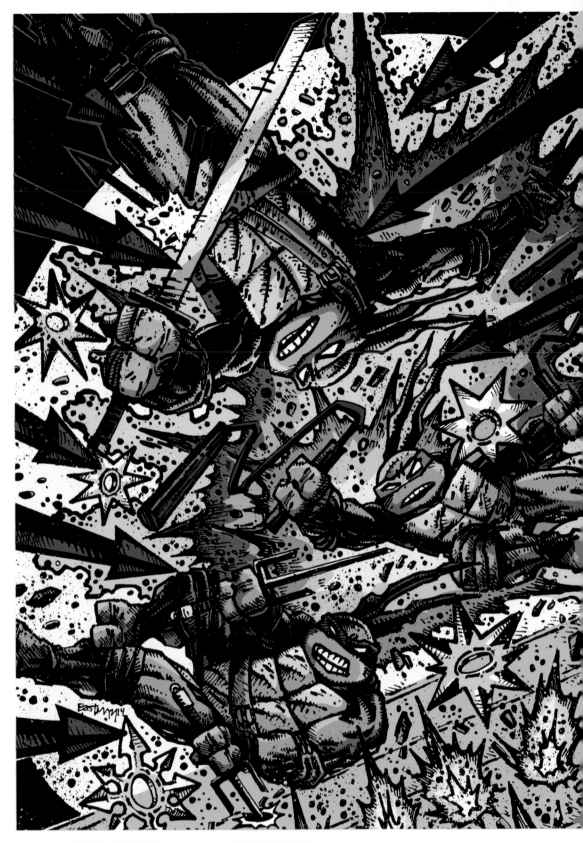

ART BY KEVIN EASTMAN · COLORS BY RONDA PATTISON

OPPOSITE PAGE: ART BY CORY SMITH

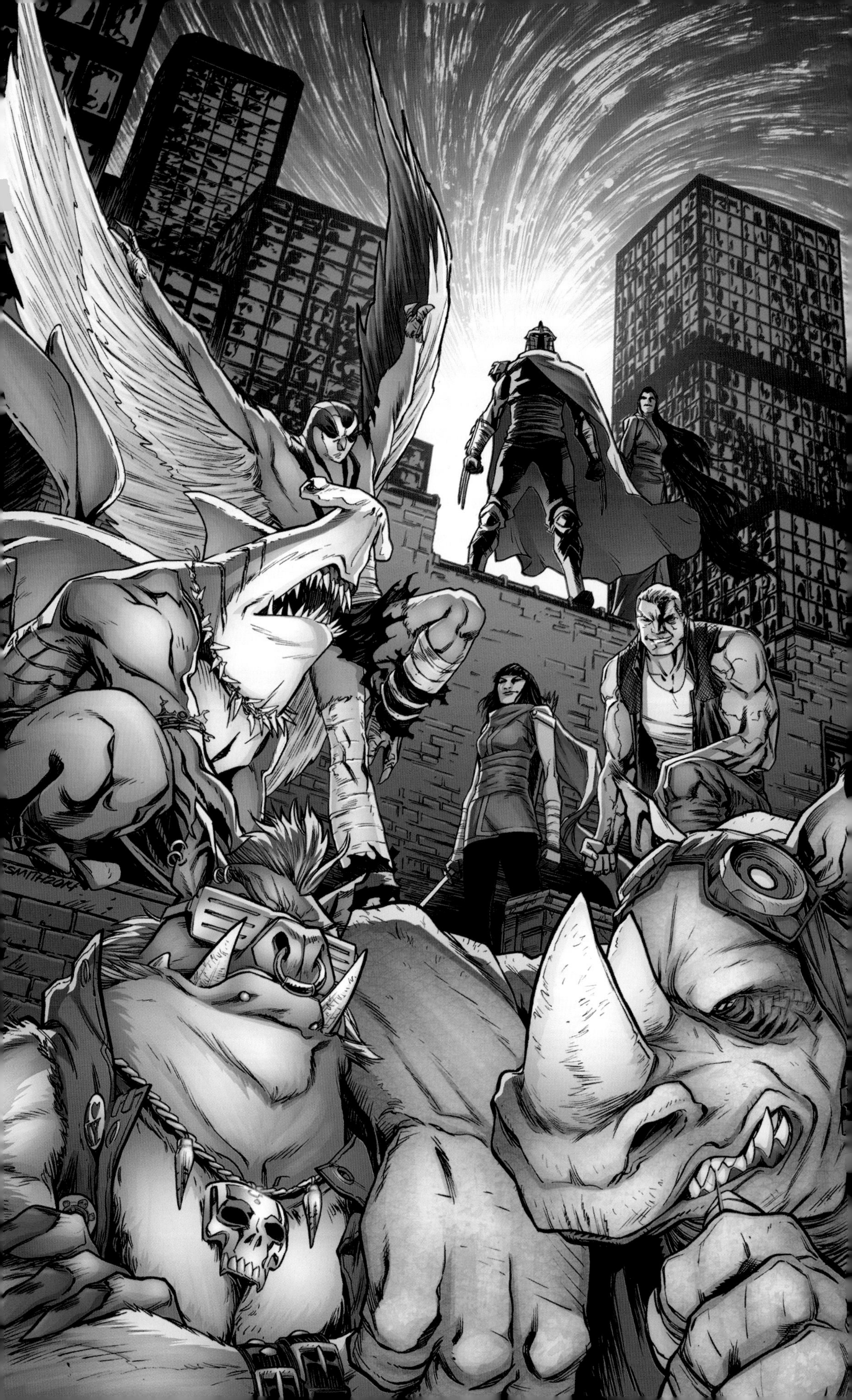
SMITH2014

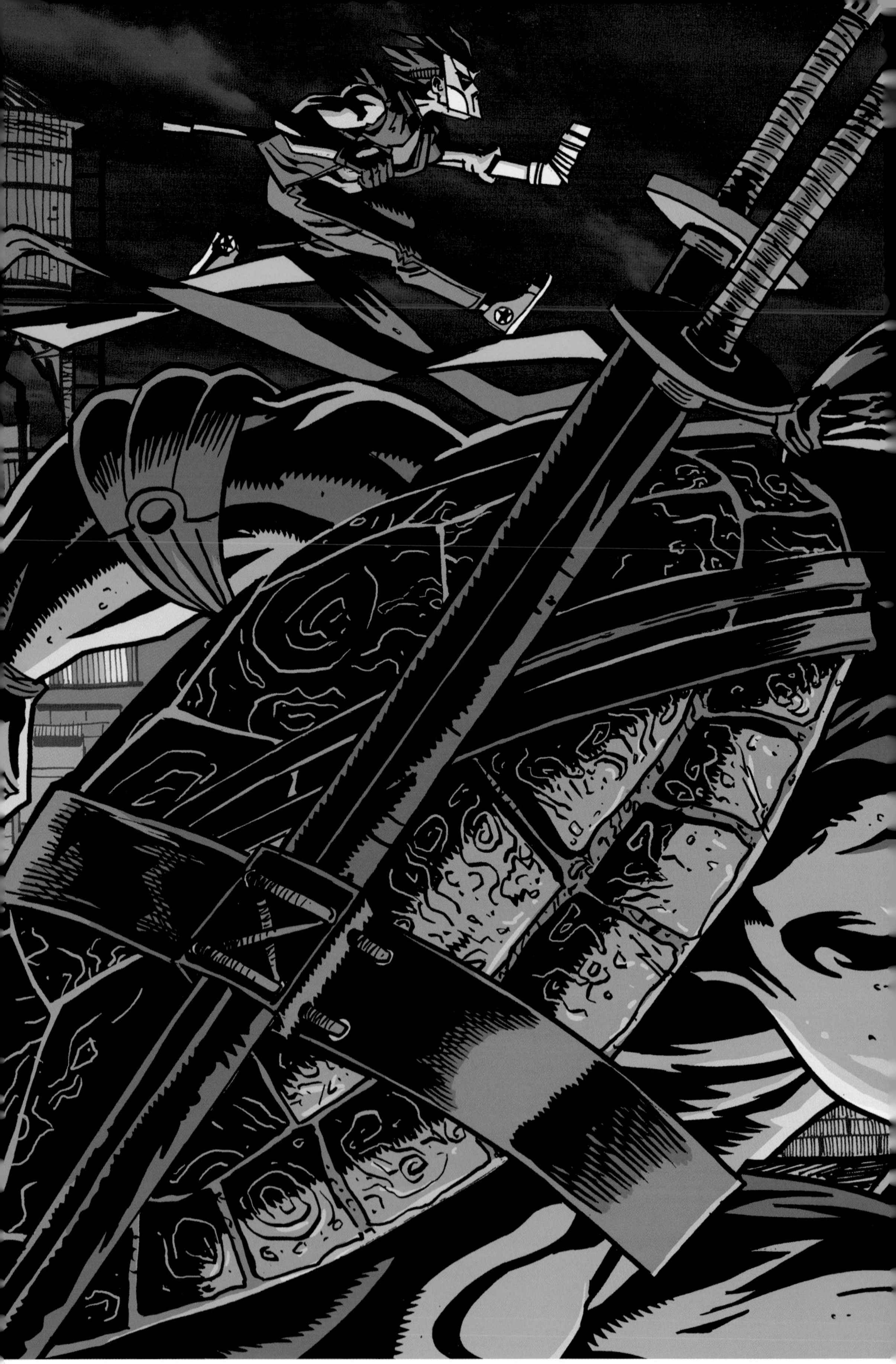

ART BY TIM DOYLE

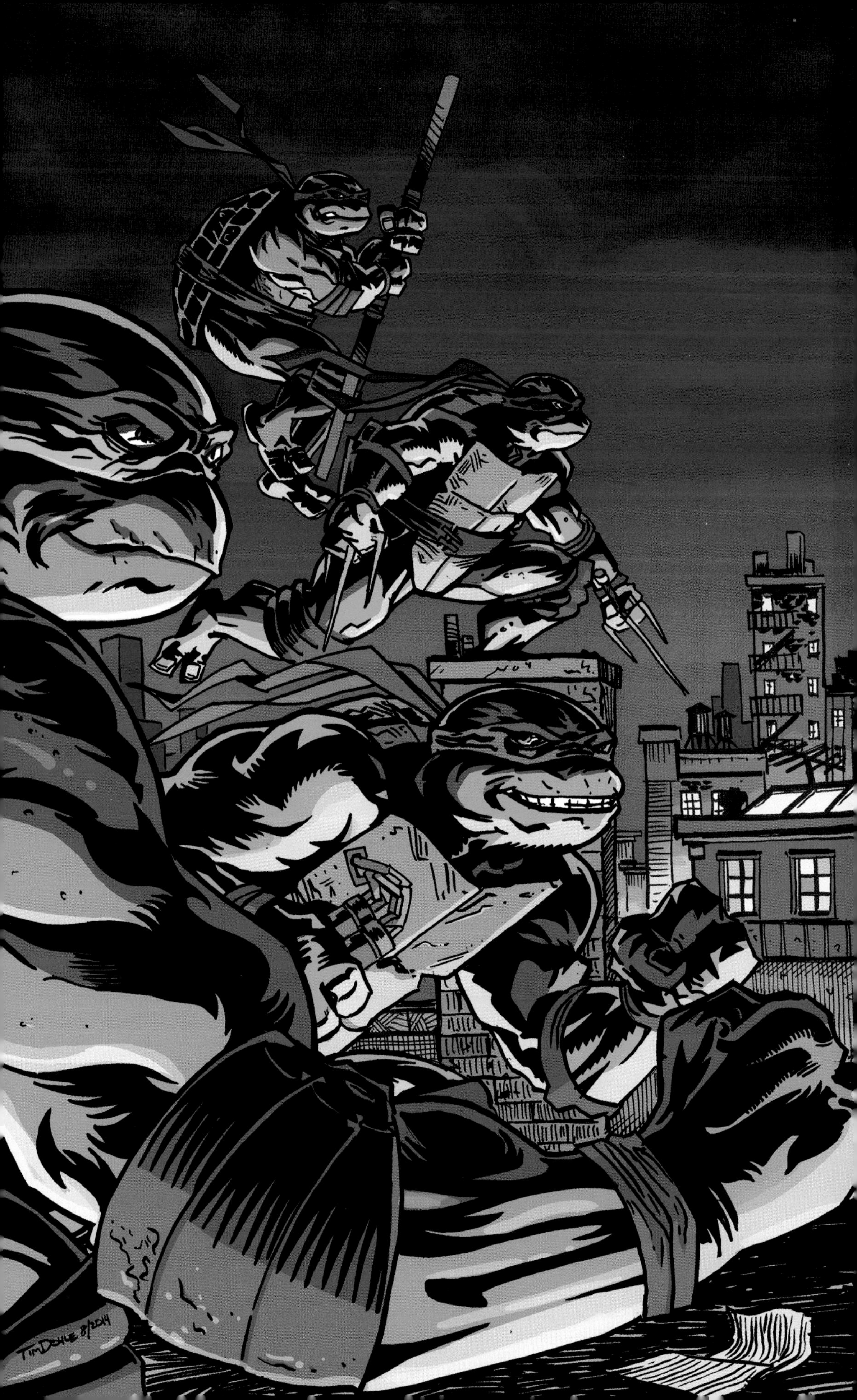
TIM DOYLE 8/2014

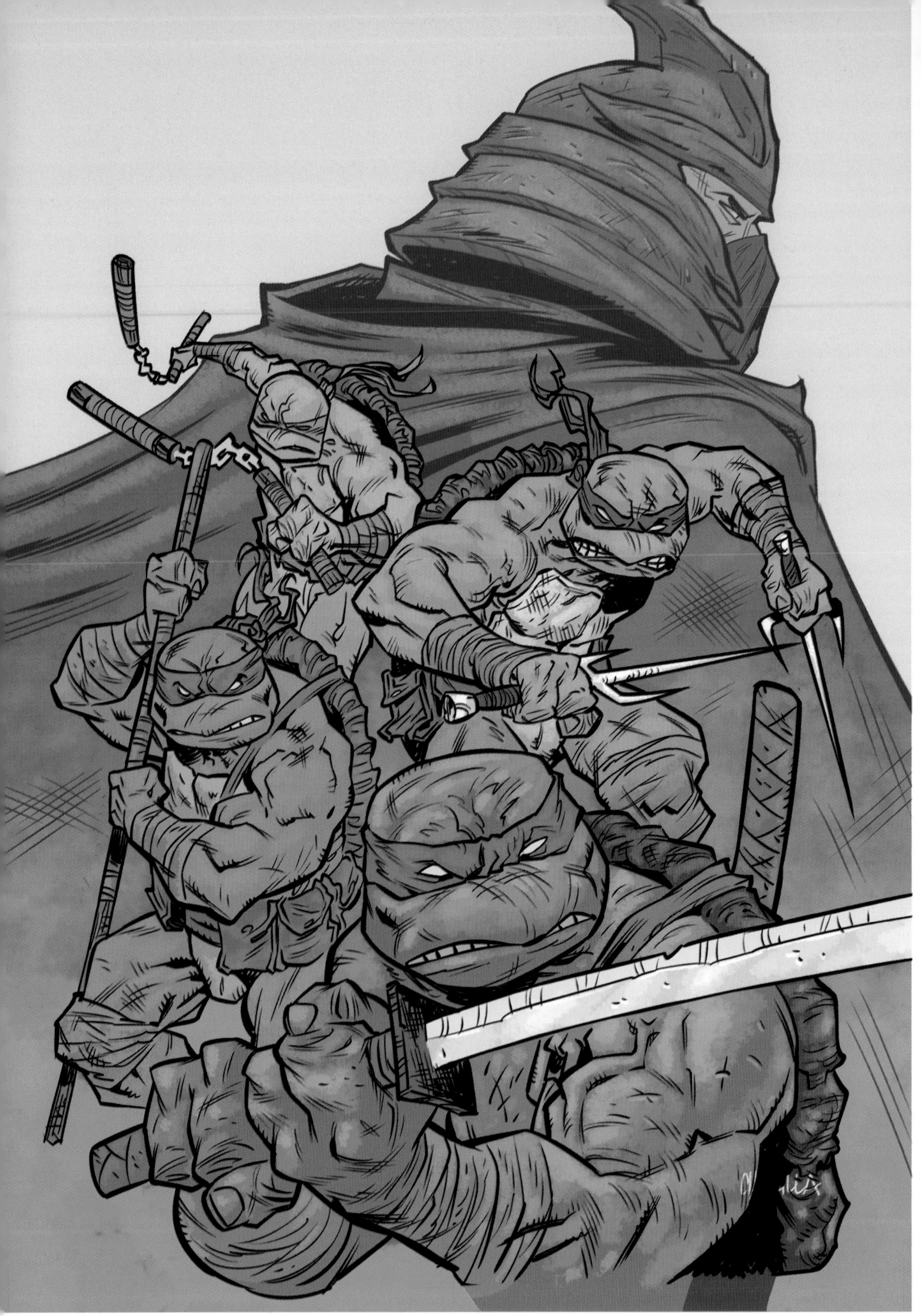

ART BY BRIAN CHURILLA

OPPOSITE PAGE: ART BY CORY SMITH · COLORS BY RONDA PATTISON

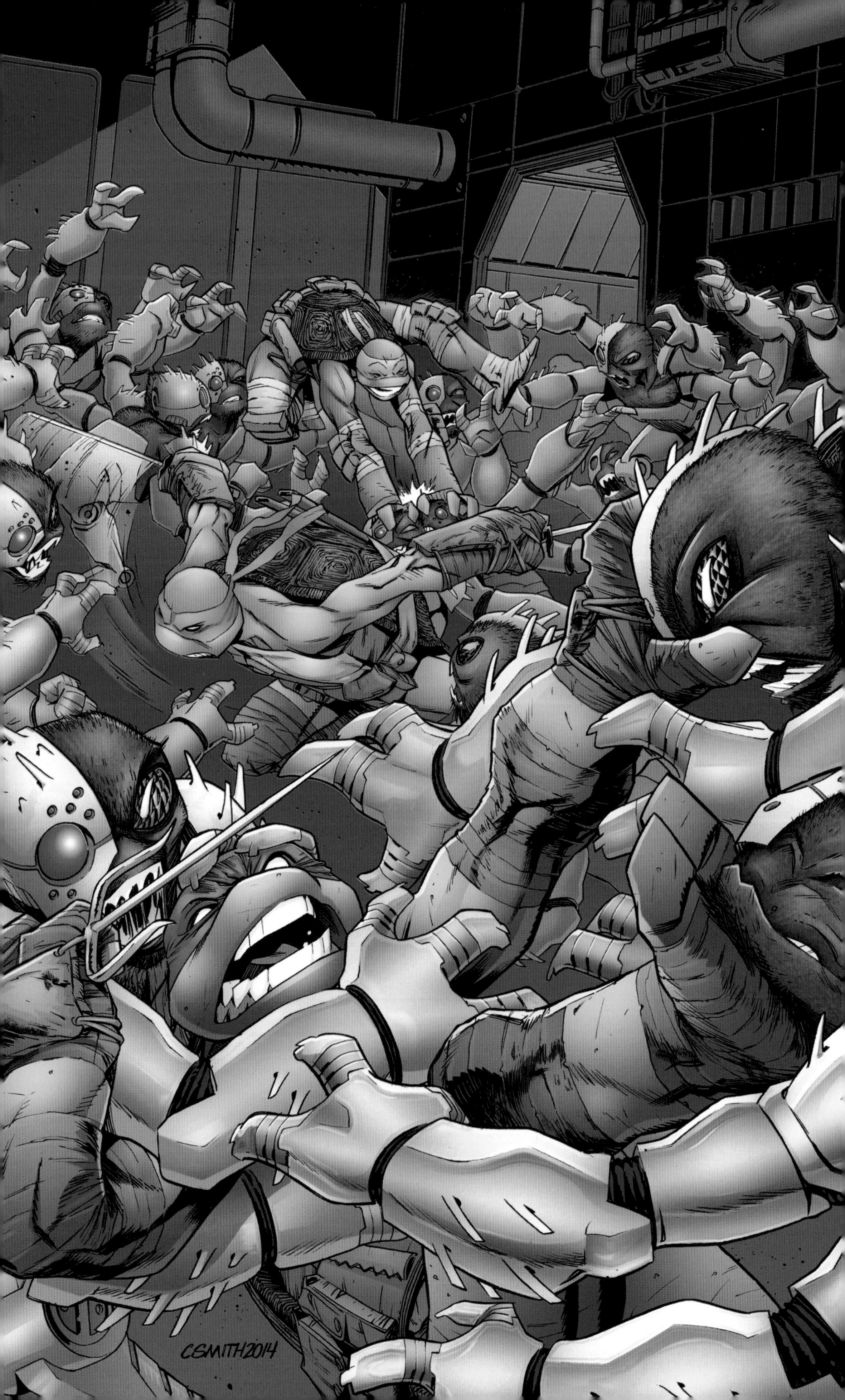
CSMITH2014

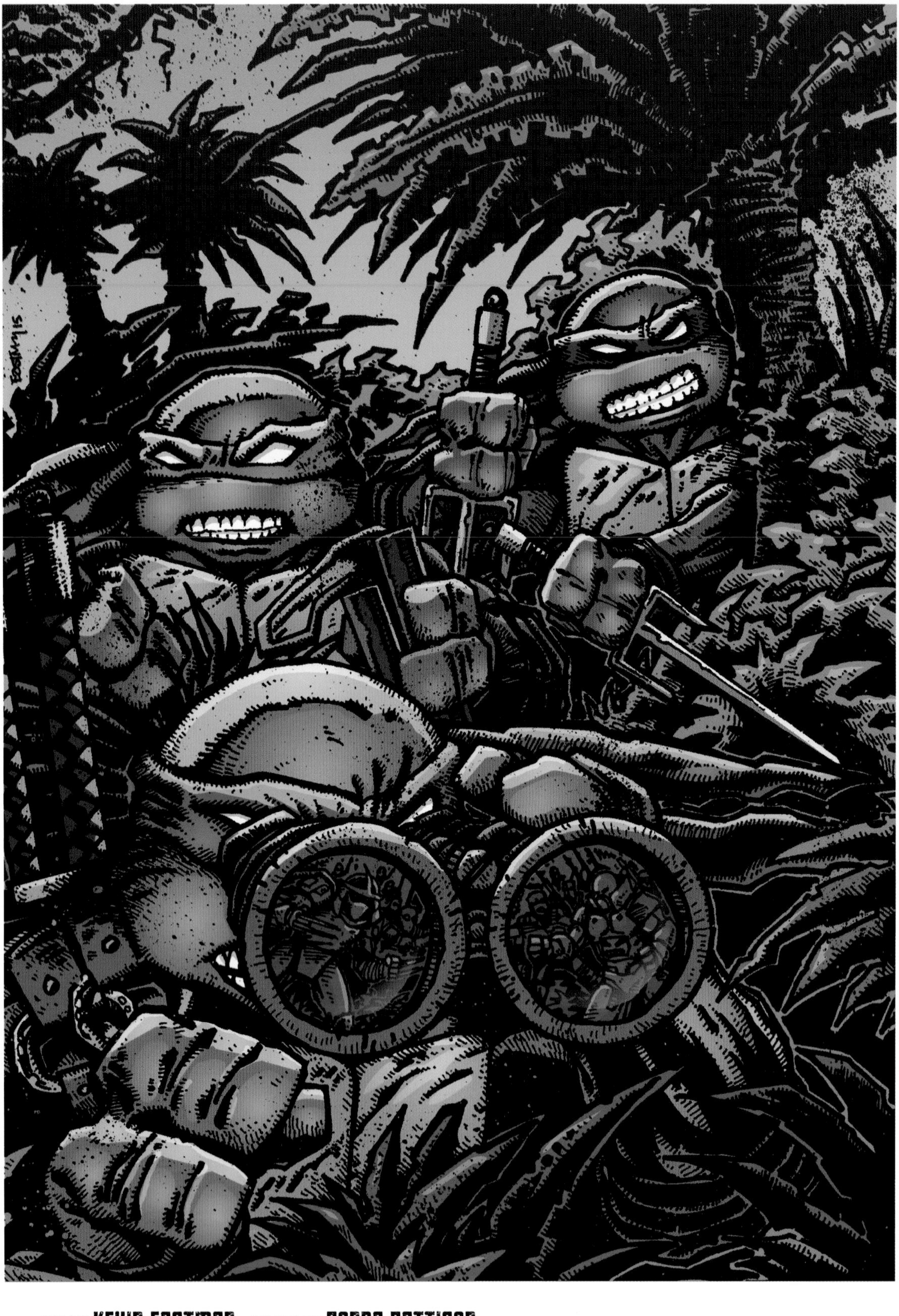

ART BY KEVIN EASTMAN · COLORS BY RONDA PATTISON

OPPOSITE PAGE: ART BY AARON CONLEY

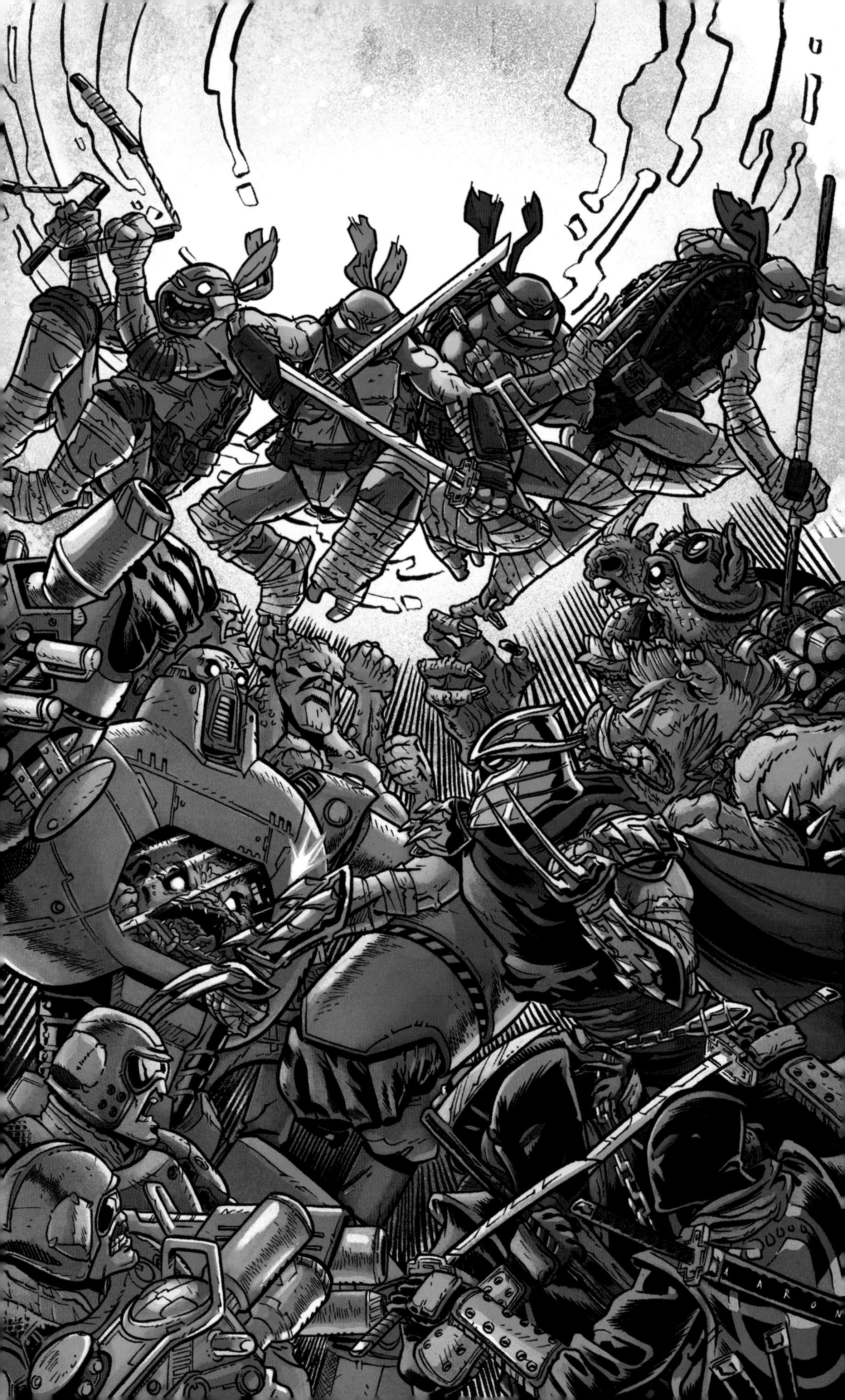

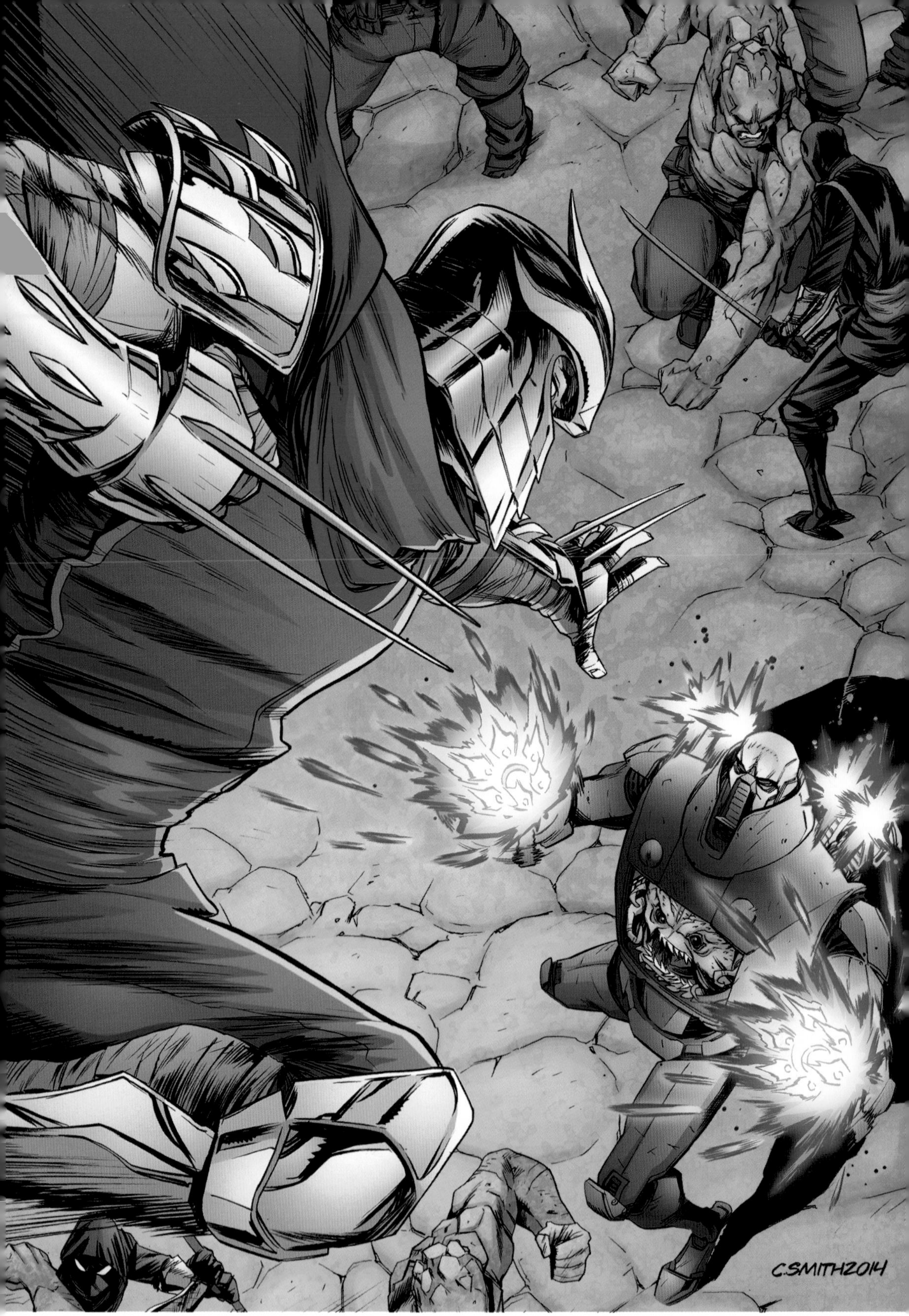
C.SMITH2014

ART BY CORY SMITH · COLORS BY RONDA PATTISON

OPPOSITE PAGE: ART BY KEVIN EASTMAN · COLORS BY RONDA PATTISON

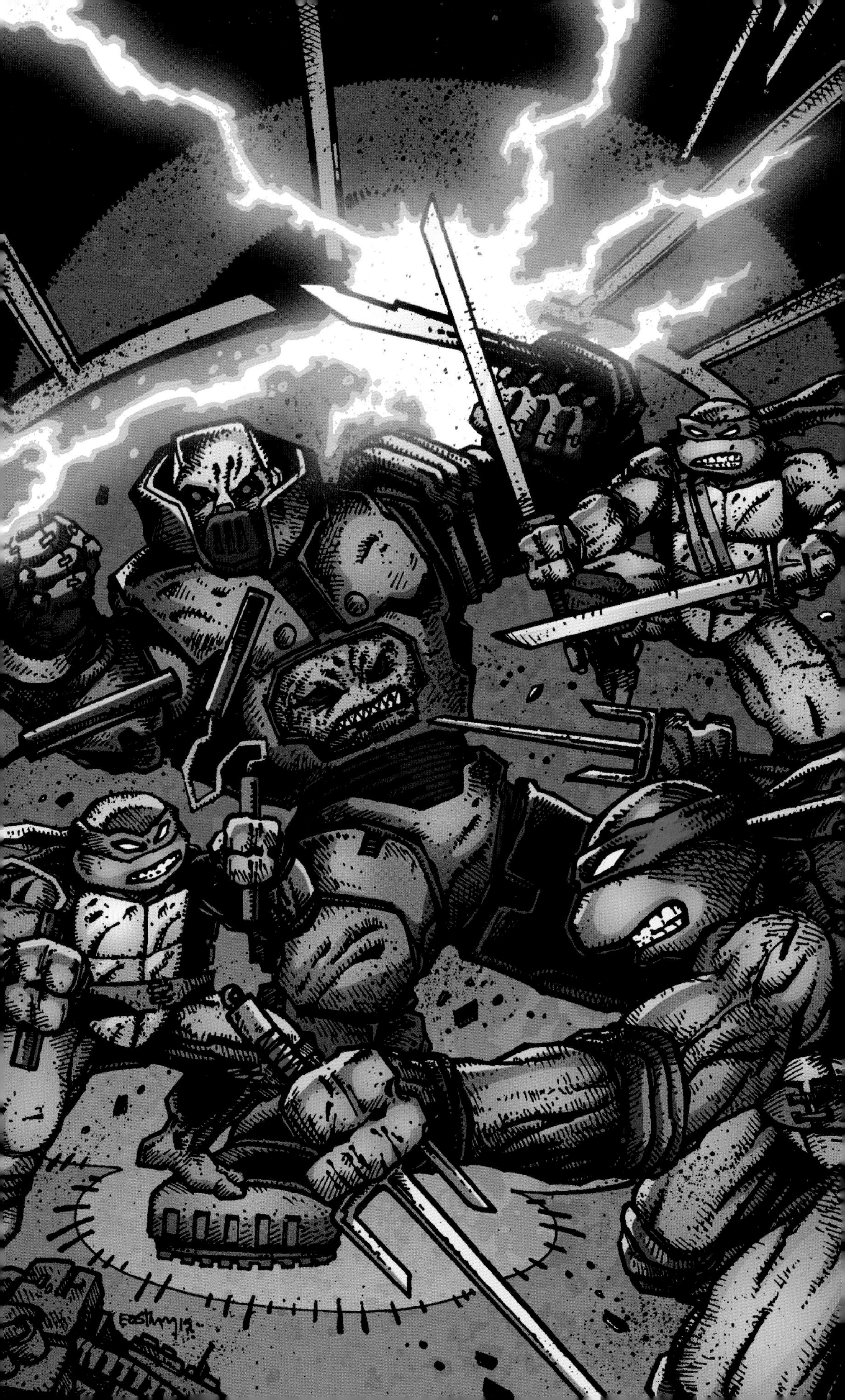

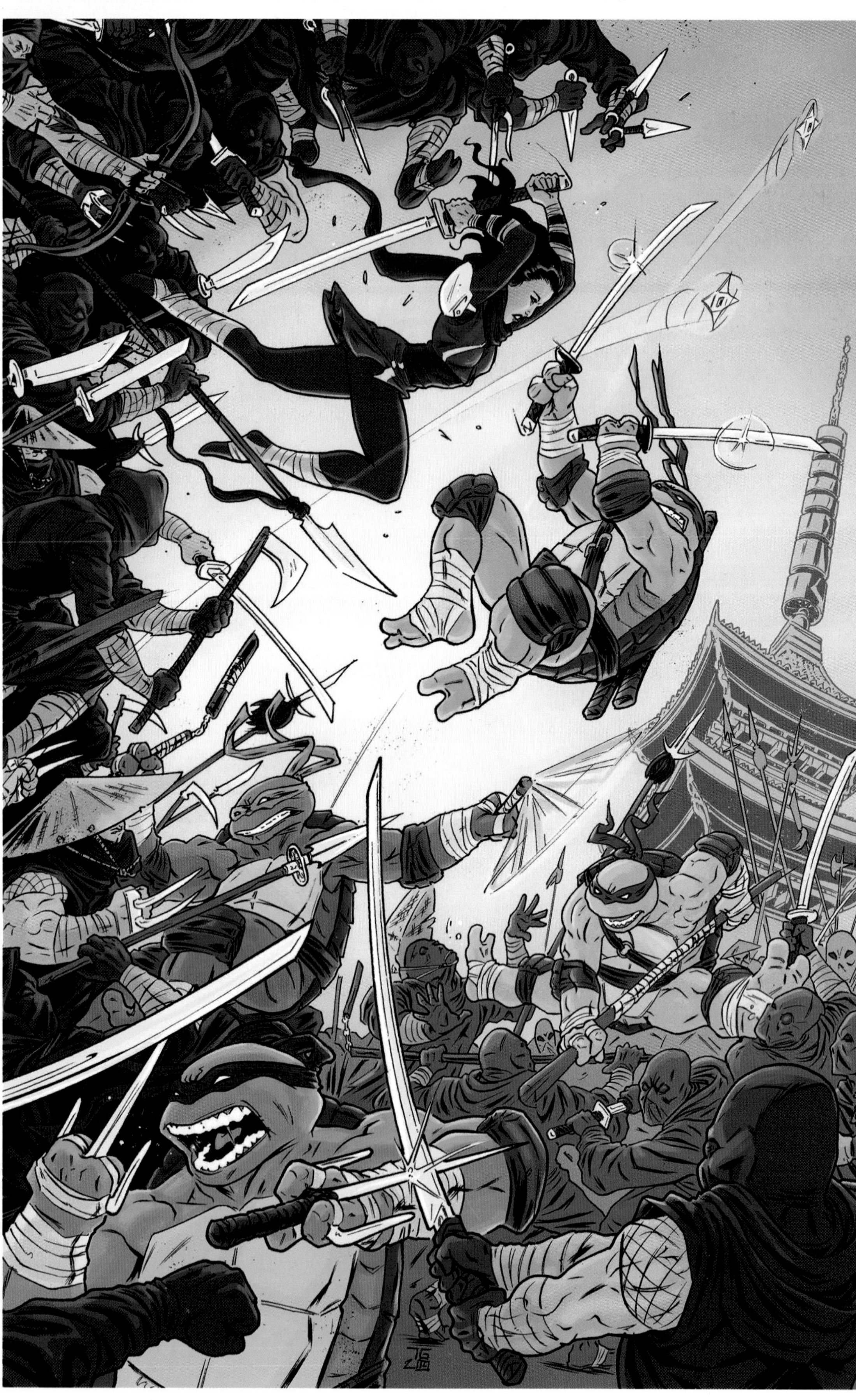

ART BY TADD GALUSHA